NIA...
SOUTHWESTERN
ONTARIO

A COLOURGUIDE

Edited by Paul Knowles

FORMAC PUBLISHING COMPANY LIMITED

CONTENTS

MAPS — 4

About This Guide — 6

Exploring Southwestern Ontario — 8

A Brief History — 13

TOURS — 19

Niagara Peninsula — 20

Caledon and Halton Hills — 31

Kitchener-Waterloo and Area — 36

Stratford and Area — 45

London and Area — 53

Lake Erie Shoreline — 58

Windsor and Area — 62

Lake Huron and Georgian Bay — 67

TOP ACTIVITIES AND ATTRACTIONS — 73

Antiquing — 74

Art Galleries and Studios — 78

Birding — 83

Boating — 87

Camping — 91

Craft Shows — 95

Cycling — 100

Festivals — 104

Food and Dining — 110

CONTENTS

Gardens	116
Golf	121
Hiking	125
Kids' Stuff	131
Museums and Historic Sites	138
Shopping	144
Snow Sports	151
Swimming	154
Theatre	157
Wine Tasting	163
Listings	169
Index	192
Contributors	207

Formac Publishing Company Limited
5502 Atlantic Street
Halifax, Nova Scotia
B3H 1G4

Printed and bound in Canada

Distributed in the United States by:
Seven Hills Book Distributors
1531 Tremont Street
Cincinnati, Ohio 45214

Distributed in the United Kingdom by:
World Leisure Marketing
9 Downing Road
West Meadows Industrial Estate
Derby, England   DE216HA

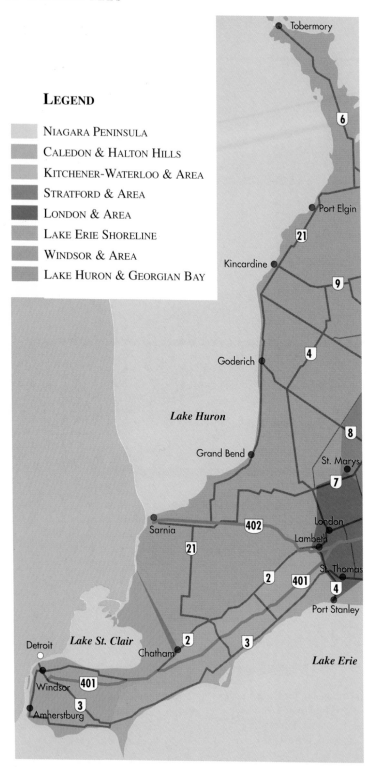

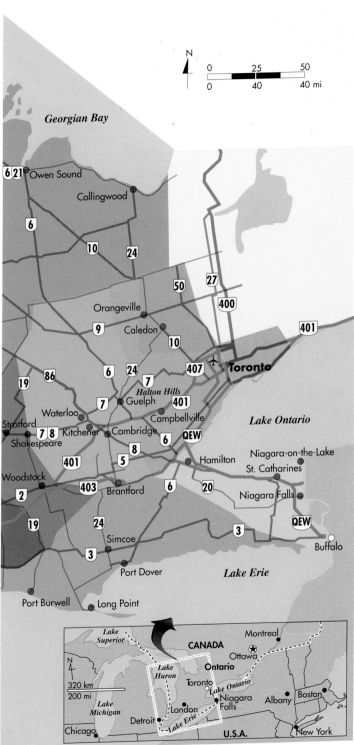

ABOUT THIS GUIDE

From Niagara Falls and the lush wine regions of the south to Tobermory and the rocky coastline of the north, southwestern Ontario offers visitors a wide range of landscapes and attractions.

This guide to Niagara and southwestern Ontario was written to help you make the most of your stay in one of the most visited areas of Canada.

The introductory chapters—"Exploring Southwestern Ontario" and "A Brief History"—provide overviews of this part of the province. The accompanying map will give you a general sense of the area as well as show you the eight smaller regions that it comprises.

NIAGARA-ON-THE LAKE

The guide itself is divided into three main sections. The first section, "Tours," contains eight chapters, each one based on a region of southwestern Ontario. These tours will offer some background about the regions as well as help you plan an itinerary that encompasses the most interesting communities and attractions. Each chapter carries a detailed regional map and many of the chapters also offer one or two community maps.

The second section, "Top Activities and Attractions," contains nineteen chapters, each built around a popular activity or type of attraction in southwestern Ontario. You will find articles on activities such as birding, golfing, and hiking as well as pieces on the best art galleries, theatres, and seasonal festivals to visit. There is a chapter devoted to food and dining as well as one dedicated to children, called "Kids' Stuff." These chapters are alphabetized to make them easy to use.

The third section of this guide contains selected listings with practical information on almost everything you might want to do in this part of Ontario. This section begins by offering general travel information before moving on to provide selected listings of accommodations, restaurants, activities, and attractions.

This book is an independent guide. Its editor and contributors have made their recommendations based solely on what they believe to be the best, most interesting, and most appealing things to see and do in southwestern Ontario. No payments or contributions of any kind are solicited or accepted by the creators or the publishers of this book.

In an area as lively and diverse as southwestern Ontario, things are bound to change. We have done our best to check that the information presented here is accurate and up to date at the time of publication. Nevertheless, it is always smart to call ahead to confirm details whether you are planning a tour or simply choosing a restaurant in which to dine.

If your experience doesn't match ours—or if you believe we've missed one of the area's best features— please let us know. Write to us at the address at the bottom of the "Contents" page.

This book is the work of a team of talented writers, editors, and photographers. You can read about the people associated with this colourguide by turning to the "Contributors" section.

We hope this guide helps you enjoy your stay in this beautiful part of Canada.

—The Publishers

GOLF COURSE, VINELAND

EXPLORING SOUTHWESTERN ONTARIO

PAUL KNOWLES

Southwestern Ontario is a large triangle of land west of Toronto, bounded on all sides by the Great Lakes. With the shoreline of Lake Erie as its base, it is defined on one side by the edge of Lake Huron and on the other by an imaginary line that runs from the Niagara Peninsula and Lake Ontario north to Georgian Bay. Bisecting the triangle is the Niagara Escarpment, a spiny ridge of elevated land, running from Niagara to Tobermory.

SHORELINE, BRUCE PENINSULA

Getting to southwestern Ontario is easy; getting around it can require a little more planning, because of the size and the rural nature of large parts of the district.

The easy part: visitors to southwestern Ontario arrive by car, plane, bus, train, or boat, or even—although this is not recommended—on foot. Highways and bridges connect the region to other parts of Canada (most typically from the Toronto area, via Highway 401), or to the United States (crossing points include bridges or tunnels at

Windsor and Sarnia in the west, and from upstate New York to the Niagara Peninsula).

Canada's busiest airport, Pearson International in Toronto, is only minutes from the easterly border of this region. There is rail and bus service from all directions, as well. Some travellers arrive by boat, either pleasure craft or ferry service in the western reaches and in the extreme north of the region, where the *Chicheemaun* ferry connects Tobermory to Manitoulin Island and other points north and northwest.

Once visitors have reached southwestern Ontario, they find that getting around is both much of the fun, and much of the challenge. Although the region is only part of the vast province of Ontario, it is still a significant size, stretching between four hundred and five hundred kilometres to each of the three points of the roughly equilateral triangle that makes up the region. This fraction of a province is actually larger than any of the three smallest Canadian provinces—Prince Edward Island, Nova Scotia, and New Brunswick.

CAMELOT, STRATFORD FESTIVAL

As the expanse of the region might suggest, there is tremendous variety within this district. Southwestern Ontario includes sophisticated cities offering a wide variety of cultural events and facilities. There are world-class theatres at Stratford and Niagara-on-the-Lake; internationally renowned concert

NIAGARA-ON-THE-LAKE

facilities such as the Centre in the Square in Kitchener; and many university communities, including London, Hamilton, St. Catharines, Waterloo, Windsor, and Guelph, all offering the range of entertainment and culture that this implies. However, visitors should be aware that even these culturally aware cities pride themselves on their friendly, small-town character.

Southwestern Ontario has several industrial centres, including Hamilton, with its steel industry, and Sarnia, with its chemical plants. But it also has dozens of resort communities, where tourism is the biggest business, from Niagara-on-the-Lake to Bayfield to Wiarton.

TRAVEL

The size and the personality of southwestern Ontario mean that most tourists make their visit by car. This leaves all of the intriguing back roads and whimsical detours available to them. To receive a free map of the province of Ontario, and for other tourist information, visit any Ontario Tourist Information Centre or call 1-800-ONTARIO.

Ask specifically for information about Ontario's "Heritage Highways," routes that will take you through the heart of the region's history, such as the Huron Road or the Talbot Road.

Travelling by car allows for the greatest freedom and flexibility. However, the size of the area means that you would still be wise to plan an itinerary, always leaving room for spontaneity. This guide is a useful tool when planning your trip—it details the best of southwestern Ontario, from campgrounds to antiquing areas, from theatres to hiking trails.

TRANSPORTATION OPTIONS

If you do not wish to use a car, many of the communities in southwestern Ontario can be reached by train or bus—although southwestern Ontario is notorious for its  infrequent service, and compares quite poorly with countries like the United Kingdom or France. For train service, contact Canadian National Railways (1-800-601-7630). For bus service, one major company is Greyhound (1-800-661-8747).

There are several travel companies in southwestern Ontario that offer bus tours (one-day, overnight, or longer) within the region. One specialist in this area (with modern buses beautifully decorated with murals of Canadian scenes) is Travel Ventures in Kitchener (519-896-8687, or contact your travel agent for other options).

Most of the larger communities (Niagara Falls, Hamilton, Guelph, Kitchener-Waterloo, London, Windsor, and Sarnia, for example) have good municipal bus services.

One final option for those looking for quality over quantity is a cycling holiday; the cycling section in this book suggests a good number of fine cycling options around the region, including bike trails that will take you through sections of the Niagara Escarpment.

Many of the communities (including Niagara-on-the-Lake, Acton, and Owen Sound) offer self-guided walking tours. You can pick up a walking tour brochure at local information centres. For the more serious, out-in-the-wilds hiker, one of the most highly regarded hiking trails in the world runs down the spine of southwestern Ontario—the Bruce Trail.

The Niagara Escarpment is covered at length in our hiking section; let us simply note, here, that it is one of three important geographical assets of southwestern

HIKERS IN SOUTHWESTERN ONTARIO

Ontario which make this one of the top tourist destinations in the world; the other two are Niagara Falls (one of the seven natural wonders of the world, and always the first on any out-of-province visitor's "must-see" list), and the Great Lakes shorelines. Only about one hundred kilometres of the boundary of southwestern Ontario is *not* water.

NIAGARA FALLS

PRINCE OF WALES HOTEL, NIAGARA-ON-THE-LAKE

Obviously, then, boaters also have plenty of options when it comes to travel, although the accessible boating areas are on the edges of the district so it is not possible to visit the heartland of southwestern Ontario that way.

ACCOMMODATIONS

When arranging accommodations in southwestern Ontario, the choice is as broad as your imagination. There are dozens of campgrounds, located in almost every community in the region (see the camping section). There are also hundreds of bed and breakfast establishments and many fine historic inns and small hotels. The large hotel chains are also represented in the cities of the region. See the listings section or contact 1-800-ONTARIO or the tourist information bureaus in the communities you plan to visit.

LANGUAGE

Ontario is a very multicultural province, although the focal point for multiculturalism is Toronto, east of our region. While southwestern Ontario offers plenty of opportunity to sample the culture and cuisine of many cultures, and several cities celebrate multicultural festivals (including Kitchener, Chatham, and Windsor), most people speak English as their first and often their only language. Small sections of this part of the province are French speaking, and many government employees and others who deal with the public (at tourist centres or provincial and national parks, for example) speak French as well as English. You are likely to hear many languages spoken from time to time (German and Pennsylvania German in Waterloo Region, for example), but almost everyone speaks English as well.

Whatever your language, as a visitor to southwestern Ontario you can be assured of a warm welcome. Tourism is both a major business and an enjoyable way of life for many people in this region. Vacationers can expect to be treated well both in tourist and resort towns like Stratford or St. Jacobs, in larger, more sophisticated cities like London or Hamilton, or in villages where they simply stop for pop and a fill-up of gasoline.

JAKOBSTETTLE HOUSE, ST. JACOBS

A BRIEF HISTORY

PAUL KNOWLES

Archaeologists have discovered evidence of settlement by native Canadians in southwestern Ontario dating back eleven thousand years. The transient people who first lived here were hunters and gatherers; thousands of years later, they constructed more permanent dwellings, and eventually longhouses and villages. Several historic sites in the region feature archaeological evidence and reconstructed longhouses and other structures from this period—the Crawford Lake Conservation Area near Campbellville, and the Museum of Indian Archaeology in London are only two examples.

LONGHOUSES, CRAWFORD LAKE CONSERVATION AREA, MILTON

Southwestern Ontario was mainly inhabited by the large group of Amerindians known as Iroquoians. The local subgroups were known as Huron, Neutral, and Petun Indians. These peoples were largely wiped out by war and by the diseases brought to the region by the first Europeans to arrive in the seventeenth century.

It is ironic that the Indian group most familiar to visitors, and the group that now bears the responsibility for much public education about native Canadian history, actually came to Ontario from the United States only about two hundred years ago. The Six Nations were granted land, including what is now the Six Nations Reserve on the Grand River, after they fought with the British against the Americans in the American War of Independence.

The first Europeans to come to southwestern Ontario arrived in the early 1600s. Among the first was famed explorer Samuel de Champlain, who with his colleagues claimed the region as part of the French territory, New France.

French occupation lasted more than a century, as Britain, France, and to a lesser extent Holland fought one another

13

FANSHAWE PIONEER VILLAGE, LONDON

(and any of the native population drawn into the conflict) for this portion of the New World. However, despite its claims on the land, France failed to populate southwestern Ontario in large numbers. In 1763, Great Britain gained the ascendency, and France withdrew from Ontario and all of Canada. But although France was gone, the French were not—Canada remains a bilingual country because the French Canadians kept their culture and language. Although they are most prominent in Quebec, French-speaking communities exist in several provinces, including southwestern Ontario. Welland is just one example of a community in this area with a sizable Francophone population.

The treaty between the French and English did not eliminate local hostilities, however, because within less than two decades, a new enemy had emerged—the United

SOLDIERS AT FORT GEORGE, NIAGARA-ON-THE-LAKE

States, which declared its independence from Great Britain. Canada continued as a British colony until Confederation in 1867, and even now is a member of the British Commonwealth. (Royal visits from members of the British Royal Family continue to be a celebrated event in Canada.)

In 1812, southwestern Ontario became a battleground for the ongoing hostilities between Britain and the United States. Battle sites and forts abound along the frontier, especially on the Niagara Peninsula and in the Windsor area. Many are now tourist spots where Canadians and Americans—and people from around the world—walk side by side through the exhibits.

EUROPEAN SETTLEMENT

It was not until the end of the eighteenth century that European settlement took hold in Ontario (then Upper Canada). The earliest settlers built their log cabins in the latter years of the 1700s in the Niagara Peninsula and the Windsor area. But expansion came quickly—immigrants arrived from Europe seeking refuge from the Napoleonic wars and other hostilities, and United Empire Loyalists opposed to American independence moved across the borders from the United States.

The names of southwestern Ontario communities bear witness to their history—Indian names like Niagara and Ontario; European names like London, Scotland, Berlin (now Kitchener), New Dundee, New Hamburg, Vienna, and Stratford; names in honour of southwestern Ontario pioneers like Talbotville, Tillsonburg, and Galt. And it seems that every community has a King Street and a Queen Street, a clear statement of loyalty to the British Crown.

Once settlement began, it took hold quickly. The few, small communities along the borders multiplied inland and to the north; within thirty years, the central part of southwestern Ontario was settled; by the 1850s, the furthest northern reaches of the Bruce were home to pioneers.

DUNDURN CASTLE, HAMILTON

Often, the settlers received their land free or for a small price, provided they built a road allowance and a log home on their property. Many of those roadways exist still, and southwestern Ontario has designated a number of Heritage Highways, including the Huron Road, the original stagecoach road through the heart of the region.

It is not rare to discover communities where the first log cabin was built around 1830, but where, within only thirty or forty years, large Victorian mansions had been constructed to take their place.

CULTURAL IDENTITY

Many communities took on the characteristics of the original homes of their settlers; there were mini-Scotlands, and bits of England throughout the district. These traditions took root, and today it is not hard to find Robbie Burns celebrations, Highland Games, and Victorian Teas.

One unique district is the Kitchener-Waterloo region, where Kitchener was named Berlin until confronted with the

LAMBTON HERITAGE MUSEUM, GRAND BEND

HORSE-DRAWN STREETCAR, ST. JACOBS

difficulties such a name presented during the First World War. Much of this region was purchased from the Six Nations by Mennonites—Pennsylvania Germans who brought German culture to the heart of southwestern Ontario. Joined later by many ethnic Germans from Europe, these settlers planted a permanent culture in the area that is strongly celebrated today, including during the huge Oktoberfest celebration.

In the Chatham and Amherstburg areas, there are also annual celebrations by black Canadians, descendents of some of the thirty thousand former slaves who escaped to freedom in Canada on the "underground railway" before and during the American Civil War.

GRAND RIVER CHAMPION OF CHAMPIONS POW WOW

The more recent history in southwestern Ontario is diverse. Canada is frequently lauded as one of the best countries in the world in which to live, and the twentieth century has brought many newcomers from every part of the globe. While Toronto has attracted the largest number of new immigrants, most of the communities of southwestern Ontario have become home to a varied community of residents. Many of our towns and cities now have significant Asian populations, large groups from the Caribbean, and new residents originally from the Middle East, from eastern Europe, and many other parts of the world.

Today, in many communities, annual multicultural festivals see fifth-generation Canadians with genealogical roots in England celebrating side by side with native Canadian Indians, and new Canadians from Asia and Africa. Communities that have cheered on their hockey teams for decades now watch cricket and soccer matches as well, while those hockey teams are now multiracial squads. One of the first places one sees the impact of a newly diverse community is in the wide variety of dining establishments; many communities now have Thai, Greek, Jamaican, Portuguese, and Arabic restaurants, to name a few!

COMMERCE

For centuries before the arrival of the European soldiers and settlers, the Iroquoian inhabitants had been farmers. This was continued by the newcomers, and farming became the way of life for most southwestern Ontario people.

However, the farmers needed supplies, and services, and soon businesses ranging from blacksmith shops to grocery stores opened at convenient crossroads. Stagecoach routes and then the extremely important railways were built, and those crossroads communities thrived with hotels and shops, or dwindled, depending on their locations with regard to the new transportation routes.

With the cessation of hostilities with the United States (the last battle on that boundary was in 1814), southwestern Ontario entered a time of peace that has lasted to this day. Although Canada has played important roles in World Wars I and II, and although those wars had an immeasurable impact on the population and economy of all parts of the country, including southwestern Ontario, at no time since 1814 have enemy soldiers been on or threatened the land.

RAILWAY STATION, WATERLOO

This has allowed unprecedented growth and prosperity. Cities have prospered with diverse pursuit of industry, commerce, education, and cultural endeavours represented in most towns and cities. Southwestern Ontario is known for its wide range of industry and commerce. This is the manufacturing heartland of Canada (southwestern Ontario is home to much of Canada's automotive industry). This is a hotbed of educational institutions. Almost every southwestern Ontario city has a university, and Waterloo has two! This is also a centre of innovation, where technology is king, with chemical companies in Sarnia; cutting-edge

UNIVERSITY OF WESTERN ONTARIO, LONDON

medical research in London; information technology in Kitchener-Waterloo; and aerospace endeavours in Cambridge.

The fruits of this prosperity are here, today, for the visitor to enjoy as well—theatres, entertainment centres, galleries, restaurants, and vacation resorts.

Visitors can also enjoy southwestern Ontario's history, because many historic buildings have been preserved, from forts to Victorian mansions, and many museums exist to explain and illuminate that history.

But while we can celebrate all of these human endeavours, visitors to southwestern Ontario will be forgiven if, as they gaze at Niagara Falls, marvel at the sunsets over the Great Lakes, or hike on the Bruce Trail, they conclude that southwestern Ontario was a wonderful place even before the farmers, the builders, and the shopkeepers arrived.

HURON COUNTY PLAYHOUSE, GRAND BEND

NIAGARA PENINSULA

PAUL KNOWLES

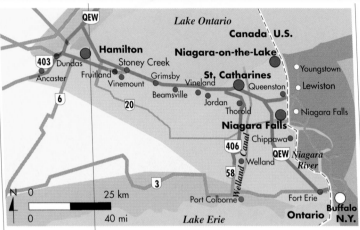

Southwestern Ontario is home to what may be the most popular tourist destination anywhere in the world—the legendary Niagara Falls. Talk to any potential visitor to Canada and the falls are almost always their number-one destination. And the falls *are* magnificent, well worthy of the attention that continually comes their way.

The problem for visitors is that if their itinerary reads only the falls, they are in danger of missing many of the most intriguing attractions and features in Ontario. The Niagara Region is rich in history, entertainment, and natural beauty. It is home to one of the country's finest theatre festivals; lies at the heart of Ontario's excellent wine region; is only a bridge and a border crossing away from excellent shopping in the United States; and has many of the top entertainment features in the country, from Marineland to Casino Niagara.

In fact, the major challenge confronting visitors to the Niagara Region is that there is just too much to do. The good news is, there is something—many things—for everyone. The bad news is, even the most dedicated visitor will have trouble doing it all. This is an area where your visit should be measured with a calendar, not a wristwatch.

NIAGARA SPANISH AERO CAR RIDE, NIAGARA RIVER

NIAGARA FALLS

The centrepiece is, and always will be, the falls. So let's begin there and then work our way out in all four directions.

Visitors who come to Niagara Falls from anywhere in Ontario usually arrive via the Queen Elizabeth Way.

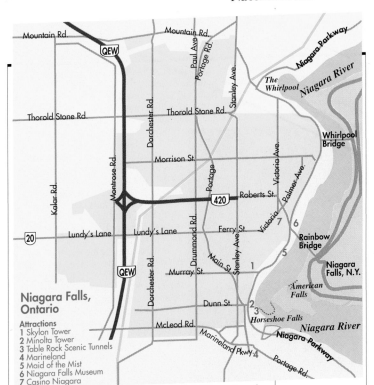

Niagara Falls, Ontario

Attractions
1 Skylon Tower
2 Minolta Tower
3 Table Rock Scenic Tunnels
4 Marineland
5 Maid of the Mist
6 Niagara Falls Museum
7 Casino Niagara

Directions to the falls are clearly marked, as are park-and-ride areas and stops for the excellent public transit system, the "People Mover." The main People Mover terminal is at the south end of Niagara Falls, along the Niagara Parkway, known as River Road within city limits. Use of public transit, which runs from the southern terminal north to Queenston Heights, is encouraged because parking can be a problem for anyone visiting the falls. Visitors from the United States may cross at any of four bridges spanning the Niagara River—the Rainbow Bridge between Niagara Falls, Ontario and Niagara Falls, New York; the Queenston-Lewiston Bridge and the Whirlpool Bridge to the north; and the Peace Bridge between Buffalo and Fort Erie.

There are many options for viewing the falls—which are actually two waterfalls, the American falls, to the north, and the Horseshoe, or Canadian falls. The first stop for most visitors is at Table Rock, right on the lip of the Canadian falls. Here visitors hear the roar, feel the spray, and get close to the Horseshoe Falls, while enjoying a great view of the American falls.

Visitors often stroll along the river to the north—each few feet covered offers a new scenic perspective. During the day, a rainbow can often be seen; at night, the falls are lit in a dramatic light show.

There are plenty of other vantage points, including Queen Victoria Park, which offer many fine viewing spots.

Two of the most popular Niagara attractions offer spectacular, bird's-eye

**TABLE ROCK
RESTAURANT,
NIAGARA FALLS**

CASINO NIAGARA, NIAGARA FALLS

views—the Skylon Tower (5200 Robinson Street) and the Minolta Tower (6732 Oakes Drive). Both include observation decks and several restaurants (one of the Skylon's revolves), as well as entertainment—Minolta offers Yuk Yuk's comedy and state-of-the-art electronic adventures.

While the towers will take you high above the falls, your options have only just begun. You can experience the falls from below—by taking a voyage on the famous *Maid of the Mist* boats that carry visitors breathtakingly close to the foot of the falls. The *Maid of the Mist* offers a half-hour ride, with departures every fifteen minutes, May to late October.

You can actually get under the falls through the Journey Behind the Falls, which takes you through tunnels, under the Table Rock, to a view directly behind the cascading water. You can soar high above the falls by helicopter, with Niagara Helicopters (Victoria Avenue at the Niagara Parkway).

You can even experience the feeling of plunging over the falls—as a number of lucky or ill-fated daredevils and accident victims have done over the years—since several attractions offer a simulation of this death-defying experience, from the Niagara Falls Imax Theatre to Ride Niagara, an amusement ride under the Rainbow Bridge.

Or perhaps you can simulate that same feeling of going over the falls in a barrel by trying your luck at the gigantic, state-of-the-art Casino Niagara. The casino is the most popular new attraction at Niagara Falls, with its three thousand slot machines, 144 gaming tables, and other

features drawing crowds twenty-four hours a day, seven days a week—the only attraction whose hours of operation exactly match those of the falls.

Casino Niagara opened its doors in December 1996 and was a huge hit from the beginning, hosting thirty thousand

CLIFTON HILL, NIAGARA FALLS

people in the first twenty-four hours. The stream of visitors continues to pour in—the busy casino provides ninety-six thousand square feet of gaming space, featuring slot machines, blackjack, roulette, baccarat, and more. It also offers restaurants and bars, including a Hard Rock Cafe and Marilyn's, featuring live entertainment.

Niagara Falls has every conceivable type of entertainment, from the natural wonder of the falls to the glitz and glamour of the other entertainment hotspots in the city. One block south of the casino is the famous Clifton Hill, which contains so much neon per square foot that it is hard to discern whether it is day or night there; in fact, night may be brighter. This is the other Niagara Falls, the fun-filled entertainment district, home to such well-known stops as Louis Tussaud's Waxworks, the Guinness World of Records Museum, and Ripley's Believe It or Not Museum.

These venerable attractions have been joined by dozens of others in the Clifton Hill district—the Rock Legends Wax Museum, the Movieland Wax Museum, the Haunted House, Castle Dracula, the House of Frankenstein, Dazzleland Family Fun Centre, Adventuredome, Ripley's Moving Theatre, and Rumours Night Club (along with the requisite "and many more").

One block north of the Rainbow Bridge is the Niagara Falls Museum, established in 1827, featuring standard museum fare spiced up with the spirit of Niagara adventure—artifacts of journeys over the falls and exhibits of "freaks of nature."

All of this lies within a few blocks of the falls, and we haven't yet mentioned the most-advertised attraction at Niagara Falls—Marineland, an amusement park, game farm, and home of a spectacular water show featuring killer whales, dolphins, and sea lions. This is family fun—kids love the sea creatures, andthe rides are geared for all age groups, from young children to thrill-seeking teenagers and adults.

THE NIAGARA PARKWAY

For those looking for more sedate entertainment, Niagara Falls offers excellent gardens along the Niagara Parkway. Of special interest are the Niagara Parks Commission Greenhouses, half a mile south of the falls, along the rapids section of the river (in the midst of which you will see the long-stranded "old scow," a landmark in the river that has rested mid-stream since 1918;

NIAGARA PARKS GREENHOUSE

two crewmen spent twenty-nine hours on the barge before being rescued). The Greenhouses, free and open year-round, allow visitors to wander among tropical plants and seasonal displays. As well, this is home to exotic birds allowed to fly free, to the delight of visitors. By the way, about 420,000 people visit the greenhouse each year!

Although we have only touched on the attractions to be enjoyed in Niagara Falls, let's head north along the Niagara Parkway, en route to the picturesque town of Niagara-on-the-Lake.

NORTH ON THE PARKWAY

The Niagara Parkway, which connects Niagara-on-the-Lake with Fort Erie, is probably the most beautiful drive in Canada. Stretching about fifty kilometres, it runs along the Niagara River Gorge, with gardens, grand homes, historic sites, orchards, and vineyards along the way.

NIAGARA RIVER

As you drive north from the falls, you will see a number of scenic lookouts—opportunities to stop and take in the highlights of the Niagara Gorge. Two stops offer special features—the Spanish Cable Ride, which carries you across the river high in a cable car, and Whirlpool Jet Boat Tours, based in Niagara-on-the-Lake (905-468-4800), which takes visitors by jet boat to the famous whirlpool. The whirlpool can also be enjoyed from a fine scenic outlook.

North of the whirlpool are two of the best attractions in the Niagara Peninsula—the Niagara Parks Botanical Gardens and the Niagara Parks Butterfly Conservatory, located within the gardens. The botanical gardens are free; there is a charge for the butterfly conservatory.

NIAGARA PARKS BOTANICAL GARDENS

The Gardens were begun here in 1936 as a school for apprentice gardeners. They now cover forty hectares, and include rose, sunken, natural, herb, and perennial gardens.

The butterfly conservatory opened in 1996 and immediately

became one of the premier attractions in the district. Visitors wander through the largest fully enclosed butterfly dome in North America, containing a tropical rain forest and more than two thousand butterflies of more than fifty species. The butterflies fly free, and may land on visitors. It is a place of high-flying magic. One visitor said she could not imagine anyone of any age who would not be delighted by the butterfly conservatory. Paths carry visitors through the building. We recommend you follow the route at least twice.

NIAGARA PARKS BUTTERFLY CONSERVATORY

A mile and a half further north is the Floral Clock, one of the world's largest at forty feet. Formed by fifteen thousand plants, it has told blooming time since 1950. Admission is free.

Queenston Heights Park has picnic areas, playgrounds, and a wading pool. It boasts monuments to two Canadian heroes—General Isaac Brock, whose tall memorial is visible for many miles, and Laura Secord. Both were heroes of the War of 1812, during which military forces based in Canada defeated the forces from the United States. The Brock Monument can also be reached by climbing from the village of Queenston, which lies to the north.

At the foot of the path to the Brock Monument is the Mackenzie Printery, where radical William Lyon Mackenzie first published his newspaper, the *Colonial Advocate*, on May 18, 1924. The printery is now a print museum, which opens in mid-May for the summer season.

WINE ROUTE

Not far north of Queenston are two of the many fine wineries of the Niagara Region—Inniskillen, just a block off the parkway and clearly marked, and Reif Winery, on the parkway, just south of Niagara-on-the-Lake.

Both are important stops on the popular Ontario Wine Route, a carefully designed journey that will take travellers to thirty-one Ontario wineries. Most of the wine route wineries are on the Niagara Peninsula, but five are located in the far west of southwestern Ontario on the north shore of Lake Erie and on Pelee Island.

Wine lovers should pick up a brochure, and venture to discover at least several of the other area wineries (also see Wine Tasting).

Ontario Wine Route brochures are available at any Ontario winery, and at Tourist Information Centres. The wine business is a growth industry, so don't be surprised to find a winery not listed in your brochure. Visitors will discover that a wine route tour can occupy several pleasurable days; the Niagara wineries, with their lovely locations and interesting shops and amenities, thoroughly reward such an itinerary.

Several of the established wineries are fine starting places for a wine tour, offering interpretive centres, regular tours, tastings, gift shops, and, in some cases, dining facilities.

As visitors drive north on the Niagara Parkway from

PICNIC AREA, NIAGARA RIVER

the falls, Inniskillen is the first winery they'll encounter; this large facility offers a wine-tasting bar (with a fee charged for tastings), tours (both guided and self-directed), a beautiful wine and gift shop, and a gallery on the second floor that usually features a hands-on display of artifacts from the Shaw Festival theatres. A short hop away is Reif, also well worth stopping at, with tastings (a fee is charged), a gift shop, tours, and special programs.

All of the Niagara wineries are situated among orchards and farm markets, making picnicking along the parkway or in other area parks tempting and delicious.

NIAGARA-ON-THE-LAKE

The next stop along the parkway from the falls is the town of Niagara-on-the-Lake. (Some confusion has been caused by a governmental decree that refers to both the larger area and the old town by the same name. In this section, Niagara-on-the-Lake refers to the town.)

As you travel the Niagara Parkway, you will see a collection of large wooden structures on your right, between the road and the river. This is Fort George, now a Parks Canada attraction. Fort George, open April 1 to October 31, is a full reconstruction of the fort circa 1812. It features guides in period costumes, and military and domestic demonstrations. This fort was built near the end of the 1700s, and featured prominently in the War of 1812, which pitted the United States against Canada (at that time, the British colony of Upper Canada). At the Battle

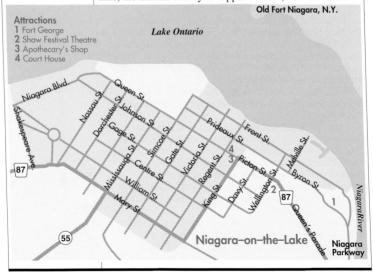

Attractions
1 Fort George
2 Shaw Festival Theatre
3 Apothecary's Shop
4 Court House

Old Fort Niagara, N.Y.

Lake Ontario

Niagara—on—the—Lake

Niagara Parkway

of Fort George, in 1813, an American fleet arrived at the mouth of the Niagara River, bombarded the fort, and captured it. Eventually, the British took it back. The Niagara Peninsula was the site for a number of battles during this war, which was a side skirmish in the international conflict of the times. Peace was restored with the Treaty of Ghent.

THE SHOP AT SLY CORNER, **SHAW FESTIVAL**

Just past Fort George, on the left, is the Shaw Festival Theatre, one of three theatres in Niagara-on-the-Lake operated by the Shaw Festival, the only theatre company in the world devoted to the works of George Bernard Shaw and his contemporaries. The playbill typically features three plays by Shaw and another three to five by Shaw's contemporaries (1-800-511-SHAW).

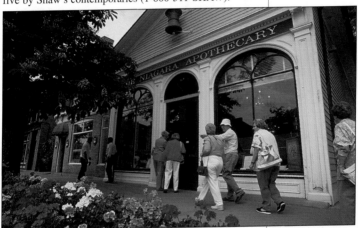

Niagara-on-the-Lake has—with considerable justification—been called the prettiest town in Canada. It is also one of the oldest settlements in southwestern Ontario, built on land purchased from the Mississauga Indians in 1781, and then granted to Lieutenant-Colonel John Butler.

NIAGARA-ON-THE-LAKE

The town, originally known as Newark, was the first capital of Upper Canada; the legislative assembly first met there in 1792. Upper Canada's first newspaper was published in Niagara-on-the-Lake, and a plaque marks the spot by a gazebo near the waterfront.

The entire downtown area has been faithfully restored in heritage mode. Many of the buildings in the blocks around the core have plaques bearing the early dates of their construction. On the main street, visitors will enjoy the restored Apothecary's Shop, the Court House (with a useful historic plaque), and, on a boulevard in the centre of the street, the unique clock tower.

Other highlights include many excellent historic inns—

THE NIAGARA APOTHECARY

the Prince of Wales, the Oban Inn, the Olde Angel Inn, the Kiely Inn, and the Pillar and Post to name a few. The Oban has the distinction of being a new old inn—a terrible fire caused serious damage a few yeas ago, but it was faithfully reconstructed. In addition, there are eighty-two bed and breakfasts listed as members of the Niagara on-the-Lake B&B Association.

Niagara-on-the-Lake is known for its shopping district, with dozens of speciality stores featuring high-end clothing, art, and souvenirs. The shopping district extends beyond the main street—be sure to duck down the side streets and explore the cul-de-sacs and back alleys. There are many fine dining establishments in town. The downtown core is only two blocks from the river front, where the Niagara River empties into Lake Ontario, and the warmer microclimate of the area makes this a pleasant place to visit year-round.

Visitors can take a self-guided walking tour of the historic town, available from the Visitor and Convention Bureau on Queen Street at King Street (905-468-4263). Of special note is the Niagara Historical Society Museum, at

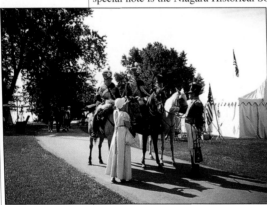

HISTORIC FORT ERIE

43 Castlereagh. Several antique dealers can be found along Highway 55. Antique lovers who enjoy well-stocked shops with an emphasis on quantity and varying quality will especially enjoy the large Red Barn Antique Mall, east of Hillebrand. This is a large co-op with thousands of items on offer, from very fine antiques to bargain-hunters' treasures.

This is the last stop on this section of the tour. Let's go back to our starting point, the falls, and travel south on the Niagara Parkway.

SOUTH ON THE PARKWAY

There are fewer attractions on this stretch, but the route is equally beautiful, this time along a river and not a gorge, since you are above the falls and heading upstream toward Lake Erie.

One caution—following the parkway out of Niagara Falls proper requires close attention, because at the adjoining town of Chippewa, you must turn left and then left again to continue along the riverbank and the parkway; watch for signs. The route from Niagara Falls to Fort Erie is about thirty kilometres.

Fort Erie is one terminus of the Peace Bridge, a busy Canada–U.S. entry point connecting Fort Erie with Buffalo, a city with its own full menu of attractions.

Key features of Fort Erie include Historic Fort Erie, the restored fort open from May through September, and operated by the Niagara Parks Commission.

Unlike the other communities on the Niagara Parkway, Fort Erie offers beautiful beaches along its Lake Erie shoreline and is also home to the Fort Erie Racetrack, with live horse racing weekdays, from mid-May through August. Fort Erie will soon feature another gambling venue—a charity gambling casino with 40 gaming tables and 150 slot machines.

VAN GOGH'S *THE OLD MILL*, ALBRIGHT-KNOX GALLERY, BUFFALO

THE UNITED STATES

There are many reasons for travellers to make the international hop across the Niagara River to Buffalo, Niagara Falls (New York), or Lewiston. Tourists can visit historic sites such as Old Fort Niagara in Youngstown, just across the mouth of the Niagara River from Niagara-on-the-Lake. There are attractions ranging from the Aquarium of Niagara, in Niagara Falls, New York, to Artpark, the visual and performing arts complex in Lewiston. There is lots of entertainment, especially in Buffalo's theatre district, fine dining throughout the area, and lots for sports fans, as Buffalo boasts both the NFL Bills, and the NHL Sabres.

Buffalo is also home to the world-renowned Albright-Knox Art Gallery, which houses one of the world's top surveys of contemporary art and sculpture. The Albright-Knox specializes in American and European art of the past fifty years, but also has a permanent collection of art through the centuries that dates back to 3000 B.C., and includes works by impressionists such as Degas and Renoir. The gallery has six thousand works in its collection; two hundred are on view at any given time (716-882-8700).

As attractive as these features are, the number-one reason travellers head east from southwestern Ontario is the shopping. The American communities across the Niagara River are known

STONEY RIDGE CELLARS, VINELAND

as shoppers' paradises, with outlet malls galore, including the Rainbow Centre Factory Outlet in Niagara Falls, New York, and the Niagara International Factory Outlets.

WEST ON THE PENINSULA

The attractions of Niagara continue when the traveller turns west from the Niagara River. Wineries abound (the Ontario Wine Route lists twenty-six wineries on the Peninsula, more than half of them west of the Niagara and Niagara-on-the-Lake area). Orchards, farmers' markets, museums, and antique shops exist in almost every community.

The largest city is St. Catharines, on the shore of Lake Ontario. The Welland Canal—the key shipping route that allows ships, including enormous lake freighters, to bypass Niagara Falls—meets Lake Ontario here, and Locks 1, 2, and 3 are located within the city limits.

A fine view of the operation of the Welland Canal can be had at Lock 3, where there is an elevated viewing platform. This is also the site of the St. Catharines Museum.

Visitors following the Welland Canal can travel south through Thorold, home to Locks 4, 5, 6, and 7 (the first three of these are "twin flight locks," allowing ships to move up and down the canal simultaneously). The final lock, just before the Lake Erie shore, is located in Fountainview Park in Port Colborne, another fine viewing location (1-800-263-2988).

The current Welland Canal was officially opened in 1932. The first of several Welland Canals opened in 1829, and it, along with the next three incarnations of the waterway, began in Port Dalhousie, now part of St. Catharines. This harbourfront village offers a treasure trove of heritage structures, and interesting shops and galleries.

ST. CATHARINES

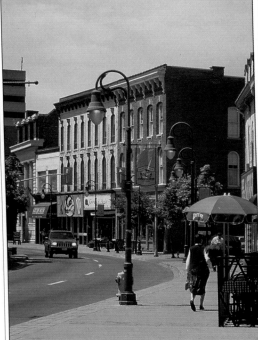

And is there still more to do on the Niagara Peninsula? Of course. Perhaps your final activity on this tour should be to pick up all the tourist information you can find, so that you can plan your next visit to one of the most picturesque areas in the province.

Besides, the supply of wine you will undoubtedly take home will certainly be gone in a few months time, so you will simply have to come back!

CALEDON AND HALTON HILLS

PAUL KNOWLES

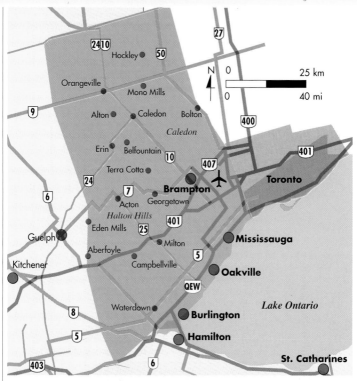

The Halton Hills and Caledon area, located northwest of Toronto and northeast of Guelph, is one of the most scenic sections of southwestern Ontario. With lovely, rolling hills, many woodlot and bush areas, streams and river valleys, immaculately maintained country estates, and picturesque small towns and villages, the landscape has been compared to that of Vermont. This area is beautiful at all times of the year, but everyone agrees it is at its best during the autumn show of colour.

This tour will take you from Mountsberg Conservation Area, west of Campbellville, northeast to Caledon East, and back to Erin. Along the way, you can hike scenic trails, creep along a rock face behind a waterfall, drop in at friendly antique stores, visit a gigantic leather store, browse in a bit of Britain, stop at a country store, and get a quick lesson in restoring and creating stained glass. There may even be time for a picnic or a play.

CALEDON

HALTON REGION CONSERVATION AREAS

Mountsberg Conservation Area is one of several Halton Region Conservation Areas that ring the village of Campbellville. These parks are special because of their location on or near the Niagara Escarpment, southwestern Ontario's most impressive geological feature.

While this section describes a one-day trip around the Halton Hills and Caledon Hills area, visitors can spend entire days at any of these conservation areas, enjoying fine walking, biking, or cross-country skiing trails, and unique features.

Mountsberg, for example, is a wildlife centre specializing in "raptor rescue." The staff care for raptors—hawks, owls, eagles, and turkey vultures—injured or captured in inappropriate environments. One Mountsberg trail passes pens that house birds that cannot be released because of injury—your chance to be face to face with a bald eagle or snowy owl. Programs include raptor demonstrations, and visitors are often invited to watch when a bird, recovered from injury, is set free. Mountsberg is also a bird-banding centre and a good place to view all types of birds (905-336-1158; 905-854-2276).

South of Campbellville is Crawford Lake Indian Village and Conservation Area, with a boardwalk around a pristine lake atop the Niagara Escarpment, and a reconstructed fifteenth-century Iroquoian Village, set on an original site. The deep lake is a rare, meromictic lake—there is no life on the bottom of the lake because nothing can survive in the unusually low oxygen levels, and everything on the bottom is perfectly preserved. This means Crawford Lake has provided scientists with a detailed account of southwestern Ontario's ecological history.

This detail is echoed on land, as well, where the Woodland Indian settlement that has been discovered and reconstructed may be the most accurately dated Indian village in the country. The reconstruction of the village includes a complete longhouse, open to visitors.

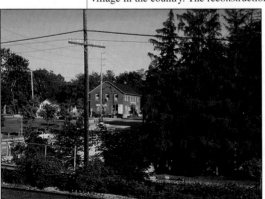

CAMPBELLVILLE

North of Campbellville is Hilton Falls, with a ten-metre waterfall where visitors can clamber over the rocks and stand behind the cascading water.

West of Campbellville is Kelso/Glen Eden Conservation Area, with a wide range of traditional recreational activities—swimming, fishing, canoeing, sailboarding and, on the slopes overlooking the lake, skiing on eleven runs geared for every level of skier (905-336-1158).

CAMPBELLVILLE

Visitors who have travelled all around the village of Campbellville may now wish to stop there awhile. Guelph Line south takes you right into town from the 401.

Campbellville's charm is its shops. It is a good place for shoppers to browse from store to store, picking up an ice-cream cone along the way. There is a small picnic area beside the pond at the south end of the downtown. This is also one of the finest antiquing areas in southwestern Ontario. More than a dozen antique stores can be found here, and there are gift and craft stores too. Most of the shops are in the downtown section. Excellent antique stores include Regency House Antiques and Village Antiques, both dealer co-ops.

Leave Campbellville on Guelph Line North (Road One) and head to Acton.

ACTON

Acton ("Canada's Leathertown") is best known for its huge leather shop, the Olde Hide House, on Highway 7. This acre of retail space features everything from coats to couches. If it can be made from leather, it's probably here.

Just across the street is a much less prepossessing shop, but one still worth a visit—Wetherby's, a store featuring all things British, from Coronation Street collectables to chutney. A tourist information section has a good selection of local brochures, including a historic walking tour (519-853-1031).

Leave Acton on Highway 7 and turn left on Road 3 (Trafalgar Road N) to the tiny village of Ballinafad, which has a general store with a difference—it's also a tack shop, reflecting the enormous interest in horseback riding in this area. Just west of Ballinafad is the hundred-acre Wildwood Manor Ranch, offering accommodation, year-round horseback riding, and other programs (905-877-6852).

TERRA COTTA

Follow Ballinafad Road, and turn right on Road 19, to Terra Cotta. The scenery here is typical of this entire region—woods, hills, and waterways abound. On your right is the Terra Cotta Conservation Area, featuring a leisurely, one-and-a-half-kilometre walk around Spring Pond.

The village of Terra Cotta is known for fine dining at the excellent Terra Cotta Inn, as well as shops like the Brass Thimble, and the Forge Studio Galleries.

Leave Terra Cotta on Peel Road 9, heading northeast across Highway 10, and on to Road 7 (Airport Road), where you turn left towards Caledon East. By now, you

CALEDON

may be lost; don't worry, there is no prettier area to be lost in. Enjoy the views, marvel at the estates, and stop at the first friendly shop you find to ask directions.

Caledon East is a pretty town. Highlights include a well-marked walking trail that starts at the main road, and some good farm markets and garden centres, just north of town.

Continue to Mono Mills and turn left on Highway 9 to Orangeville. Hockley Valley Ski Resort is on your right, along with Hockley Valley Provincial Nature Reserve.

ORANGEVILLE

Stay on Highway 9 into downtown Orangeville, a much larger town than the villages we have been visiting. Orangeville is often characterized as a gateway to cottage country, a halfway point for people heading north to their summer homes. That may explain the huge selection of fast-food outlets at the entrance to town.

But while there are certainly eat-and-run restaurants

FORKS OF THE CREDIT PROVINCIAL PARK

and stores where one can find basic supplies for a week at the cottage, there are also more interesting opportunities to eat and shop. Book lovers enjoy Readers' Choice, a used-book store that is bright, cheerful, and accessible. Especially interesting is Glasscraft, featuring stained glass and other unique glass and giftware, where the working studio is open to visitors. Owner Bill Adler happily shares the secrets of his craft; you may see him adapting a Tom Thompson painting to a stained glass design, or restoring a century-old window. Nearby is Theatre Orangeville, opened in 1994 in the beautifully restored Orangeville Town Hall Opera House, and already known as one of southwestern Ontario's best summer theatres (519-942-3423).

Leave Orangeville on Highway 136 and head south to Alton, where a fine country hotel, the Millcroft Inn, features one hundred acres of magnificent outdoor trails and the unique dining option of enjoying excellent cuisine and fine wine suspended over the falls in a glass pod (519-941-8111).

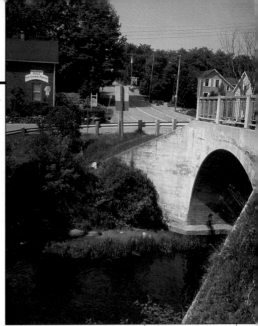

FORKS OF THE CREDIT

When you reach Highway 24, turn left. This takes you to Forks of the Credit Provincial Park, a wonderful, 262-hectare park on the Niagara Escarpment named for the "forks" of the main Credit River and the Credit River West Branch. The Forks is an exceptionally beautiful nature conservancy, with carefully developed trails through meadows of wildflowers, marshes where children catch frogs and turtles in the spring, picnic areas, the ruins of a power plant, and the remnants of a pioneer settlement. The park's excellent trails, including sections of the Bruce Trail, will take you to all of the scenic features of the park including the dramatic Cataract Falls (705-435-4331).

BELFOUNTAIN

Proceed east to Caledon Village, to enjoy Tall Stories Antiques, with a fine selection of elegant antiques, and Wooden Bucket Antiques, with primitive wooden pieces.

Retrace your route along Highway 24, turning right at the sign to the pretty hamlet of Belfountain, which has an old-fashioned general store, an ice-cream shop, restaurants, and antique stores.

Now return to Highway 24, and turn left to continue to Erin, another picturesque town typical of this area, with some nicely restored downtown shops. An unlikely stop is

ERIN

at a garage on the outskirts, where the Motor Vehicle Inspection Station shares quarters with Rainbarrel Antiques. The antique store, although packed to the rafters, has interesting small antiques.

A highlight of downtown Erin is the Boston Mills Press, which shares space with A Day in the Country. The latter features intriguing statuary and giftware; the press sells books published by this successful, small Canadian publisher, and new, bargain books of all varieties can be found on the shelves in the basement.

If your day trip is approaching the supper hour, the perfect gastronomic conclusion may be found to the southeast, in Georgetown, or to the southwest, in Guelph—although personally, we'd slip back to the Millcroft Inn in Alton and enjoy dinner and the view above the falls.

35

KITCHENER-WATERLOO AND AREA

CATHY WILLIAMS

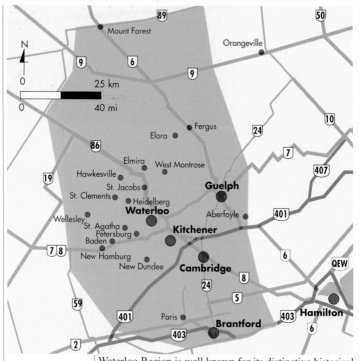

Waterloo Region is well known for its distinctive historical flavour, especially the living history of its Mennonite and German residents. The region is proud of its heritage and honours its original settlers, who were Mennonite, German, Scottish, and English, through tourist sites which enhance and explain the uniqueness of "old Waterloo County." Lots of contemporary fun is also available: golfing, fun parks, bargain shopping at factory outlets, and farmers' markets.

Waterloo Region likes to celebrate. In fact, every month, somewhere in the region, there is a festival you can attend—from beer to buskers, quilts to string quartets.

For those who want to view Waterloo Region's history and beauty from the water, several companies operate canoeing, rafting, and guided water tours along the magnificent Grand River, which is, with all of its

FARMERS' MARKET, ST. JACOBS

tributaries, one of Canada's heritage rivers. Tourist centres in most Waterloo Region communities have full information regarding ways to enjoy this aquatic perspective.

CAMBRIDGE

Cambridge is a city of riverfront parks, with attractive recreational areas along the waterways that flow throughout the community. For local residents, Cambridge is not its real name—it is the product of an amalgamation in 1973. The three original communities— Galt, Hespeler, and Preston (residents still use those names)—share a rich architectural heritage. Most of its public, and indeed many of its private, buildings were constructed with the local limestone, which gave each community the sobriquet "the city of stone." The settlements grew along the banks of the Grand River and its tributary the Speed.

CAMBRIDGE (TOP);
KITCHENER
FARMERS' MARKET

Consequently, each area of the city has attractive riverside parks to explore, with both summer and winter festivals to attend. Cambridge's factory outlets, as well as its historic farmers' market, are well worth visiting.

Close by to the west, in the historic village of Blair, is the magnificent Langdon Hall, a colonial Georgian mansion built in 1898 for Eugene Langdon Wilks, a descendent of John Jacob Astor. Sitting among two hundred sculptured acres, Langdon Hall is now a four-star hotel with a fine restaurant. Indulging in high tea in the hall's library is an unforgettable experience (1-800-268-1898).

KITCHENER

Kitchener is Waterloo Region's largest city, a prosperous, bustling community that offers visitors an interesting mix

Attractions
1 University of Waterloo
2 Wilfred Laurier University
3 Woodside National Historic Park
4 Centre in the Square
5 Doon Heritage Crossroads
6 Kitchener Farmers' Market

37

of activities and attractions: fine heritage sites and museums, a busy farmers' market, and an excellent local concert hall, the Centre in the Square.

As you head into Kitchener from Cambridge, the Pioneer Memorial Tower just off Highway 8 commemorates the 1806 arrival of the first settlers to the interior reaches of Upper Canada. Mennonites from Pennsylvania purchased sixty thousand acres of Canadian wilderness to escape religious persecution. A graveyard on the site has fascinating grave markers.

Another tribute to the area's original settlers is the Joseph Schneider Haus, on Queen Street South in the heart of the city. Joseph Schneider's land holdings included what is now most of downtown Kitchener. Built circa 1816, the home has been restored to 1856, when the second generation of Schneiders farmed and operated a sawmill. An interpretive "living" museum, it holds activities demonstrating early farming life almost year-round (519-742-7752).

JOSEPH SCHNEIDER HAUS, KITCHENER (TOP); PIONEER TOWER

Doon Heritage Crossroads, a living museum where visitors walk through stores, shops, and homes, represents life in "busy Berlin" before its name was changed to Kitchener in 1914. Many original buildings were moved to the site, and include a smithy, general store, farmsteads, and homes where weavers, tailors, and spinners "live." The historic Freeport Church holds regular services at this large site on Homer Watson Boulevard in the southeast end of Kitchener (519-748-1914).

In 1886, the family of William Lyon Mackenzie King moved to what is now Woodside National Historic Park, near central Kitchener. Canada's tenth prime minister spent his boyhood in the comfortable, fourteen-room house, which was built in 1853. Now restored to represent life in 1891, its interpretive program and holiday celebrations make it a popular attraction for visitors (519-742-5273).

The Homer Watson House and Gallery, not far from Doon Heritage Crossroads, was the home of Homer Watson, Canada's first noted landscape painter. It displays works by Watson and by contemporary artists and has an extensive interpretive program (519-748-4377).

CENTRE IN THE SQUARE

Downtown Kitchener is a mixture of both old and new. Walking tours run year-round. Check with the Visitor and Convention Bureau for details (1-800-265-6959). Among the places you will want to see is the Kitchener Farmers' Market, which operates year-round with indoor and outdoor vendors.

Kitchener's award-winning city hall is the centre for festivals and celebrations. The acoustically perfect Centre in the Square, home of the Kitchener-Waterloo Symphony, has concerts, road shows, and entertainers for all tastes. Across its foyer is the Kitchener-Waterloo Art Gallery, whose exhibits change monthly. Right by downtown Kitchener is Victoria Park, with its restored clock tower, concert band pavilion, swans, and even a gondola ride.

For fun of a more physical variety, visit Sportsworld, a modern recreation park with indoor and outdoor driving ranges, batting cages, indoor rock climbing, miniature golf, and waterslides (519-653-4442). At Bingeman Park, there are loads of activities for children and adults—including waterslides, go karts, bumper boats, and more, plenty of camp sites, and a chance to sample Waterloo County food at its restaurant (519-744-1555).

WATERLOO

WATERLOO

WATERLOO

Kitchener's next door neighbour, Waterloo, is clearly a university city. As a small city that is home to thousands of students at two universities, the University of Waterloo and Wilfrid Laurier University (both on University Avenue), the community revels in concerts, theatre, and excellent bookstores. WLU's noted music program provides visitors with free, noon-hour faculty and student recitals at the Maureen Forrester Recital Hall, the Theatre Auditorium, and Keffer Memorial Chapel (519-884-1970).

UNIVERSITY OF WATERLOO

The University of Waterloo has three interesting gardens and four museums. A geological garden displays a collection of rocks representing the geology of Ontario, including jasper, gold, and amethyst. The Robert Starbird Dorney ecology garden features trees, shrubs, and wildflowers common to the Carolinian forest. A botanical garden includes a woodlot with a walking trail.

UW's Museum and Archive of Games is the only museum in the world dedicated to the study of games and game playing. In the Biology and Earth Sciences Museum, visitors can meet Albert and Perry (two completely cast dinosaur skeletons), plus many other fossils. The Visual Science and Optometry Museum displays antique optical instruments, spectacles, and stereoscopes. Brubacher House Museum is a restored 1850s Mennonite farmhouse.

UW is also the home of two performing arts theatres, with year-round performances by both students and

WATERLOO-ST. JACOBS RAILWAY

SHRINE OF THE SORROWFUL MOTHER, ST. AGATHA

professionals (519-885-1211).

Waterloo has two other performing arts theatres, near the uptown area. The Waterloo Stage Theatre was recently restored from its former incarnation as a movie house and features live theatre productions (519-745-8451). The Waterloo Community Arts Centre is also affectionately known as The Button Factory—the 1840 building's original purpose. Now restored and renovated, it features performances by talented local performance artists (519-886-4577).

The Canadian Clay and Glass Gallery, just a block from uptown, is Canada's first centre for works in clay, glass, stained glass, and enamel, all the work of twentieth-century Canadian artists. Its displays are visually stunning (519-746-1882).

Just behind the gallery is the Waterloo terminus of the Waterloo-St. Jacobs Railway. Running daily, Waterloo's first tourist train, the Fifties Streamliner, is restored to all its 1950s glory. It's a nostalgic way to travel to historical Mennonite country (519-746-1950).

At the Waterloo-Woolwich Township border, on

Highway 86 North, are two huge farmers' markets, the Waterloo Farmers' Market and the Waterloo County Farmers' Market. Everything you could want, from blueberries to blue jeans, can be found in these environs, open year-round (1-800-265-6959).

Leave Waterloo heading west on Erb's Road towards St. Agatha, and then follow a circular route that will take you through the communities of Wilmot, Wellesley, and Woolwich township, ending up in the Wellington County communities of Elora and Fergus.

ST. AGATHA

St. Agatha is perched on a hill; its church is on the brow of that hill and the steeple is a landmark for miles around. St. Agatha's Catholic cemetery is home to the Shrine of the Sorrowful Mother, a splendidly decorated Gothic shrine that is visited by thousands yearly. The religious pictures decorating the shrine's walls and ceiling were imported from Germany by Father Eugene Funcken, who constructed the edifice in 1857. Also impressive is the soaring St. Agatha Roman Catholic Church.

BADEN

Baden is a little village with a big Victorian mansion dominating its main street. Castle Kilbride is a National Historic Site. Built in 1877 by the town's leading citizen, James Livingston, the castle is Italianate in design and is capped by a belvedere from which visitors can see far into the countryside. Castle Kilbride's most stunning feature is its magnificent *trompe l'oeil* paintings, executed by H. Schasstein. The entrance-hall columns, the elaborate crown mouldings throughout the mansion, and the elaborately painted library are breathtaking (519-634-8444).

NEW HAMBURG

The town of New Hamburg is Wilmot Township's architectural treasure. It was founded in the early 1830s by German immigrants, who settled along the banks of the Nith River. Now a splendour of Victorian buildings, more than 60 per cent of its downtown buildings have been declared historically and architecturally significant. The town is a designated Heritage Conservation District.

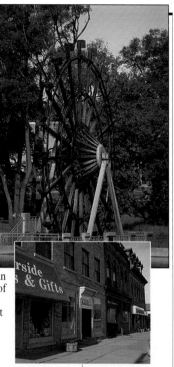

WATERWHEEL, NEW HAMBURG (TOP); NEW HAMBURG

New Hamburg's extensive waterfront park areas provide many scenic views, along with the company of swans and Canada geese. Among its tourist attractions is North America's largest operating water wheel, built in 1990 to commemorate the mills, which were New Hamburg's first industry.

New Hamburg is also home to the yearly Mennonite Relief Sale and Quilt Auction, held the last Saturday in May, and attracting thirty thousand or more visitors. Sponsored by the Mennonite Relief Committee, all proceeds support the Central Committee's relief efforts in countries in need.

Also in New Hamburg is the head office, and a large retail outlet, of Ten Thousand Villages. One of the Mennonite Central Committee's ongoing world-wide projects, Ten Thousand Villages imports and sells handcrafted gift items made by artisans in more than two dozen developing countries. All proceeds go directly back to the artisans and the co-operatives of which they are members. Ten Thousand Village stores can be found in many Waterloo Region and southwestern Ontario communities, including Elmira, St. Jacobs, Kitchener, Stratford, and Niagara-on-the-Lake.

WELLESLEY

One of the best ways to explore Wellesley Township is by following the Culture Trail, a sixty-mile journey deep into the heart of Mennonite country. Off the beaten tourist track, the trail leads to small villages where home-baked goods are readily available and traditional quilts can be bought directly from the homes of their makers. The trail is marked by signposts; group bus tours are also available (519-699-4611).

One intriguing stop along the trail is the country village of Wellesley, home of the annual Wellesley Apple Butter and Cheese Festival, which draws up to forty thousand people early in the fall. Noted for its private gardens, Wellesley has a fully restored carousel, a mill that has been in continual operation for nearly 150 years, and two splendid roadhouses: the Queen's Hotel, built in 1855 by the brothers of the village's founder, John Smith, and the Wellesley Inn (originally called the Royal Hotel), built in 1857.

ST. CLEMENTS

St. Clements was settled originally by Catholics from Alsace and Lorraine who wanted to preserve their faith and heritage. The residents built a stunningly beautiful church with a square bell tower. The interior carvings, paintings, and stained glass windows are magnificent. The attached cemetery has intriguing iron cross markers.

HAWKESVILLE

The hamlet of Hawkesville, although settled and still populated by more than a dozen different Mennonite groups,

ST. JACOBS

was the home in the 1860s to a significant number of blacks, successful travellers of the underground railway from the South during the U.S. Civil War. They held "Emancipation Day" meetings on Temperance Island. Hawkesville's 1850s architecture and its famous summer sausage, made locally, are worth stopping for.

ST. JACOBS

St. Jacobs nestles in a river valley, its buildings jammed with boutiques and its main street jammed with an odd assortment of upscale tourists in four-wheel-drives and Old Order Mennonites in one-horse buggies. This is a small village packed with things to do and see, one of the most popular tourist destinations in southwestern Ontario. Its farmers' market includes arts and crafts, a petting zoo, and a flea market. More than thirty manufacturers are represented at the St. Jacobs Factory Outlet Mall. Antique collectors will be delighted with the Waterloo County Antique Warehouse. The village is a quilter's, and quilt collector's, heaven. The village blacksmith has a steady

clientele of Mennonite farmers. The recently renovated Schoolhouse Theatre is home to stage shows and recitals throughout the year. For those who are interested in history, the Meetingplace, a museum and interpretive centre downtown, presents an accurate and respectful examination of this county's Mennonite heritage.

MENNONITE BUGGY

ELMIRA

Elmira has some of the ambience of St. Jacobs, but is much lower key. It was part of the original 1806 Pennsylvania Mennonite land purchase, which established Waterloo County. First-settler Edward Bristow arrived in 1834 and was faced with the arduous task of clearing the land of its native forest in order to till the rich soil, still vital to the region's local economy. First named Bristow's Corners, then West Woolwich, the settlement that grew from Bristow's original fifty-three-acre purchase adopted the name Elmira in 1853.

Elmira's famous Maple Syrup Festival, held in April, celebrates one of the early businesses in this enterprising community. Now boasting three factory outlets, plus a justifiably famous reputation for authentic Waterloo County food that "schmecks" (a uniquely Pennsylvania German term that means, roughly, "tastes tasty and just like it should"), Elmira offers fine examples of early settlement architecture. An especially interesting bit of local history is the town's bandstand. Built in 1912 from a design presented by the Elmira Musical Society, it was restored as Elmira's Canadian Centennial project in 1967 and is historically designated.

WEST MONTROSE

Just east of Elmira is the tiny hamlet of West Montrose, famed throughout the county for its "kissing" bridge, Ontario's sole remaining covered bridge to serve a public throughway. Built in 1881 and originally lit by gas lamps, it gained a reputation as one of the few places where "sparking" couples could steal a kiss in an environment otherwise closely monitored.

ELORA

Elora, a beautiful limestone village nestled along the Grand River, is justly famous for its spectacular Elora Gorge Park and the Elora Quarry. Each year, the Elora Music Festival sponsors concerts in the quarry, a natural amphitheatre.

FERGUS

GORGE PARK,
ELORA

Its main street shops and boutiques, which back directly onto the Grand River, are especially fine examples of the limestone architecture for which the area is known. Past the ruined mill are studios where artisans and craftspeople work and display their wares.

The Elora Mill Inn, a nineteenth-century grist mill overlooking the river, is a good place to enjoy a fine meal or while away a relaxing autumn weekend.

FERGUS

North of Elmira, in Wellington County, is Fergus, incorporated in 1857. Home of the internationally respected Fergus Highland Games, Fergus displays its Scottish heritage in the limestone buildings in its downtown. Among the most notable are the 1874 James McQueen building, the town's original post office; the Commercial Hotel Building, constructed in 1883; the 1862 St. Andrew Presbyterian Church; and Temperance Hall, built in 1852 by the Fergus Branch of the Sons of Temperance—the oldest building in downtown Fergus. All these buildings are on St. Andrew Street, which boasts many historical plaques.

The historic Fergus Market, housed in a century-old foundry, and the fascinating display at Richlyn Nurseries' botanical exhibition gardens, featuring traditional and historical British garden plants, are both worth a visit.

Theatre on the Grand is housed in a former 1920s movie theatre and has a full summer season of live stage plays (519-787-1981). Fergus also boasts North America's best brown trout fishing, as the avid fly fishermen (and women) who line the Grand River's banks during fishing season will attest.

ELORA MILL

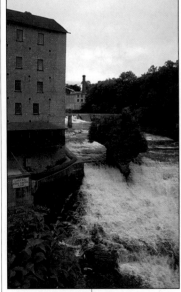

Between Fergus and Elora is the Wellington County Museum and Archives. Erected in 1877, the Wellington County House of Industry and Refuge provided shelter for the "deserving poor" for nearly a century. The building now houses an impressive collection of artifacts illustrating the history of Wellington County (519-846-0916).

The Kitchener-Waterloo area is one of southwestern Ontario's most popular regions—second only to the Niagara Peninsula. It has a wealth of sights, sounds, and events to reward visitors, particularly during the summer and fall months. Travellers to the area will have no trouble finding activities to fill a pleasant autumn weekend or even a week-long summer holiday.

STRATFORD AND AREA

KELLY DAYNARD

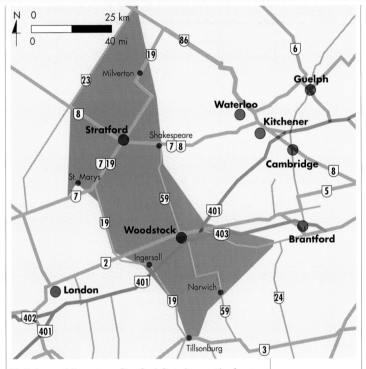

If all the world's a stage, Stratford Ontario must be front row, centre. Situated at the hub of southwestern Ontario, the Stratford area is a treasured discovery for any visitor— world-class theatre, exciting shopping, fine dining, scenic countryside, beautiful gardens, and historic museums.

The area features several communities of interest to visitors: Stratford, home of the world-renowned Stratford Shakespearean Festival; St. Marys, famous for its historic stone buildings; and Shakespeare, well known for its antique shops.

CAMELOT, **STRATFORD FESTIVAL**

STRATFORD

Located an hour and a half from Toronto and only slightly farther from Niagara Falls, and two and a half hours from Windsor, Stratford can easily be visited in a day, but that would be a mistake—its attractions will keep visitors entertained for a weekend or more.

The community was first known as

45

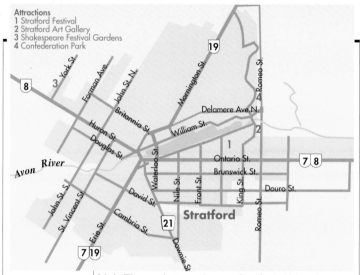

Attractions
1 Stratford Festival
2 Stratford Art Gallery
3 Shakespeare Festival Gardens
4 Confederation Park

Little Thames, but soon became Stratford. Although surveyed by the Canada Company in 1827, it was not settled for another four years; the first hotel was built in 1832, and saw mills and grist mills soon followed.

In 1854, the community reached village status, and two years later Stratford received the boost it needed when it became a railway town with the arrival of the Grand Trunk and Buffalo Lake Huron Railways. A year later, the first town hall was built, and by 1859 the settlement had grown so much that it was incorporated as a town. In keeping with its name, the town was divided into five wards named Avon, Falstaff, Hamlet, Romeo, and Shakespeare.

The railway continued to play a key factor in Stratford's development. In 1871, locomotive repair shops for the Grand Trunk Railway were moved to Stratford, substantially increasing the population. Stratford was incorporated as a city in 1885, and in 1889 another major expansion of the GTR repair shops led to a second influx of craftsmen. In the meantime, furniture manufacturing had also become one of the city's major industries.

By 1923, the railway was losing its popularity and the Grand Trunk Railway was amalgamated with the Canadian National Railways. In 1964, the CNR shops closed and other industries were introduced in an attempt to stabilize Stratford's economy.

PERTH COUNTY COURTHOUSE, STRATFORD

The community had carried the name of William Shakespeare's British birthplace since 1831, but it took more than a century for that connection to be culturally exploited. In July 1953, the Stratford Festival Theatre opened to the public with a performance by Sir Alec Guinness in the title role of Richard III. Critics assumed that the theatre would be a short-lived venture. After all, performances in those early years were held in a tent, and at the time Stratford was a farming community of less than twenty thousand.

The idea for the theatre was that of

FESTIVAL THEATRE, STRATFORD

Stratford native and journalist Tom Patterson, for whom the third stage has been named. After years of tireless promotion, Patterson finally convinced the rest of the world that there was indeed a future for theatre in Stratford. When the early success of the festival became apparent, local authorities knew that a permanent theatre was necessary. The giant canvas tent was dismantled for the final time at the end of the 1956 season and by January 1957, the current Festival Theatre was under construction.

Today, Stratford is North America's largest classical repertory theatre company, generating an estimated $125 million in goods and services annually. While the festival is best known for its performances of William Shakespeare's plays, it also offers productions of dramas by other playwrights.

Plays are now performed on three stages: the Festival Theatre, overlooking the Avon River, was renovated for the 1997 season, and the project saw the development of beautiful perennial gardens. The Avon Theatre has been a landmark in downtown Stratford since the turn of the century and part of the festival since 1963. Also on the Avon River is the Tom Patterson Theatre. Performances run from May through to November (1-800-567-1600).

AVON RIVER, STRATFORD

Of course, Stratford is much more than its famous theatre. Along the beautiful Avon River, there are plenty of picnicking areas. Both sides of the Avon feature walking paths. The Avon Boat Rentals, located below the Visitors' Information Centre in downtown Stratford, allows visitors the

opportunity to explore the river on their own, either by canoe or pedal boat (519-271-8681). There are also guided boat tours of the river.

In early spring, the official Parade of the Swans is a popular attraction, as the swans march from their winter quarters to the Avon River. The first pair of swans was introduced to Stratford parks in 1918; in 1954, Australian Black Swans were added. The swans are now among the most photographed birds on the continent. The collection includes White Mute Swans, Black Swans, and an assortment of white fronted geese, Canada geese, Chinese geese, and mallard ducks. In 1973, the city exchanged two white swans with Ottawa for two that are descendants of the Royal Swans given to Canada's capital city by Queen Elizabeth.

AUSTRALIAN BLACK SWAN

SHAKESPEAREAN GARDENS, STRATFORD

Stratford has one of the largest parks systems per capita in Canada. An amazing 17.5 per cent of the city's area consists of parkland, including Queen's Park and Confederation Park. The award-winning Shakespeare Festival Gardens feature more than twenty-seven thousand plants on beautifully manicured grounds. Nearby, the Shakespearean Gardens specializes in the more historic plants—herbs, roses, and English flowers, many of them referred to in Shakespeare's plays.

Confederation Park, next to the Gallery Stratford, has a waterfall, beautiful birch and evergreen trees, and extensive plantings of flowers.

Throughout the summer, Art in the Park in Stratford runs every Wednesday, Saturday, and Sunday, weather permitting. Meet the artists and craftspeople who display and sell their unique Canadian-made art and craft work along Lakeside Drive and Front Street.

STRATFORD

Jazz on the River is also a popular summertime attraction. Enjoy the sounds of the 1939 Casino Band and local musical groups as they travel Lake Victoria on the *HMS Raazzaamajazz.*

Visit Stratford's public art gallery on Romeo Street, only a short walk east of the Festival Theatre through Queen's Park. The gallery features exhibitions of Canadian art and is open early June to September.

Special walking tours through many private studios of Stratford artists also give art lovers the chance to meet local artists (519-273-7523).

Stratford boasts more than five hundred downtown shops and two indoor malls. Unique shops cover all districts of the city. Whether you are in the market for antiques, books, clothing, or original gifts, Stratford's shops can take visitors days to explore. Take a leisurely stroll through the city or consult the tourism offices for lists of stores and restaurants. Stratford boasts many fine dining establishments ranging from quaint "British-style" pubs and

cafes to elegant French cuisine. There are dozens of places to eat. Among the dining opportunities in the city are the Church Restaurant (elegant dining), Lindsay's (quiet and classy), Down The Street (adventurous cuisine and enthusiastic ambience), and Fellini's (fun Italian food).

STRATFORD

Accommodations may be found in small hotels, motels, and dozens of attractive, inviting bed and breakfasts. Many of the villages around Stratford also have thriving and interesting B&B establishments.

Free walking tours of Stratford's historical areas are led by trained guides during July and August. Walks begin at the Visitors' Information Centre on Mondays through Saturdays at 9:30 a.m. Special group walks can be arranged through Tourism Stratford (519-271-5140). The city features many beautiful Victorian homes and downtown stores. Highlights of the downtown core include Stratford's City Hall, constructed in 1900, and the majestic Perth County Courthouse opened to the public in 1887. While staying in Stratford, you might want to venture out of town on one of Perth County's Agri Tours. Stratford is surrounded by the county's rich farmland and visits to traditional and non-traditional farms can be set up by appointment. Farming is a big business in Perth County. Farmers have more than $1.5 billion invested in their operations. This investment pays off in yearly production in excess of $336 million, making the area the number one agricultural producer in all of Canada. For information about tours, call Tourism Stratford (1-800-561-7926).

ST. MARY'S TOWN HALL

Tourism Stratford is eager to help visitors plan their visit or guide them during their stay. Drop into the Information Centre on York Street or the main office at 88 Wellington Street. Pick up your free parking pass for the day. Discover racks of information on the area or call 1-800-561-SWAN.

ST. MARYS

Located only twenty minutes from Stratford at the junction of Highways 19 and 23, St. Marys is a beautiful country town featuring magnificent local architecture. Established in 1841, St. Marys became known as Stonetown for its many buildings constructed from limestone, all quarried locally.

Outstanding examples of the workmanship of early stonemasons can be seen on many buildings. The majestic Opera House is one of the most remarkable nineteenth-century stone buildings in Ontario. The neo-Gothic building was built by the local Oddfellows Lodge and opened in 1880. In its heyday, it staged featured performances by entertainers and travelling theatrical groups. Canada's first prime minister, Sir John A. Macdonald, made one of his last campaign speeches in the eight hundred seat theatre. The building was threatened with demolition in 1986 before it was transformed into eighteen apartments. The exterior of the building has been restored.

The town hall, constructed in 1891 at the heart of the community, is one of the most impressive of St. Marys' stone buildings; its bell tower is the town's best-known symbol. As well as being the headquarters for the local government, the town hall boasts a large auditorium, used by the local theatre group.

The water tower, built in 1899 at a cost of $40,000, was part of the town's first water system. In 1977, the local Public Utilities Commission spent many thousands of dollars repairing the stone structure, repointing the stone work, and refurbishing the interior. It is now painted with

TRAIN STATION, ST. MARYS

the proud slogan The Town Worth Living In.

Most of the downtown buildings are also stone. Some are made of smooth-faced stone while others contain a rough- or rock-faced variant. The old post office, now

ST. MARYS QUARRY

Damon's Restaurant, built in 1907, is a good example of the rough-faced stone-sided buildings.

Other buildings, while not as spectacular in appearance, still have intriguing histories. One was the site of Timothy Eaton's general store in the 1860s, before he established the Eaton's empire in Toronto. Another, the Creamery Restaurant, is situated in a beautifully restored old structure that was once the base of the community's dairy industry.

Complete walking tours featuring all of the unique "Stonetown buildings" are available at the community's tourist centre.

The railway station, located beside Trout Creek, is another heritage building worth seeing. The railway arrived in St. Marys in the late 1850s with Junction Station being built in 1858. A Save-the-Junction-Station campaign several years ago ensured that the station remains—probably the only one in the country from its era that still maintains many of its original features. The station is now also used as a tourist facility. Newspaper articles from the 1860s refer to the importance of the town as a shipment centre for grain and other goods.

In June 1998, St. Marys became home to the Canadian Baseball Hall of Fame and Museum, located on a plateau at the southern edge of town. Included in the first stages of this multi-million dollar project will be a ballpark stadium and a showplace for a large collection of artifacts.

WILDWOOD INN RESTAURANT, ST. MARYS

Near the Hall of Fame is the well-known Quarry, said to be Canada's largest natural swimming pool. The facility was a limestone quarry in the early 1900s but excavation opened up an underground spring and it was eventually filled with water. It was developed into a town-operated swimming facility in the 1940s and now features a well-maintained park, beach volleyball, washroom and change room facilities, and is staffed throughout the summer by qualified lifeguards. It is also adjacent to the town's tennis courts and Centennial Park. The Quarry opens to the public on the first weekend of June and closes on Labour Day.

The St. Marys Museum, located in one of the community's oldest limestone houses, offers exhibits, programs, and an archival collection of photographs, local newspapers, maps, and genealogical files. The home is so impressive that it has been nicknamed "the Castle in the Bush." Adjacent buildings house a collection of farm implements and even some early forms of transportation including a 1902 Baker Electric car and a 1913 motorcycle.

St. Marys offers more than forty-five acres of beautiful parks along the Thames River, excellent recreational facilities, and a variety of good restaurants—from casual to formal.

The St. Marys community also offers three first-class golf courses including the St. Marys Golf and Country

Club, the Science Hill Golf Course, and the River Valley Golf and Country Club.

For hikers, the Avon Trail runs for one hundred kilometres from St. Marys to Conestogo in Waterloo Region. The hiking trail links the Thames Valley Trail and the Grand Valley Trail and membership is open to anyone willing to abide by the Trail User's Code.

McCully's Hill Farm, located just outside St. Marys, features fresh produce, wagon rides, mixed livestock, maple production, and farm forestry. Tours are available year-round by appointment. The market is open in March and April and late July through Halloween.

For information about St. Marys, visit the community's tourist office (519-284-3500).

SHAKESPEARE

TWO VIEWS OF SHAKESPEARE

Once or twice a year, the rumour will go around that a major celebrity has come to Shakespeare to shop for antiques. Almost invariably, the rumour will be true. The picturesque little town of Shakespeare has come to mean "antiques" to discriminating buyers all over North America.

Located ten minutes east of Stratford, on Highways 7&8, Shakespeare is filled with antique and craft shops. The hamlet, home to only 750 people, has more antique shops per square mile than any other place in the province.

Antique hunters will find everything from museum-quality pieces to affordable collectables. And those who love country crafts, collectables, and quilts will also enjoy Shakespeare's small-town hospitality. Shops feature everything from fine furniture, ladies' wear, and original art, to fresh produce. The village also features a tea room (with an authentic English Cream Tea), a hotel, and several bed and breakfasts.

Stratford and the nearby towns of St. Marys and Shakespeare are pleasant destinations for a weekend getaway, particularly from May to November when the theatre festival is operating. Visitors can enjoy dinner and a play one evening, stay overnight in one of the many hotels or small establishments in Stratford, and then spend the next day exploring the area's sights and shops.

LONDON AND AREA

ELLEN ASHTON-HAISTE

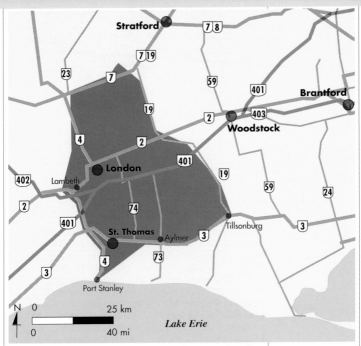

Stratford 7 8
7 19
23 7
59
19 401 Brantford
4 2 2 403
Woodstock
London 401
402 Lambeth 19
2 59 24
74
401 3
St. Thomas Aylmer 3 Tillsonburg 3
73
3 4
Port Stanley

N 0 25 km

0 40 mi

Lake Erie

The London area is the heartland of southwestern Ontario. Located almost exactly halfway between Toronto and Windsor, the city of London dominates a geographic district that includes large stretches of the coastline of Lakes Huron and Erie.

The district was settled by European pioneers in the early decades of the nineteenth century; it was part of the Talbot settlement, developed under the leadership of Colonel Thomas Talbot. London was named for the capital of England; not coincidentally, it is on the Thames River. St. Thomas was Talbot's patron saint.

The London area was largely exempt from the historical conflicts in the first decades of the nineteenth century along the Canada–U.S. border. Rather than playing a military role in the history of the district, the area is important for its role in education (the University of Western Ontario in London is well respected), in transportation (St. Thomas was a key railway city, and Port Stanley an important Lake Erie port), and in business and industry.

SPRINGBANK PARK, LONDON

LONDON

In London, it's easy being green. The "Forest City" certainly has its share of

53

London

Fanshawe Lake

Fanshawe Park Rd

Thames River

Oxford St.

Dundas St.

York St. / Florence St.

Southdale Rd.

Wharncliffe Rd.

Attractions
1 Guy Lombardo Museum
2 Banting House Museum
3 Fanshawe Pioneer Village
4 Eldon House
5 London's Museum of Archaeology
6 London Regional Children's Museum
7 St. Paul's Cathedral
8 St. Peter's Cathedral
9 Grand Theatre
10 University of Western Ontario

trees—more than 160,000 of them on public property alone—along its streets and in thousands of acres of parkland and green space. This wealth of greenery makes Canada's eleventh largest metropolis appear smaller than its 2,105 square kilometres and population of 326,000.

The city's commitment to history is apparent. Well known as the home town of big-band king Guy Lombardo, London offers a documentary of the band leader's life and a wealth of big-band era memorabilia at the Guy Lombardo Museum (519-473-9003), right next to nostalgic Wonderland Gardens, one of the few remaining dance pavilions from the 1930s (519-471-6320).

Also known as the place where Sir Frederick Banting (1891–1941) discovered insulin, London is home to the Banting House Museum, where the Queen Mother lit an eternal flame during her 1989 visit. The flame will burn until a cure for diabetes is found. Inside, the museum includes the fully furnished office where Banting lived and worked when he made his life-saving discovery, paintings by the scientist, who was also an artist, and other exhibits depicting Banting's life and times (519-673-1752).

Fanshawe Pioneer Village presents a glimpse into early Ontario life with more than two dozen restored homes and businesses. Costumed interpreters guide visitors through life as their ancestors experienced it. The village is located in Fanshawe Conservation Area, which features a large lake and a modern campground, in the northeast corner of the city (519-457-1296).

FANSHAWE PIONEER VILLAGE, LONDON

Eldon House on Ridout Street is operated by the London Regional Art and Historical Museums. It's the city's oldest surviving private dwelling and offers a glimpse of lifestyles circa 1834, and frequent special programs (519-661-5169).

Harking back to earlier times,

London's Museum of Indian Archeology, in the northwest of the city, offers tours of on-site excavations of a fifteenth-century Neutral Indian village with its longhouse, palisade, and gardens. As well, a gallery traces the eleven-thousand-year history of native peoples in Canada (519-473-1360).

Future generations are not forgotten. The London Regional Children's Museum offers hands-on exhibits exploring the past, present, and future of culture and science. Here, kids can dig for dinosaurs, crawl through caves, or experience a journey to the stars. Gallery themes include the Inuit, "Science in Your World," and "Child Long Ago" (519-434-5726).

A tour of the downtown area highlights local history in the architecture of many of the buildings. The Middlesex County courthouse in the heart of the city is said to emulate Malahide Castle, the Irish ancestral home of the area's founder, Col. Thomas Talbot.

ST. PETER'S CATHEDRAL, LONDON

But nowhere is the historic element more evident than in the religious centres of London's core. St. Paul's Cathedral, on Richmond Street, is a Gothic Revival-style structure erected in 1846 and extended twice during the second half of the nineteenth century. The church, which became the cathedral of the Huron Diocese in 1857, has two Tiffany stained-glass windows.

St. Peter's Cathedral, completed in the late 1880s, is built in the thirteenth-century French Gothic style favoured by Ontario Roman Catholic churches in the late nineteenth century. Notable is the rose window imported from Innsbruck, Austria.

The downtown Grand Theatre, rebuilt in 1901 to replace the Grand Opera House which was destroyed by fire, boasts its own resident ghost, a nod to things past that has survived several renovations.

GRAND THEATRE

CRONYN OBSERVATORY

The Grand is now known as one of the leading professional theatres in the country. It presents a main-stage playbill of six or seven productions in the full range of drama and comedy from September through May, with alternative productions and theatre for young audiences presented at the McManus Theatre (1-800-265-1593).

London is also home to the historic University of Western Ontario, noted for its stone buildings, in the north end of the city. The parklike campus is a lovely place for a

stroll (accessed from Richmond Street). The university campus plays an important cultural role, especially at Talbot Theatre (519-661-3391).

ST. THOMAS

St. Thomas, in neighbouring Elgin County, was one of the key centres along the Talbot Road, an important pioneer roadway from Long Point to Detroit built by Colonel Thomas Talbot. Talbot County was first settled between 1814 and 1837. The Talbot Road is signposted today as one of Ontario's "Heritage Highways."

St. Thomas is a typical small southwestern Ontario city: pleasant for its residents, but with no long menu of attractions to offer visitors. Perhaps the oddest thing about the city is its obsession with a long-dead elephant! The first thing most visitors to this municipality see is a larger-than-life-size replica of P.T. Barnum's star elephant, Jumbo. Erected in 1985, the statue commemorates the hundredth anniversary of Jumbo's death in St. Thomas when the pachyderm was hit by a Grand Trunk locomotive while being led along the tracks by his trainer.

ST. THOMAS (TOP); JUMBO

Jumbo stands at the apex of the city's historic district, anchored by pioneer and military museums and the Old English Church and cemetery. These sites are among the few that have survived from the early days of the Talbot Settlement. Between them are several heritage homes that may be examined on a self-guided walking tour. This area is home to the Elgin County Pioneer Museum (519-631-6537), with three pioneer buildings and room vignettes.

Perhaps Jumbo's departure by rail was pre-ordained: St. Thomas thrived as a railway terminus in the early days of the century and efforts are being made to preserve that heritage with a railway museum, in the planning stages, and various themed events.

Those efforts have already paid off in the revival of the L&PS (London and Port Stanley) Railroad, which once carried commuters daily between London and St. Thomas and the Lake Erie village of Port Stanley, sixteen kilometres south. Now a tourist train, it carries passengers to Port Stanley through the lush farmland of the Kettle Creek valley.

SPARTA

SPARTA

The valley produces mixed farms, orchards, and even a winery, Quai du Vin, near the village of Sparta, about halfway between St. Thomas and Port Stanley and slightly east. An early nineteenth-century Quaker village,

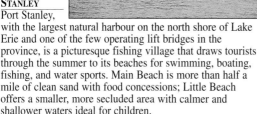

Sparta resembles a living museum with several preserved buildings that house antique shops, tea rooms, and the studio of artist Peter Robson.

PORT STANLEY

Port Stanley, with the largest natural harbour on the north shore of Lake Erie and one of the few operating lift bridges in the province, is a picturesque fishing village that draws tourists through the summer to its beaches for swimming, boating, fishing, and water sports. Main Beach is more than half a mile of clean sand with food concessions; Little Beach offers a smaller, more secluded area with calmer and shallower waters ideal for children.

HARBOUR, PORT STANLEY

Special events here include the Port Stanley Fish Fest on Victoria Day weekend, and the Port Stanley Hawk Festival in September. The Port Stanley Festival Theatre offers light summertime drama from June through August.

The village is home to a host of boutiques, art galleries, and eateries, many of them along Main and Bridge Streets.

Shops especially worth a visit include the antique boutiques on Main Street (especially the large and well-stocked Harbour House Antiques & Uniques), Darbyshire House, with a large selection of bears, and Kettle Creek Clothing Co. As well, there are five art galleries in the village, more than half a dozen clothing shops, and plenty of gift shops.

BEACH, PORT STANLEY

Port Stanley is also the home of Moore Water Gardens, a retail garden centre specializing in water plants, with beautiful display gardens, and Floridel, specializing in orchids. Both gardens have gained national recognition for their exotic tropical and aquatic plants and elaborate fountains.

Fine dining is available at the Kettle Creek Inn; for something exotic, try the San Saba Cafe; and for a great view of the harbour, dine or quench your thirst at the Wharf Restaurant and Bars.

London and the surrounding area offers visitors many attractions and sites to explore. While the area is not as richly diverse as some of the others in southwestern Ontario, London is an attractive and appealing small city and Port Stanley, in particular, a pleasant destination for visitors looking for a place to while away a summer's afternoon.

LAKE ERIE SHORELINE

ANITA HANSON

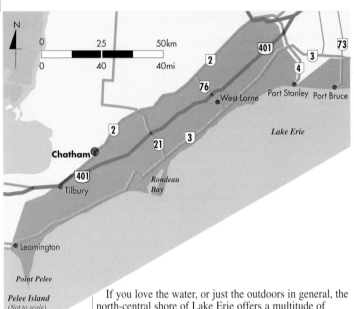

If you love the water, or just the outdoors in general, the north-central shore of Lake Erie offers a multitude of pleasures.

From Port Dover to Port Bruce, beautiful, sandy beaches abound along the shoreline, some of them large and open to the public, others tiny and secluded. This is a swimmer's paradise—the water is clear and clean, the bottom sandy. And Lake Erie has another major advantage for swimmers—since it is a shallow, southern lake, it heats up more quickly and reaches higher temperatures than many of Canada's deeper and more northerly lakes.

Not a swimmer? Perhaps you'd like to try boating instead. Some of the best boating in the province can be found here. Long Point, a sandy peninsula extending thirty-two kilometres south from the village of the same name, provides a natural windbreak for the bay it creates, keeping wind and waves under control. Pop into the little fishing villages and tie up for a look around; find an appealing beach and lower the anchor for the afternoon; find out where the fish are running and throw in a line; or get more physical and try out the water skis. It can all be done here.

PIER, PORT DOVER

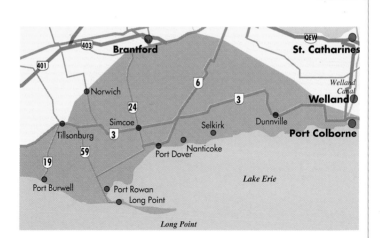

PORT DOVER

Port Dover makes an excellent first stop, with a little bit of everything to offer—shopping, with an emphasis on beachwear and nautical gifts, restaurants serving up famous Lake Erie perch, a museum, and even a summer theatre series.

TURKEY POINT

Turkey Point has one of the best beaches on the lake, and plenty of beach lovers to go with it—every weekend is a party. This stretch of shoreline boasts some of the province's most beautiful provincial parks, including Turkey Point (unusual in that it has its own golf course), Long Point, Port Burwell (famous for its springtime song birds), and Port Bruce (day use only). Forest, beach, hiking, swimming—whatever your preference, one of these parks will give you what you're after. Reservations are generally recommended. To obtain a park guide, or for more information, call 1-800-667-1940.

PORT ROWAN

Port Rowan, home of the annual Tomato Fest, serves as an example of a true Ontario small town—don't expect anything trendy or "touristy" here.

For a lesson in history dating back two centuries, check out the Backus Conservation Area just north of Port Rowan, where you'll find twenty historic buildings lovingly restored, including the John Backhouse Mill from 1798. John Backhouse, a pioneer in the area, was a miller, a

MILL, BACKUS HERITAGE VILLAGE, PORT ROWAN

LONG POINT

businessman, and, unusual for his time, a conservationist. The buildings on-site include a rare octagonal schoolhouse from 1866, barns, and outbuildings that contain vast collections of antique farm tools and implements, and the restored Backus farmhouse, furnished to the era.

Backus also comprises an arboretum, a lake for fishing, picnic and camping facilities, and 650 acres of Canada's largest remaining Carolinian forest, which includes many examples of unique plant and animal life that exist here because of the moderate microclimate. In Canadian Carolinian forests, these exotic flora and fauna (from the Louisiana Waterthrush to Tulip trees) co-exist with more common Canadian plants, animals, and birds. Other rare trees found here include sassafras, hickory, sycamore, and even Kentucky Coffee trees and Cucumber trees.

MONARCHS, LONG POINT PROVINCIAL PARK

LONG POINT

The most significant feature in the area is the unique Long Point World Biosphere Reserve, a twenty-seven-thousand-hectare expanse of land and water surrounding Long Point, designated a Biosphere Reserve in 1986, thus joining other unique world environments such as the Everglades, the Serengeti, and the Galapagos Islands.

The point itself is the largest and finest example of sand spit and dune formation in the Great Lakes, home to an impressive array of distinctive flora and fauna in and around its pools, creeks, and marshes. More than seven hundred species of plants have been recorded, ninety of which are rarely found in Ontario, and four of which are found nowhere else in Canada. This is an important feeding area for many species of migratory birds, and about a hundred species breed here. The marshes provide a spawning ground for many of Lake Erie's fish, and a large variety of Canada's reptiles and amphibians make their home here.

Although this is protected territory, designated for the purpose of preservation and study rather than tourism, wildfowling, sport fishing,

BEACH, PORT BURWELL

canoeing, walking, and wildlife viewing are permitted in most of the "buffer area" outside the central core. The "zone of cooperation" outside the buffer area includes developed areas such as the villages of Long Point and Turkey Point and all the amenities they provide. There are also Wildlife Area Officers on regular duty at the Big Creek National Wildlife Area Headquarters at the base of the point.

Tragic marine history abounds in the waters around Long Point, "the graveyard of the Great Lakes," providing a utopia for modern-day divers. An estimated two hundred wrecks lie in the sand beneath the surface, most from the nineteenth century, before a lighthouse was built at the end of the point. And yes, there are stories of buried treasure.

This part of southwestern Ontario is important for its history, as well as its geography. Archaeological digs have shown that the shores were settled by the Iroquois, with traces of villages dating from 700 A.D. Artifacts dating from as long as five thousand years ago have been discovered.

SAND HILLS PARK, PORT BURWELL

PORT BURWELL

Further west, you will encounter the famous Sand Hills Park, a privately operated park featuring towering sand dunes overlooking the beach. Next comes a stop at Port Burwell for a look at Canada's oldest wooden lighthouse (built in 1840), rising seventy-five feet and now housing the tourist information centre.

Whatever your outdoor tastes, and whether you come for a day, a weekend, or an entire summer holiday, Long Point and its neighbours will never allow you to run out of things to see and do.

WINDSOR AND AREA

SUE BAILEY

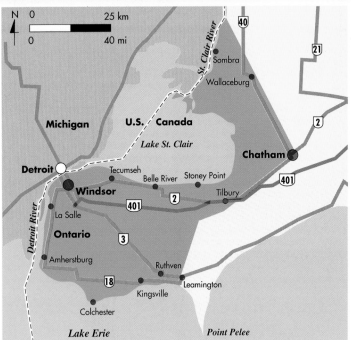

Windsor may be best known as Canada's automotive capital, but it also offers a wide range of cosmopolitan attractions on the doorstep of America's ninth-largest metropolis. The bustling city of 200,000, along with Amherstburg, Point Pelee, and Pelee Island are among the highlights of the nation's southland—a sprawling peninsula and island on Lake Erie with excellent fishing, boating, nature walks, and birding. The balmy climate means hot summers and mild winters, creating ideal conditions for a bounty of fruits, vegetables, and some of Canada's most celebrated wines.

WINDSOR

WINDSOR

For those with a taste for city life, Windsor is famous for introducing Ontario to casino gaming and boasts an impressive array of cafes, restaurants, theatres, shops, and night life.

The ribbon of road tracing the Detroit River east and west is Riverside Drive, home to the new, $505-million Casino Windsor at the corner of McDougall Street. It's

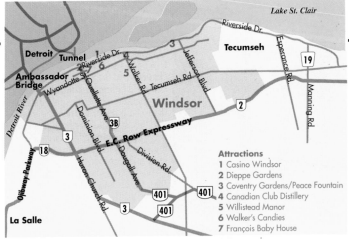

Lake St. Clair

Detroit — Tunnel

Ambassador Bridge

Tecumseh

Windsor

E.C. Row Expressway

La Salle

Attractions
1 Casino Windsor
2 Dieppe Gardens
3 Coventry Gardens/Peace Fountain
4 Canadian Club Distillery
5 Willistead Manor
6 Walker's Candies
7 François Baby House

impossible to miss the glittering white and blue building from almost anywhere on the downtown waterfront.

No expense was spared to make it one of Ontario's premier tourist attractions. Aquatic themes flow throughout the dramatic interior, which features an eighteen-metre waterfall, connecting streams and ponds, a Mediterranean indoor garden, and a rotunda soaring twenty-three metres high and thirty-six metres across. There are nine thousand square metres of gaming space on two floors, including 2,770 slot machines and 136 gaming tables. Fine dining and more casual restaurants and bars are also found throughout the complex, which is attached to a four-hundred-room hotel.

Casino Windsor is worth a peek regardless of whether you try your luck, and many other points of interest abound in Canada's Motor City.

More than eight million people visit the region each year and many are surprised to learn they must look north to see the United States. (Windsor is that far south!) Newcomers also gape when they drive north into the city for the first time along Ouellette Avenue and mistake Detroit's skyscrapers for downtown Windsor. The optical illusion fools many, but Motown's looming buildings are just across the scenic Detroit River—one of the world's busiest international waterways.

AMBASSADOR BRIDGE, WINDSOR (TOP); PEACE FOUNTAIN

Windsor's spectacular waterfront is a good place to start your visit. It illustrates why the city is renowned for vast stretches of unspoiled riverfront and rambling inland parks.

Dieppe Gardens, at the foot of downtown Windsor, is an immaculate collection of blazing colours in summer and fall, featuring a great view of the Detroit skyline. The gardens were named to honour hundreds of Essex Scottish Regiment members killed while attempting to land in Dieppe, France, in 1942, and are home to several memorials. Ambassador and Assumption Parks run west along the river to the Ambassador Bridge—the world's longest international suspension bridge—offering closeup views of giant freighters and numerous pleasure craft.

JACKSON PARK, WINDSOR

Head several miles east along Riverside Drive to see Coventry Gardens and the Peace Fountain. The latter is a computer-controlled, twenty-one-metre fountain blasting sixty-eight thousand litres of water per minute into the air while vibrant lights cast patterns changing every twenty-four minutes. It's in action from late May until mid-October.

Just outside the city centre, Jackson Park shows why Windsor is also known as the City of Roses. It's a fragrant wonder in bloom, with dozens of varieties growing in gardens around a vintage Second World War Lancaster Bomber.

In addition to its physical beauty, Windsor has a rich heritage. The historic Canadian Club Distillery—home of Hiram Walker & Sons Ltd., makers of Canadian Club whiskey—is found on Riverside Drive East at Walker Road. The distillery dates back to 1858 and tours are available all year. You can see and hear how the liquid gold is made, while learning about the founding of one of Windsor's most successful enterprises (519-254-5171).

A short distance south, Willistead Manor and Walker's Fine Candies also recall times past. The Tudor–Jacobean manor, built between 1904 and 1906, showcases thirty-six rooms including an elaborate drawing room, white marble fireplace, ornate staircase, and many other elegant features (519-253-2019).

WILLISTEAD MANOR

Its manicured grounds host a popular outdoor craft show each spring, and the Willistead Classic and Antique Car Show is held there in August (519-253-2365).

Your sweet tooth can be soothed the old-fashioned way at Walker's Candies, where tradition is as much a part of the candy-making process as sugar. Enjoy the enticing aromas as rich chocolates and other treats are finished by hand. The cravings sure to follow can be satisfied at a store located on-site.

Before leaving the downtown area visit François Baby House, built in 1812 by François Baby, a member of the Upper Canada Assembly. The house, which almost immediately upon construction served as headquarters to General William Hull during the 1812 invasion by the Americans, offers exhibits and programs to answer your questions on local history (519-253-1812). And for an original keepsake, try Ontario's only Wood Carving Museum at the Windsor Public Library on Ouellette Avenue. The museum is open Tuesday to Saturday all year and group tours are by appointment (519-977-0823).

You can explore downtown Windsor on foot or by car, bus, taxi, limousine, or bicycle, but Carriages To You also offers tours by horse-drawn buggy. Pickup can be arranged from May to September across from the Windsor–Detroit Tunnel exit (519-252-8449). Pride of Windsor Cruises run during the spring, summer, and early fall for sightseeing tours on the water. Trips begin at Dieppe Gardens and sunset dinner cruises can be arranged in advance (1-800-706-2607).

Windsor features many options for shoppers, including the boutiques along Ouellette Avenue and Ottawa Street, and Devonshire Mall (also home to the Art Gallery of Windsor, 519-969-4494) on Howard Avenue. There are scores of good restaurants, as well. Some stand-outs include Alabazam Tap & Watery (New Orleans cuisine) on Ottawa Street, Il Gabbiano (classic Italian) on Erie Street, The Mini (authentic Vietnamese) on University Avenue, and the Windsor Hilton Park Terrace restaurant (fine dining) on Riverside Drive West. Reservations are recommended.

Hot night spots include the Aardvark Blues Cafe, Patrick O'Ryan's Irish Pub, and the Amsterdam Lounge, all located in the heart of downtown.

Detroit is easily accessed using the Ambassador Bridge or the Windsor–Detroit Tunnel, but citizenship documents must be available for border officials. It's also important to have clear directions because some areas of Detroit can be dangerous. Carry a cell phone.

AMHERSTBURG

Back on the Canadian side, follow Highway 18 to leave Windsor for historic Amherstburg. Wine Route signs along the way lead to local vintners offering tours year-round.

Amherstburg was one of the first southwestern Ontario communities to be settled by European pioneers, with some of the earliest settlers arriving before 1800. Some houses from that earliest era are preserved. The community was also an important terminus for the Underground Railway, which brought former slaves to freedom in Canada.

Today, this town on the Detroit River features a parkland waterfront, and lots of historic ambience.

Visitors should explore the spartan digs of the nineteenth-century soldiers at Fort Malden National Historic Park, an eleven-acre strategic military site built beside the Detroit River in 1796. It was used during the War of 1812 and the Rebellion of 1837, and features restored living quarters, exhibits, and demonstrations. On-site is Park House, an early Amherstburg home and now a museum (519-736-5416).

FORT MALDEN, AMHERSTBURG

A short distance away is the Gordon House, Amherstburg's oldest original building. The refurbished

home was built in 1798 and offers a great view of the Detroit River and a display of the town's marine history (519-736-1133). And at the North American Black Historical Museum, learn about the Underground Railroad (519-736-5433).

Farther south along Highway 18 you will find Colasanti's Tropical Gardens—a 1.4 hectare indoor wonderland of plants, flowers, cacti, and crafts. There are also a petting zoo and restaurant.

PELEE ISLAND

POINT PELEE/PELEE ISLAND

Follow Highway 18 or take scenic country roads for a shortcut to Point Pelee National Park. The Visitor Centre is open all year to help newcomers enjoy the birding, nature walks, canoeing, and hiking that have made the area famous (519-322-2365).

To top off your visit to Canada's southland, catch the ferry from nearby Leamington or Kingsville to Pelee Island, the nation's most southerly settlement. This patchwork of earth and greenery in Lake Erie is just fourteen and a half kilometres long and five and a half kilometres wide. Visitors often choose to travel by bicycle only during their stay (bikes can be rented on the island).

The island, one of southwestern Ontario's three wine-producing areas, is well known for its wines (red-wine lovers should be sure to sample the award-winning Pelee Island Pinot Noir, with the characteristics of the full-bodied red wine of Burgundy; white-wine drinkers will enjoy Pelee Island Gerwurtztraminer, the Canadian version of the famed Alsace wine). You'll want to visit the Wine Pavilion (519-724-2469).

The Island boasts spectacular beaches, nature trails, and marina facilities. Bird watchers will love Pelee Island: top-rated places for birding including Lighthouse Point, Fish Point Nature Reserve, and Stone Road Alvar, a prairie-like nature preserve. Pelee Island Festival of Birds is a month-long affair from the end of April through late May.

The island offers a number of dining options, including

Gooseberry's, at the hundred-year-old Victorian Tin Goose Inn, which also offers elegant accommodations at reasonable prices, and the Island Restaurant at the Anchor & Wheel Inn (a bed and breakfast). Accommodations on the island range from camping to luxury suites with jacuzzis.

The most southwesterly part of Ontario is a picturesque destination to visit. Windsor is a

THE VINTAGE GOOSE, KINGSVILLE

small, gracious city with a variety of attractions for the visitor while Amherstburg, Point Pelee, and Pelee Island all have their own distinctive charm.

LAKE HURON AND GEORGIAN BAY

PAUL KNOWLES

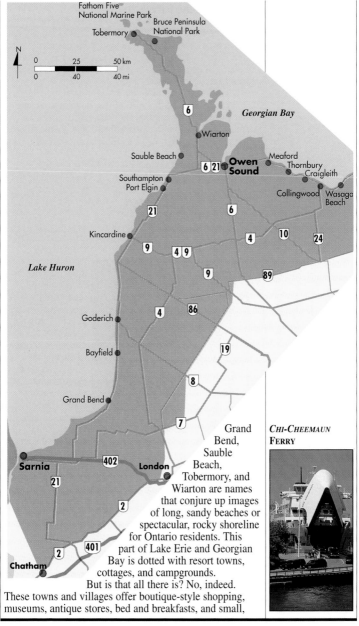

CHI-CHEEMAUN FERRY

Grand Bend, Sauble Beach, Tobermory, and Wiarton are names that conjure up images of long, sandy beaches or spectacular, rocky shoreline for Ontario residents. This part of Lake Erie and Georgian Bay is dotted with resort towns, cottages, and campgrounds. But is that all there is? No, indeed. These towns and villages offer boutique-style shopping, museums, antique stores, bed and breakfasts, and small,

BRUCE PENINSULA

comfortable hotels. This is one of the most scenic regions of southwestern Ontario, from the sunsets on the water at Goderich to the cliffs and caves north of Owen Sound.

It is here that southwestern Ontario meets the north, as the traveller ventures up the Bruce Peninsula toward Tobermory. And although thousands flock to this popular area every summer, the sheer size of the region minimizes the crowds. With the exception of a few beaches like Grand Bend and Sauble Beach, where people go because they like crowds and plenty of action, long stretches of the shoreline are peaceful and uncrowded.

The trip from Grand Bend to Owen Sound, on Highway 21, covers about 175 kilometres if you travel north from Grand Bend to Southampton, and then east to Owen Sound. It can be more than twice that if you choose to continue north on Highway 6 to Tobermory and then meander back to Owen Sound.

Of course, almost no one goes to Tobermory in the summer without catching a ride on the *Chi-cheemaun*, the car and passenger ferry that makes the one hour, forty-five minute trip to Manitoulin Island.

GRAND BEND

BEACH, GRAND BEND

Grand Bend, known for its beautiful beach, has long been a popular day-trip destination for southwestern Ontario

residents, attracting visitors of all ages, but recognized as a mecca for young people. Easily accessible from almost anywhere in the region, it offers everything a summertime visitor could want—fine beaches, ample camping and accommodation, and plenty of shops, entertainment venues, and night life. Tens of thousands of visitors come to Grand Bend every weekend in the summer. Most hit the beaches, or browse in the shops, but others discover the wider variety of entertainment, from golf to horseback riding to skydiving at the Grand Bend Sport Parachuting Centre (519-238-2001).

SHOPPING IN BAYFIELD

Theatre-lovers will enjoy the Huron Country Playhouse, three kilometres east of Grand Bend, which runs from early June through August, with more than half a dozen plays and a concert series presented in two playhouses (1-800-706-6665).

Just south of "the Bend" is the

outstanding Pinery Provincial Park, one of the most popular provincial parks in Ontario, with a ten-kilometre beach, a thousand campsites, and a variety of nature-oriented programs (519-243-2220).

Near the Pinery is the Lambton Heritage Museum, which traces the natural and human history of the region. The wooded area is home to galleries and restored historic buildings including a chapel, a pioneer log cabin, a blacksmith shop, and a school house. The main gallery has Canada's finest exhibit of pressed glass (519-243-2600).

BAYFIELD

North of Grand Bend on Highway 21 is the picturesque village of Bayfield, an upscale tourist destination. Bayfield offers a fine variety of accommodations, including the acclaimed Little Inn of Bayfield, in operation since 1832. Unlike many Ontario small towns, Bayfield's main street is tucked away behind the highway and ends at a bank leading down to the lake, making it quieter than most. This wide, tree-lined street boasts unique and historic storefronts.

GODERICH

There are dozens of boutiques and shops, including some fine antique stores, clothing stores, toy shops, and bakery/cafes. Gammages of Bayfield, a shop on the main street, has elegant garden and home statuary and planters. Many restaurants have patios, excellent for people-watching. Bayfield is also home to four beaches, as well as two marinas, and a number of businesses catering to boaters (519-565-2021).

GODERICH

Goderich is a delightful, heritage-minded town, from the eight-sided downtown square to the harbourfront views of Lake Huron. It claims the title "prettiest town in Canada," which is partly attributable to its tree-lined streets and historical residences. The community sits on a bluff overlooking the lake, and the sunsets there are beautiful. According to National Geographic, this is "the best sunset-viewing spot in North America." The town's harbour is the only seaway-depth harbour on the east side of Lake Huron, and thus is visited by hundreds of huge ocean vessels that sail the

HURON COUNTY HISTORICAL GAOL

Great Lakes from Thunder Bay in the west to the mouth of the St. Lawrence. Visitors enjoy watching the tugboats manoeuvre the giant lakers and ocean freighters into harbour.

Goderich also has three public beaches (with swimming, windsurfing, and sailing), all connected by an old-fashioned boardwalk.

Downtown Goderich is constructed on an eight-sided "square," with

Point Clark Lighthouse, Kincardine

dozens of shops, including quaint gift boutiques and craft stores, surrounding the grand courthouse. And just off the square on West St. stands Culbert's, a 121-year-old bakery offering the world's best cream puffs and other delights. (519-524-6600).

Historic highlights are well presented at the Huron County Museum and the Huron Historic Gaol. The Museum is impressive, with twenty-thousand square feet of exhibition space, far more than one would expect in a community of this size. Its History Hall includes a number of authentic storefronts from the late 1800s, and a steam locomotive. Other exhibits focus on military history, agriculture, and fully furnished rooms of antique furniture (519-524-2686). A tour of the gaol, a national historic site, guarantees the visitor a chilling glimpse into penal servitude from 1842 on; the attached Governor's House is restored, furnished, and open to visitors (519-524-6971).

A few miles inland is the unique Benmiller Inn, where accommodations, a restaurant, recreation facilities, and conference rooms are housed in five restored pioneer mills and millers' homes (1-800-265-1711).

KINCARDINE

Kincardine was founded in the 1850s, and the town has proudly preserved the architectural evidence of its Scottish heritage. Guided walking tours take visitors to the historic homes and other buildings. One treasured landmark is the Point Clark Lighthouse, built in 1881.

Like its Lake Huron shoreline neighbours, the town of Kincardine offers a beach, fishing charters, and other fun on and in the water. Of special note is the opportunity to dive to a large number of wrecks only a short distance

Southampton

offshore (519-396-2731). The trip north from Kincardine carries the traveller to other beautiful beach areas, including MacGregor Point Provincial Park, and Port Elgin (1-800-387-3456). For something completely different, the nearby Bruce Nuclear Power Development offers tours and has a visitors' centre.

SOUTHAMPTON

Southampton bills itself as "the oldest port on the Bruce Coast," and it is clear that the waterfront is the town's best feature. One famous landmark is the tall, white lighthouse, built in 1855 on Chantry Island. The most scenic spot here is at the beach at sunset, as the sun sinks behind the island (which is also a bird sanctuary). The lakefront also features the unique Chantry Dunes. The Chantry Dunes are a protected zone with trails to allow visits to the unique ecosystem. There is also a beach, and the town is home to the Bruce County Museum and archives. The town itself has pretty, tree-lined streets with historic homes bearing plaques with the name, profession, and year of the original occupants.

And while the community may be a historic Lake Huron port, it is equally well known for another body of water—this is the mouth of the Saugeen River, one of the finest salmon and trout rivers in Ontario, with part of the river offering year-round open season.

Near Southampton is the Saugeen First Nations Reserve, with the spectacular Saugeen Amphitheatre and Rock Gardens (519-797-2215).

SAUBLE BEACH

Further north lies Sauble Beach, with twelve kilometres of sand beach. Sauble has everything a beach resort should offer—amusement park, mini golf, and water slides.

FLOWERPOT ISLAND

BRUCE PENINSULA

From Southampton, the traveller can head east to Owen Sound, or north into the beauty of the Bruce Peninsula, with five hundred miles of rocky shoreline, fantastic views, and few people. The Bruce is formed by southwestern Ontario's defining geological formation, the Niagara Escarpment. This is heaven for nature-lovers and photographers, with dozens of rare species of wildlife and plants.

At the very tip of the Bruce is the Bruce Peninsula

TOBERMORY

National Park; off the tip is Fathom Five National Marine Park, Canada's only underwater park, where shipwrecks can be explored by divers.

Tobermory, the village of 1,900 people on the tip of the peninsula, offers Tour Boat

Cruises to Flowerpot Island in the National Marine Park. It is also the southern terminus for the *Chi-cheemaun*, which carries travellers to Manitoulin Island (May through Canadian Thanksgiving). Tobermory is also the northern terminus of the Bruce Trail, which runs from Tobermory all the way south to Queenston on the Niagara Peninsula, and is featured in the hiking section of this guide (519-596-2452; *Chi-cheemaun*, 1-800-265-3163).

Follow Highway 6 south to Wiarton, famous in Canada as the home of Wiarton Willie, the albino groundhog who predicts the weather with much pomp and circumstance on Groundhog Day, February 2. From Wiarton, follow Road 26, the meandering shoreline route that leads to caves open for exploration at the Bruce's Caves Conservation Area, and Keppel Croft Gardens at Big Bay, *Canadian Gardening* magazine's 1995 Garden of the Year (519-534-1090).

OWEN SOUND

Road 26 links with Road 1 into Owen Sound, a city with the look and feel of a Georgian Bay port and fishing community. Although Owen Sound sees more than its share of visitors, the city has never lost the rough-and-tumble ambience of a frontier community. There are not many yuppie bars or upscale nightclubs here, and most restaurants are unlikely to sacrifice quantity for gourmet cuisine.

This is not to say that there is nothing here to interest the tourist. Highlights include the Tom Thomson Memorial Art Gallery, a superb gallery featuring Thomson and his colleagues, who formed the Group of Seven after his mysterious death. There are other museums and galleries in the city—the County of Grey-Owen Sound Museum, with

INGLIS FALLS

restored historic buildings including an automobile garage; the Billy Bishop Heritage Museum, dedicated to the World War I aviation hero; and the Owen Sound Marine and Rail Heritage Museum.

Two beautiful natural areas near Owen Sound are Inglis Falls, an eighteen-metre falls beside the ruins of a grist mill (Inglis Falls Road, south of the city), and Indian Falls, Grey County Road 1, north of the city (1-888-675-5555).

Lake Huron and Georgian Bay are cottage and resort country for Ontario residents and for many Americans, too. This stretch of the Lake Huron shoreline is home to many resort towns, each with its own distinctive character. Those visitors who like a more rugged landscape will prefer the southern shore of Georgian Bay where they can swim, boat, or simply sit on an enormous granite boulder and gaze out over the sparkling blue water.

Top Activities
and Attractions

UPSTAIRS AT THE BUTTERY

HENRY VIIIth Feeste

FRIDAY & SATURDAY EVENINGS ALL YEAR

Open

ANTIQUING

BRET EVANS

Antique hunting is an arcane art, combining the thrill of the chase and the excitement of a treasure hunt with the talents of shopping for a bargain. The fun is in the find. Southwestern Ontario is a particularly rich field for antiquing; almost every community has a shop or two, ranging from "everything and the kitchen sink" shops piled to the rafters with the good, the bad, and the ugly, to the finest in high-end boutiques featuring the rare and the unique.

RED BARN ANTIQUES, NIAGARA-ON-THE-LAKE

NOTHING NEW ANTIQUES, NIAGARA-ON-THE-LAKE

NIAGARA PENINSULA

Niagara-on-the-Lake is noted for its well-preserved buildings, most dating from the 1800s. It's also a good place to start or finish a day of antiquing, especially if you want to combine some other activities with your search. Most of the dealers are located in the two-storey Red Barn Antique Mall (905-468-0900). The area is particularly good for glassware, china, and accessories.

Nearby, in the historic village of Queenston, a local dealer specializes in four-posters, making it a great place to pick up beds. Another shop has English and European antiques, as well as barometers, clocks, stained glass, and leaded windows. Nothing New Antiques, Olde Coach House Antiques, and Queenston Antiques are all interesting places to browse.

The small town of Fonthill has several shops; most have furniture, but a number also specialize in glass. See Lakeshore Antiques, Pelham Antiques, and Treasure Trove.

Another area gem is Jordan, where the main street has a large grouping of antique stores. Many specialize in lighting and decorating items, but you can also pick up a complete dining or bedroom suite. The Antique Centre is a multi-dealer shop with plenty of variety, including china, glass, collectables, and clocks (905-562-7723). Also visit Brittanic Antiques, Creighton House Antiques, Mrs. Audrey E. Griffith, and J. Hageraats Antique Lighting.

CALEDON AND HALTON HILLS

The Caledon area is noted for dealers who have some degree of specialization. This is the place to come if you're interested in Carnival Glass, antique and period lighting, or accessories. Among the more interesting stores to visit are Clark House Antiques, Wooden Bucket Antiques, the Lamplighter Shoppe, and Generations Apart.

Campbellville, just south of Halton Hills, is an antiquer's dream. A dozen or more dealers, many of them grouped together in several multi-dealer venues, are within walking distance of one another. The selection is astounding, and will satisfy both the casual collector and the most discriminating antique enthusiast. Here is the place to go if you're looking for collectables as diverse as buggies, sleighs, gramophones, furniture, decorative items, books, sheet music, glass, instruments, prints, oil lamps, militaria, china, silver, and linens. You could pick out an entire suite of furniture and find all the accessories and decoratives you need in the same day. If you're looking for specialized antiques, chances are that sooner or later they will end up here. This is also a good place for reproduction eighteenth- and nineteenth-century furniture.

KITCHENER-WATERLOO AND AREA

The picturesque community of Elora was discovered by artists and artisans more than a quarter century ago. The antique crowd soon followed, and the area has become a must-see for any serious antiquer. The Antique Warehouse, just outside town, has more than forty dealers and is open year-round (519-725-2644). Other local shops have flatware, orientals, silver, furniture, accessories, china and glass, books, and art. Bernadette's Antiques, Elora's Antiques, J. Ferguson Antiques, The Elora Antique Warehouse, and Paul Noonan Antiques are good places to browse.

RUMNER'S WOBBLE, KITCHENER

Not only is this area an excellent source of well-preserved wood furniture, there is also a strong local arts and crafts tradition. Most of the antique action is at St. Jacobs Antique Market, open most of the year, a multi-dealer shop with an eclectic range of antiques, nostalgia, collectables, and unusual items (519-664-1243). Just a short distance to the south, Kitchener-Waterloo has several antique shops, offering fine art, china, brass, glass, copper, and furniture. Here you might try Rumners Wobble Antiques and Duke's Antiques Inc.

The small community of St. George sat quietly for many years before being discovered by the antique community. The combination of small-town ambience and several antique shops makes for a delightful experience. And Paris is just a few miles down the road. There, Babes in the Wood Antiques has a novel approach—it combines more traditional antiques with a selection of baby buggies and old dolls(519-442-1755). This is also a good area to hunt for pine, brass, china, glass, silver, furniture, vintage lace, and linen. See Stocks Antiques, White Horse Antiques, and the Macs Antiques.

STRATFORD AND AREA

Stratford, best known for its Shakespearean Theatre Festival, is also a good place to pick up interesting antiques, textiles, paints, china, books, and furnishings. If you arrive on the first weekend of August, you'll find your selection expanded by the dealers at the community's annual Antiques Show. See Carol Telfer Antiques, Gregory Connor Antiques, and Hidden Treasures Antiques.

Shakespeare is known for its high-end antiques. If you're a serious antiquer, you'll eventually come here. If you're more casual, you may still want to stop by, to view some of the finer antiques. More than just furniture, this is also a good area to shop for old

SHAKESPEARE

pottery and porcelain, with several shops carrying extensive inventories. The most notable shops are Jonny's Antiques Ltd. and Glen Manor Galleries; you could also visit Agnes Gillespie Galleries, J. Donald Antiques, Kathleen's Antiques, Land/Ross Antique Co-op, and Peter C. Land and Wayne W. Ross Antiques (519-625-8307; 519-625-8920).

LONDON AND AREA

London is a big place, and you're not going to get everywhere by walking, but the variety and selection of stores is well worth the extra effort. The Wortley Road area in particular hosts a cluster of shops. Dealers in this city specialize in old books, depression glass, country furniture, glass, china, primitives, refinishing supplies, with one dealer even specializing in stereo cards.

Just west of London is Lambeth. Most of the dealers there are more eclectic, often including paintings, jewellery, and collectables along with the usual furnishings. See Granny's Treasure and Gordon F. Baker Antiques (519-652-1090; 519-652-9290).

LAKE ERIE SHORELINE

This is another good area for furniture. You can also find pottery, primitives, lighting, quilts, glass, silver, and even poison and patent medicine bottles in some shops. Several shops offer possible bargains with "as found" furniture, while in Waterford, C.J.'s Antiques and Refinishing has an extensive inventory of antique furniture (519-443-4197). See also Anderson Antiques, Country Corner Antiques, The Old Country Store, The Roost, Townsend's Treasures, and Varey-Us Antiques.

LAKE HURON AND GEORGIAN BAY

Tucked away in the Bruce/Grey County area, Hanover is a small community with a surprising number of antique shops. The word here is diversity, with three stores offering a selection of everything from jewellery to furniture, and china to old clothes. The entire area is rife with isolated stores and the trip to Hanover may prove eventful for what you discover on the way. Visit Definitely Denis, Campbell's Corner Consignment Store, and Glendon Arts.

Kincardine is known for its formal furniture—several local stores feature cherry, maple, and butternut, as well as the usual selection of china, collectables, and small items. See Andrew Pratt Antiques, J&B Antiques, Jenny's Antiques, Kathleen Millard Collectables and Antiques, and the Thriving Shed (519-396-8669; 519-396-2375).

One thing you will find plenty of here is country furniture, often still with the original finish. Inventories here are usually large, so you can be assured a selection. The area is also noted for glassware and the smaller items you often need to add details to a room. Shops include Marika's Antiques, Blue House Antiques, Cottage Antiques and Collectables, Pine Plus Mirrors and Antiques, and Stayner Antiques.

TIMES AND PLACES, BAYFIELD

TIMES AND PLACES

When it comes to antiques, southwestern Ontario has both quality and quantity. By almost any measure, it is an antique-lover's dream come true.

ART GALLERIES AND STUDIOS

CATHY WILLIAMS

THE MAN OF SORROWS AND THE MATER DOLOROSA, MCMASTER MUSEUM OF ART, HAMILTON

Art lovers travelling in southwestern Ontario will have many opportunities to see exciting works by contemporary and historical Canadian artists, as well as fine examples of European art.

Almost every municipality supports at least one community gallery focusing at the very least on the works of local and regional artists and artisans. Others have the good fortune to be home to several specialized collections. This article touches on highlights from various communities; be sure to check local tourist information centres for other galleries in the area. (All galleries mentioned are fully wheelchair accessible, unless otherwise noted.)

PRESERVATION GALLERY, NIAGARA-ON-THE-LAKE

NIAGARA PENINSULA

Niagara-on-the-Lake is a haven for artists, with a number of private galleries located in the downtown area. The

Preservation Fine Art Gallery is located in a gorgeous Victorian home that was once the family home of artist Trisha Romance. The entire house is now a gallery, featuring the works of Romance (who appropriately produces works with a Victorian romantic flourish), super realist Alex Colville, and Philip Craig (1-800-667-8525). In the dock area is the Doug Forsythe

Gallery (905-468-3659), while on the main thoroughfare is the Angie Strauss Gallery, featuring Strauss's original watercolours, limited edition prints, fashions and more bearing her designs (905-468-2255).

BATHERS AT CAPRI, **ART GALLERY OF HAMILTON**

The catalyst behind the formation of the Art Gallery of Hamilton in 1914 was the donation of twenty-nine works by the widow of Canadian artist William Blair Bruce to the city of Hamilton. Influenced by the play of light and atmosphere evidenced by the French Impressionists, Bruce nonetheless brought a distinctive Canadian flavour to his landscapes and portraiture.

These works are now on permanent display at the AGH. Located in the heart of downtown Hamilton, the gallery's spacious, contemporary home contains ten galleries and a sculpture garden. Its 7,500 art works include paintings, sculpture, and large installations focusing on Canadian contemporary, modernist, and historical works; twentieth-century British and American art; seventeenth-century Dutch masters; Italian artists from the seventeenth and eighteenth century; and French art, including sculpture, from the nineteenth and twentieth centuries. Its circulating fine arts library and reference-only rare book special collection are especially impressive (905-527-6610).

GIRL UNDER A TREE, **ART GALLERY OF HAMILTON**

The McMaster Museum of Art, located at McMaster University and overlooking the Royal Botanical Gardens, is a teaching facility and a public gallery. Growing from private donations and faculty acquisitions since 1887, including a print donation from the Carnegie Institute in the 1930s, it significantly increased its holdings in the 1980s, when Hamilton businessman Dr. Herman H. Levy donated his collection of 185 European and American works of art to the museum. Now on permanent display, this collection includes fine Impressionist and Post-Impressionist works.

The museum owns the largest collection of German Expressionist prints in Canada and also has strong holdings in sixteenth to twentieth century European prints and oils, and Inuit art (905-525-9140).

Buffalo's Albright-Knox Art Gallery, just across the Canada–U.S. border from Fort Erie in the Niagara Peninsula, is one of the premier facilities in the world in which to enjoy contemporary art and sculpture. The Albright-Knox has built its excellent reputation on its definitive collection of American and European art from the past fifty years, as its

CONVERGENCE, **ALBRIGHT-KNOX GALLERY, BUFFALO**

curators have pursued (and continue to pursue) an aggressive and up-to-the-minute acquisitions policy. The gallery also has a permanent collection of art through the centuries that reaches back to 3000 B.C. and approaches the modern era through key works by impressionists such as Degas and Renoir. There are six thousand works in the Albright-Knox collection; two hundred are on view at any given time. Return visits are therefore a must (716-882-8700).

KITCHENER-WATERLOO AND AREA

Homer Watson, a self-taught landscape artist, was the country's first artist, to paint Canada from a distinctive Canadian perspective. The circa-1835 Homer Watson House and Gallery, in Kitchener's historic Doon area, was Watson's home from 1881 until his death in 1936, and is now run by the Homer Watson House foundation. His studio houses the foundation's collection of his works on permanent display. Watson's frieze, painted on the studio's walls as homage to the art masters of his time, was restored in 1991. The gallery has a continually changing exhibition of works in many media by contemporary local and regional artists (519-748-4377).

PREPARING THE BINDER, **PETER ETRIL SNYDER STUDIO, WATERLOO**

The Kitchener-Waterloo Art Gallery now houses four thousand works of art. The gallery focuses on the works of

contemporary Canadian artists, as well as an admirable Group of Seven/Tom Thomson collection. It owns the second-largest collection of Homer Watson works in Canada.

Exhibitions change almost monthly, in three gallery spaces and two print corridors. A favourite is the annual juried quilt show. Situated across the foyer from Kitchener's respected Centre in the Square, the gallery is a favourite with theatregoers (519-579-5860).

Painter Peter Etril Snyder is Canada's foremost portrayer of the unique Mennonite culture of Waterloo County. His own Mennonite upbringing, as he worked with draft horses used in his family's dairy business, gives his representations of both historical and contemporary subjects—especially the interplay between human and animal—accuracy and sensitivity. His use of light and shadow contrasts, plus unexpected details, are hallmarks of his work.

Snyder's oeuvre also includes florals and European and other landscapes and cityscapes. His Waterloo-based reproduction gallery and working studio are open to the public (519-886-9452). Not wheelchair accessible.

Waterloo's Canadian Clay and Glass Gallery is unique in Canada. Housed in an award-winning building designed by Vancouver architects John and Patricia Patkau, the gallery is Canada's first centre for works in clay, glass, stained glass, and enamel. The core of its permanent collection is the Indusmin Collection, 169 ceramic and glass pieces by Canadian artists, donated in 1989 by Unimin Canada Limited, a major glass and ceramic industry supplier. Formed to both document and preserve Canadian twentieth-century art in these media, the gallery has continually changing exhibitions. On a sunny day, the gallery is especially stunning (519-746-1882).

FLYING TRAPEZE, THE GALLERY/ STRATFORD

Guelph's Macdonald Stewart Art Centre opened in 1980, in the 1904 Sir William Macdonald Consolidated School building. An addition designed by Canadian architect Raymond Moriyama brought the gallery space up ten thousand square meters with seven galleries. Its rare collection of five hundred Inuit prints complement the art centre's fine collection of contemporary Canadian works. Donald Forster Sculpture Park contains a growing collection of works by contemporary Canadian sculptors (519-837-0010).

THREE CHAIRS, THE GALLERY/ STRATFORD

STRATFORD AND AREA

The Gallery/Stratford marvelously illustrates that small can be perfect.

Housed in a heritage building—an 1883 city water commission pump house completely renovated inside—the gallery's six-hundred-piece collection focuses exclusively on Canadian contemporary works of art on paper produced since 1967, including prints, watercolours, drawings, collages, and mixed media works.

Its year-round exhibition program includes international touring exhibits. Although the gallery specializes in contemporary Canadian works on paper, the permanent collection (more than five hundred pieces) is much broader than that, with works by Salvador Dali, Jack Shadbolt, sculptor Robert Murray, and well-known Canadians Harold Town, Ken Danby, and Christopher Pratt. Gallery/Stratford summer exhibits highlighting the theatre art of the Stratford Shakespearean Festival—costume and set design, particularly—are especially popular (519-271-5271).

LAKE HURON AND GEORGIAN BAY

Owen Sound's native son, Tom Thomson, directly influenced the artistic development of four men who would form the Group of Seven after Thomson's mysterious death in 1917: Arthur Lismer, Fred Varley, Franklin Carmichael, and Frank Johnston. Fellow employees at Grip Ltd. Photoengravers, the four men went on painting expeditions to Georgian Bay, each developing his own distinctive style.

Opened in 1967, the Tom Thompson Gallery has the third largest collection of Thomson paintings and sketches in the world, donated by Thomson's family. These works, plus many Group of Seven pieces, are on permanent display. New acquisitions are selected to enhance one of the finest collections of Canadian landscape artists in the country (519-376-1932).

WINDSOR AND AREA

The Art Gallery of Windsor offers more than thirty exhibitions each year, all in a highly innovative setting—a Windsor shopping centre, the Devonshire Mall. This location is both a cost-saving measure, and an attempt to bring art to the people.

The collection numbers nearly 2,500 works of art, all relevant to the cultural heritage of Canada. Especially strong are the collections of later nineteenth-century Canadian painting and early twentieth-century Canadian modernistic works. Included are works by artists Bertram Brooker, Group of Seven member Lauren Harris, and Detroit artist Sheldon Iden (519-969-4494).

The galleries of southwestern Ontario feature art from many eras and cultures. The real opportunity for visitors, however, is the chance to view both contemporary and historical paintings and sculptures by Canadian artists. They may even get the chance to meet local artists or watch them work.

APRIL IN ALGONQUIN PARK, TOM THOMSON GALLERY, OWEN SOUND

BIRDING

PATRICIA BOW

For birds and birders, southwestern Ontario is one of the top destinations in North America. Three natural features account for this—the Great Lakes, the Carolinian woodlands that border Lakes Erie and Ontario, and the Niagara Escarpment, a limestone ridge that angles across southwestern Ontario from southeast to northwest.

BLACKBURNIAN WARBLER, RONDEAU PROVINCIAL PARK

The lakes lie in the path of several migratory flyways. When the migrants reach Ontario's shores they find a forest with a southern flavour, lush with hackberries, sassafras, and Virginia creeper. Some of the new arrivals—Carolina wrens, red-bellied woodpeckers, and the many species of warblers—choose to summer in these warm, moist woods. Others, after a rest stop, continue north, using the escarpment as a highway. The cliffs and canyons of this great spine also make a summer home for eagles and vultures, and provide a sheltering wall for pockets of wilderness which in turn protect rare birds and plants.

NIAGARA PENINSULA

Sandwiched between Lakes Erie and Ontario, the Niagara Peninsula makes a convenient flyway to the north for migrating raptors, which dislike crossing large stretches of water. One of the peninsula's major birding events is the spring (March to mid-May) Hawk Watch, held at Beamer Memorial Conservation Area, near Grimsby. Lookouts

BIRDING AT THE PINERY PROVINCIAL PARK

high on the Niagara Escarpment are perfect vantage points for watching the hawks as they sail past. Turkey vultures and falcons also follow this flight path, as do bald eagles—which are occasionally seen by surprised tourists strolling the Niagara Parkway. In November, the Niagara River becomes a gathering place for many different species of gulls. Contact the Niagara Peninsula Conservation Authority (905-227-1013).

Continuing along the Niagara Escarpment, half an hour's drive from Hamilton or Toronto you'll find Rattlesnake Point and Crawford Lake Conservation Areas,

near Guelph Line between Highway 401 and Derry Road (905-336-1158). A drive to the top of the escarpment brings you to wild, rocky forests and hiking trails along the edge of eighty-foot cliffs. You'll be rewarded with spectacular views not only of the lowlands—on a clear day you can see the CN Tower in Toronto—but also of hawks, turkey vultures, and eagles circling at eye level in Nassagaweya Canyon.

CALEDON AND HALTON HILLS

The wildlife centre in Mountsberg Conservation Area, near Campbellville, is a good place to observe warblers and bobolinks. Here, too, you can watch migrating wood ducks splash down, make eye contact with a great horned owl, and visit a hospital for injured raptors. Live exhibits, demonstrations related to the raptor rescue program, fine interpretive facilities, and other activities make Mountsberg an excellent place to visit with children. Information regarding all three conservation areas is available at the Halton Region Conservation Authority (905-336-1158).

YELLOW-RUMPED WARBLER, RONDEAU PROVINCIAL PARK

KITCHENER-WATERLOO AND AREA

One of North America's most diversified collections of waterfowl can be seen without binoculars at the Kortright Waterfowl Park on weekends, March through October (519-824-6729). Wildlife artists such as Robert Bateman have visited the park, located in the southwest corner of Guelph, to photograph the more than ninety species of native birds, as well as exotic Brazilian teal and Australian black swans. These permanent residents are joined twice a year by flocks of migrating geese and ducks.

CANADA GOOSE, THE PINERY PROVINCIAL PARK

North of Kitchener-Waterloo, at the headwaters of the Grand River, Luther Marsh Wildlife Management Area brings you closer to true wilderness. One of southern Ontario's largest inland wetlands—fourteen hundred hectares of marsh, bog, and forest—the area is a magnet for waterfowl. More

than 230 species of birds have been sighted here, including herons and raptors. Trails, canoe routes, interpretive displays, and observation towers enhance the viewing. However, the season is limited. To protect wildlife, sanctuaries are off limits from March 15 to November 15, and the marsh itself is closed from spring break-up to July 31. Contact the Grand River Conservation Authority for details (519-621-2761).

LAKE ERIE SHORELINE

The densest concentration of birding hotspots in the province is a string of parks and conservation areas along the Lake Erie shoreline. Provincial and national parks and most conservation areas charge a moderate fee for entry. Days and times of opening will vary, so it's always wise to call ahead. Phone numbers have been provided where available.

The best known of these hotspots is Point Pelee (519-322-2365), located just south of Leamington and a forty-minute drive from Windsor. This sixteen-square-kilometre spit of land is one of the smallest of Canada's national parks, but it has the richest trove of unique plants: many of the seven hundred species growing there are found nowhere else in Canada. It's also Canada's southernmost tip of land, and the site where thousands of migrating birds, following the shortest path across the lakes, touch down.

FEMALE MALLARD, THE PINERY PROVINCIAL PARK

More than 350 bird species, many rare or endangered, have been recorded at Pelee. Nearly one hundred species nest there, and about fifty remain through the winter. Spring migration begins in March and culminates in the first three weeks in May. During peak season, Pelee is one of the few places where a birder can hope to achieve that magical "century," spotting one hundred species in one day. The park throngs with warblers (most of North America's warblers can be found here), thrushes, finches, owls, woodpeckers, vireos, cuckoos, meadowlarks, waterfowl, and shore birds. During the more leisurely fall migration, July through December, you're more likely to see the golden eagles, peregrine falcons, saw-whet owls, and sandpipers that might have been missed in the spring.

Not surprisingly, Pelee also attracts half a million people per year. The area offers plenty of accommodation, but you're advised to book at least four months ahead if you plan to arrive during the Festival of Birds in May.

Rondeau Provincial Park (519-674-1750), located about sixty-five kilometres east along the coast, is a less crowded alternative to Pelee. Almost as many, and as varied, species

**RED-HEADED
WOODPECKER**

**TUNDRA SWANS, THE
PINERY PROVINCIAL
PARK**

of birds arrive during spring migration, but the human visitors are not as numerous. A peninsula with long beaches and a particularly lush Carolinian forest, Rondeau is a good place to see endangered prothonotary warblers and Acadian flycatchers, as well as many rare species of orchids.

For hawk enthusiasts, the autumn destination is Holiday Beach Conservation Area, south of Malden Centre, about forty-five kilometres west of Pelee. During the Festival of Hawks in September, as many as ninety-five thousand broad-winged hawks have been counted in a day. Up to fourteen other hawk species have been recorded. Other visitors are falcons and bald eagles, and flocks of thousands of blue jays and hummingbirds. You can call the Essex Region Conservation Authority for more information (519-766-5209).

Heading east again along the Erie shore brings you to Long Point Provincial Park, about forty-five kilometres southwest of Simcoe. Long Point (519-586-2133) is the longest and wildest of the Great Lakes' sand spits, a forty-kilometre-long tongue of sand dunes, marshes, woodlands, and meadows, and an important stopover point for migrating warblers and wetlands birds, including tundra swans and sandhill cranes. About three hundred bird species and hundreds of species of plants, many rare and some unique, have been reported here. Long Point is now a Biosphere Reserve recognized by the United Nations. Much of the spit is restricted, but marked paths and canoes give some access, and you can watch banding operations at the bird observatory.

LAKE HURON AND GEORGIAN BAY

While the Erie/escarpment curve is prime birding territory, there are plenty of other places in southwestern Ontario to enjoy birds, including Pinery (519-243-2220), Inverhuron (519-389-9056) and MacGregor Point (519-389-9056) Provincial Parks, situated along the Lake Huron shoreline. Additional viewing sites may be found in the boreal forest that grows over much of the province, and in any of the thousands of wilderness fragments on stream, scarp, or woodlot.

The key to birding in Ontario is variety—the variety of environments and terrain guarantees a wide spectrum of species. That's why this district offers some of the best birding to be found anywhere in North America.

BOATING

ANITA HANSON

It's hard to imagine a geographic spot more perfectly suited to the boating enthusiast than southwestern Ontario. Almost completely surrounded by the waters of three of the Great Lakes (Huron, Erie, and Ontario), plus Lake St. Clair and the connecting rivers, the area boasts thousands of kilometres of shoreline, which provide a full spectrum of landscapes and boating opportunities.

HARBOUR, PORT DOVER

LAKE ONTARIO

Hamilton, the largest city at the west end of Lake Ontario, with its museums, galleries, theatres, and great shopping, is an excellent stop for an urban boater. A recently spruced-up

waterfront in Hamilton Harbour is very inviting, with lovely landscaping and walking paths, restaurants, and several marinas, including the Royal Hamilton Yacht Club (905-528-8464).

ROYAL HAMILTON YACHT CLUB

Farther along the Niagara Peninsula shoreline, in Stoney Creek, the Newport Marina (905-643-0195) also provides transient dockage, just a short walk from the elegant Edgewater Manor, an old stone house now converted to a restaurant—the perfect spot for a romantic evening.

For waterside dining in a more casual atmosphere, try Fifty Point, between Stoney Creek and Grimsby (905-643-2103). Tie up in the picturesque little marina and eat in the restaurant on the dock, or bring your own and choose a picnic table in the lovely conservation area. The park and benches make Fifty Point the ideal spot for a quiet, relaxing afternoon.

It's hard to imagine a better spot to spend the day than Port Dalhousie, on the outskirts of St. Catharines. History buffs and shoppers alike will delight in this engaging and beautifully kept little town. A marina near Lakeside Park now makes it possible to dock without having to go up the river, so it is very easy to access the boutiques, galleries, and many restaurants. And plan to stay over, so you don't miss the action when the sun goes down—Port Dalhousie is known for its night life.

The "last-stop" marina on Lake Ontario is the historic town of Niagara-on-the-Lake, where the marina is located just inside the mouth of the Niagara River. Restaurants, inns, and dozens of shops and galleries are only minutes on foot from your boat, as are historic sites including Fort George, fully restored to War of 1812 battle-readiness.

LAKE ERIE

Lake Erie has a very different personality. A shallow, sandy lake, Erie offers miles of beaches, picturesque shoreline, and tranquil coves. This is a lake to relax on—drop the anchor, go for a swim near a sandy beach, or just bob contentedly. It is also a lake to play on—warm temperatures and open water make it perfect for water

WELLAND CANAL

skiing, para-sailing, personal water craft, and any other type of water sport you can think of.

Alongside an interesting collection of small fishing villages, a few small but lively resort towns provide for those looking for a little more action. At the eastern end of the lake, Port Colborne's Sugarloaf Harbour Marina Centre has more than five hundred slips along with fine recreational and dining facilities, all within easy walking distance of the famous Welland Canal (905-835-6644). Port Dover, still an active commercial fishing centre, offers a beautiful beach, and the best Lake Erie perch around. Looking for a party? The beach at Turkey Point will provide one all weekend long.

PIER, PORT DOVER

Port Stanley, on the other side of Long Point, is a very popular stop for those travelling both on land and water. Several marinas grant access to this historic village, once the prime tourist destination on the lake, and now coming back into its own with a wide array of restaurants, galleries, boutiques, and even a festival theatre. All this, and an enormous sand beach, too.

For the above reasons, the lake attracts a lot of boating enthusiasts. The vast areas mean there's always lots of room for everyone, but there are some favourite spots that are particularly popular. A true phenomenon takes place every July, on the second Sunday, at Pottahawk Point in Long Point Bay. Pottahawk has a narrow beach, several kilometres long, and on this particular Sunday, all the boaters in the world, it seems, gather there. Thousands (yes, thousands!) of boats line the shore, five and six deep, from the smallest of dinghies to sixty-foot yachts, and everyone is there to have a good time. Don't participate if you're shy, but if you enjoy the company of other boaters, and like looking at other boats, there is no better opportunity anywhere.

LAKE ST. CLAIR/DETROIT RIVER

Between Lakes Erie and Huron, in the Windsor and Sarnia areas, local boaters boast that they have the best of both worlds—quiet islands and sand spits for anchoring (check out Peach Island near Windsor) and all the action and excitement of the city. Night-life seekers generally head for Detroit and its abundance of waterside bars and restaurants, just a quick run across the Detroit

BOATING NEAR PELEE ISLAND

River. Of course, not all the action is on the American side—the Windsor Casino is also a destination, and something no visitor to the area should miss.

LAKE HURON

"Around the corner," on Lake Huron, yet another type of boating opportunity presents itself. A more rugged landscape, this shoreline provides wilderness beauty unequalled in the world. The craggy banks do not mean an absence of beaches, however. Some of Ontario's most popular resort towns, including Grand Bend, are found along this stretch of water, so whether you're looking for a back to nature experience, or an afternoon of fun on a busy beach, you'll find it here.

Fine ports along Lake Huron include the lovely tourist town of Bayfield; Goderich, with the only harbour on the east shore of Lake Huron deep enough to serve the huge,

**HARBOUR,
GODERICH**

ocean-going vessels that ply the Great Lakes; Port Elgin, and Southampton, at the mouth of the Saugeen River.

The rocky nature of this lake creates challenges for boaters. Further north, about halfway between Oliphant and Stokes Bay, there is a most interesting geological formation known as the Chimney Reefs. They are a series of chimney-like structures that rise from the bottom, as much as ninety feet down, and come up to within just a few feet of the surface. Fascinating as this is, however, any boater who values his or her vessel is not advised to go in for a look. In fact, boaters should give the entire area a wide berth.

The main port on Georgian Bay is Owen Sound, although the shoreline from Owen Sound all the way north to Tobermory includes many launching areas both for power boaters and for sailors.

SOUTHWESTERN ONTARIO RIVERS

Impressive as the Great Lakes are, they are by no means the only source of boating opportunities in Ontario. This is a province with 100,000 kilometres of river, and many of these waterways are found in southwestern sections of the province, making this a favourite spot for canoeing and kayaking. The rivers here, sometimes gentle, sometimes exciting, wind their way through miles of scenic farmland and unspoiled wilderness. Whether a seasoned expert or an inexperienced beginner, you will find routes and resources here to make your canoe trip memorable.

**CANOEING IN
SOUTHWESTERN
ONTARIO**

The Grand River is a particularly popular route, carrying you through some of the most picturesque countryside, along with charming small towns, larger cities, and the Six Nations Reserve. Canoeing is, of course, not limited to rivers, and the many small lakes in southwestern Ontario are perfect for a tranquil ride, particularly for paddlers with less experience. The shores of the Great Lakes are becoming one of the fastest-growing destinations for sea kayaking.

Private operators throughout the area provide rental equipment, instructions, and guided excursions (which are always recommended for beginners). Go for an afternoon, or pack your sleeping bag and take a week-long holiday trip you'll never forget.

Southwestern Ontario is a travel destination with no end of things to offer the visitor. Why not see some of these sights from a different perspective? Don't just stand on the shore and gaze at the beautiful water—go out onto the water and gaze at the beautiful shore!

CAMPING

KELLY DAYNARD

The history of Ontario's provincial parks stretches back over a century. The system's first park, Algonquin, was opened in 1893. Since then, the province has expanded the park system and now has 270 parkland locations—106 of which are operating parks.

Of the 106 operating provincial parks in Ontario, 22 are located in the southwestern portion of the province. Parks are organized into categories, with each having particular characteristics. All but three of the provincial parks in southwestern Ontario are categorized as

CAMPERS AT THE PINERY PROVINCIAL PARK

Recreational Parks, featuring the three S's—sand, surf, and sun. They have good beaches, many campsites, and lots of outdoor recreation opportunities. A few are classified as Natural Environment, meaning that the park maintains a balance by protecting the local natural and cultural heritage while offering recreational activities. Most of the Natural Environment Parks have swimming and hiking trails. Several have special attractions such as museums or displays.

Most of the provincial parks in southwestern Ontario provide electricity and accommodate motor homes. All have trailer sanitary services and all have some form of maintained washroom facility. Many have laundry facilities. Pets are allowed in provincial parks providing they are on leashes, but not in swimming areas or beaches. Many of the provincial parks have an alcohol ban around the Victoria Day weekend. Fees vary according to the facilities and services provided. Ontario Parks have five fee levels. Parks with the least developed campsites have the lowest fees; those with showers, flush toilets, and other services, the highest.

Provincial parks offer discounts on day use and camping fees to Ontario residents over the age of 65 and to persons with disabilities who have a CNIB identity card or a Ministry of Transportation parking permit.

NIAGARA PENINSULA

Sherkston Shores, near Fort Erie, is one of the province's biggest private campgrounds. It has two thousand campsites, fishing, natural swimming, an outdoor pool, and many more recreational activities (1-800-263-8121).

CALEDON HILLS

Earl Rowe Provincial Park, near Alliston, is open early

May to late September and features 365 camping spots. Fishing, board sailing, and canoeing are all offered. The park has a football-field-sized swimming pool as well as a playing field. Nature trails offer picturesque views of the area. The park is located in the scenic Boyne River Valley (705-435-4331).

LAKE ERIE SHORELINE

Rock Point Provincial Park, on the shores of Lake Erie near Dunnville, is categorized as a Recreation Park and is open early May to mid-October with 135 campsites. The park offers swimming and a 600-metre-long beach. In the five kilometres of nature trails, visitors can find themselves in an ancient world. Lakeside shelves of limestone are of special interest. There, visitors can view fossilized creatures that lived on a coral reef 350 million years ago. Today's inhabitants of the campground include opossums, reptiles, and birds. The park is a popular destination for birdwatchers during the spring and fall migrations. Hikers also like the opportunity to identify trees not found elsewhere in the province, including blue beech and shagbark hickory (905-774-6642).

TWO VIEWS OF EARL ROWE PROVINCIAL PARK

Rondeau Provincial Park, about halfway between London and Windsor on Lake Erie's north shore, a Natural Environment Park, is open year round, with 258 campsites. The park offers swimming, a nature centre, and hiking trails. It is one of the few provincial parks in southwestern Ontario with boat launching facilities. Marsh waterways are great for canoes (519-674-1750).

Because of its mild climate, this region has hardwood trees more common to the east-central United States including beech and black walnut, tulip trees, sugar maple, and red oak. Birds, especially warblers, are at home in the Carolinian forest/wetland climate. Rondeau Bay is a natural harbour and, during the War of 1812, was a British naval base (519-674-1750).

Port Burwell Provincial Park, open early May to mid-September, has 232 campsites. The park features warm water swimming, a two-kilometre beach, hiking trails to the bluffs above, and nature and cultural programs (519-874-4691).

Long Point Provincial Park is open early May to mid-October, with 256 campsites, swimming, and boat launching facilities. Long Point, a World Biosphere

Reserve, is well known among bird watchers as a place to watch spring and fall migrations. More than 320 species have been recorded. The area features a sandbar which extends almost forty kilometres into the lake (519-586-2133).

PORT BURWELL
PROVINCIAL PARK

Turkey Point Provincial Park is open May to September, and has 200 campsites, all wheelchair accessible. Swimming and nature trails are highlighted activities. For much of the twentieth century, visitors to this provincial park hadn't been able to see the birds for which the park was named. In the mid-1980s, however, the Ministry of Natural Resources released nearly 300 of the birds, brought from the United States. Officials now estimate that there are several thousand turkeys on the loose in and around the park (519-426-3239).

TURKEY POINT
PROVINCIAL PARK

WINDSOR AND AREA

Wheatley Provincial Park, located near the community of the same name, is open mid-April to mid-October, with 210 campsites. The park has a two-kilometre beach. Group camping is welcome; amenities include swimming, showers, laundromat, and nature trails. Wheatley, on Lake Erie, is one of the southernmost locations in Canada. The diverse area offers excellent bird and nature watching opportunities. It isn't unusual to find turtles sunning themselves or herons fishing in the creeks. The park is near the Jack Minor Bird Sanctuary and Point Pelee National Park, a living museum of natural history, flora, and fauna. Many trees unusual to Canada, including Sassafras, thrive in the warmer climate (519-825-4659).

LAKE HURON AND GEORGIAN BAY

The most popular provincial park in southwestern Ontario is, undoubtedly, The Pinery, located on the shores of Lake Huron. The Pinery, a Natural Environment Park, is a nature-lover's paradise with over seven hundred plant species and three hundred bird species. A park guide notes "massive oaks...prairie grasses, wildflowers, shrubs and sun-drenched meadows." The Pinery has enough bogs, wildlife, animals, and birds to keep naturalists busy for days or weeks at a time. The park has ten nature trails, extensive programs, a

FISHING AT THE
PINERY PROVINCIAL
PARK

Visitor's Centre that is open year-round, and excellent cycling opportunities. Canoe rentals are available and winter campers are welcome. During the winter, there are thirty kilometres of groomed cross country skiing and walking trails. Ski and snowshoe rentals are also offered. The park features a thousand camping sites. Special events throughout the year include the Return of the Swans in mid-to-late March and the Fall Colour Weekend in mid-October. In November and December, the park also hosts Christmas events (519-243-2220).

Point Farms Provincial Park, near Goderich, is open from early May to mid-October with 200 camp sites, nature trails, and a visitor centre. At the turn of the century, visitors to this Lake Huron area stayed at the luxurious Point Farms Hotel, a European-style hotel that attracted visitors from across the province. The hotel has been demolished but the area is still a popular tourist attraction (519-524-7124).

MacGregor Point on Lake Huron near Port Elgin is one of the largest provincial parks in southwestern Ontario. It has 360 campsites and is open May to October. The area combines the unique features of wetlands, sand dunes, woodlands, and beaches. An extensive network of trails and boardwalks allows visitors a close-up view of most of the park. MacGregor Point offers cycling and swimming. Hiking trails take visitors along the edge of the bluff marking the shore of the prehistoric glacial Lake Algonquin. Cross country ski trails are available for winter visitors (519-389-9056).

Sauble Falls near Wiarton has 152 campsites and is open from the end of April to the end of October. A raised platform offers an ideal spring viewing point for the trout and salmon that travel upstream to reach their spawning grounds. The park is also close to Sauble Beach on Lake Huron, famed for its 11 kilometres of beach (519-422-1952).

Craigleith Provincial Park near Collingwood has 172 campsites and is open from the middle of April through to the end of October. Craigleith, nestled at the base of Blue Mountain, features fossils of minute animals that lived in the sea that covered the area 450-million years ago (705-445-4467).

THE PINERY PROVINCIAL PARK

There are literally hundreds of campgrounds in every part of southwestern Ontario. Many are stopover spots, perfect for the traveller who plans to move on the next day; a large number are warm-weather communities providing resort facilities for trailer-dwellers. There are some fine conservation areas, and a few exceptional private facilities. But few campers would dispute the claim that the best campgrounds are the excellent provincial parks, each offering camping facilities, unique nature programs, good supervision, and great beaches.

CRAFT SHOWS

KELLY DAYNARD

QUILT BY IDELLA
SCHWARTZENTRUBE,
ST. JACOBS
MENNONITE QUILTS

Southwestern Ontario is a hotbed of arts and crafts. Almost every community has its collection of artisans and crafters, and many host craft fairs. These exhibitions have grown in popularity. Today, virtually every church group, service club, or school hosts a local show at some time during the year, with the fall season being particularly popular.

NIAGARA PENINSULA

Celebrating Canada's birthday on July 1, Niagara-on-the-Lake puts a different spin on the Art in the Park theme and holds Artistry by the Lake featuring some of Niagara's finest artisans. The show is held outdoors in Queen's Royal Park by Lake Ontario.

Niagara Falls also changes the tone of the outdoor art show when it annually plays host to Art by the Falls, a giant arts and crafts show held at the Rapidsview parking lot across from Marineland on the third weekend of September. Although this location is actually several blocks from the falls, the Art by the Falls showcase also attracts thousands of visitors.

The Winter Festival of Friends show runs in late November at the Hamilton Convention Centre, featuring all-Canadian arts and crafts, and big band concerts (905-525-6644).

Arts in Bloom is a Christmas arts sale at the Art Gallery of Hamilton. Artisans and craftspeople are on site for demonstrations, unique gift items, and refreshments (905-527-6610).

KITCHENER-WATERLOO AND AREA

Two of the best showcases for handcrafted products in southwestern Ontario are found in Waterloo Region. The annual Mennonite Relief Sale and Quilt Auction, held on the last Saturday in May in New Hamburg and the Wellesley Apple Butter and Cheese Festival attract thousands of visitors (519-745-8458; 519-699-4611).

The town of New Hamburg, located halfway between Kitchener and Stratford, has hosted the relief sale for more than thirty years. All goods for sale are donated by individuals, businesses, and church groups. As a result, all revenue generated by the event is used to support the worldwide relief efforts of the Mennonite Central Committee. The feature sale auctions off hundreds of donated handmade quilts (embroidered, cross-stitched, appliqued, and patchworked), afghans, and wall hangings. There are also giant craft tents filled with unique articles made both locally and in Third World countries.

ITEMS FROM CRAFTWORLD CRAFTS

In Wellesley, the annual Apple Butter and Cheese Festival, on the last Saturday in September, features booth after booth of tasty delicacies. It is, however, also a craft-lover's mecca. The community's arena is filled with crafters selling everything from pottery and Mennonite furniture to decorative tole, painted items, and quilts. Other attractions at the Wellesley festival include local artisans at work making wreaths and bonsai trees, quilting, cooking, and spinning.

In Guelph, the popular Fair November craft show features one-of-a-kind items not easily found anywhere else. The well-attended show is held in the University Centre at the University of Guelph (519-824-4120).

In Kitchener, Canadian handmade arts and crafts are included in the Craftworld Arts and Crafts Show at both the beginning of November and middle of March at Bingeman Park. The show features floral items, pottery, folk art, country collectables, clothing, wood furniture, shelving, candles, and seasonal crafts (519-351-8344).

The Woodland Cultural Centre in Brantford is host to the Independent Indian Handicrafters Bazaar each November, featuring native crafts (519-758-5444).

STRATFORD AND AREA

Throughout the summer, Art in the Park in Stratford runs every Wednesday, Saturday, and Sunday, in the parks along the Avon River between the Festival Theatre and the Tom Patterson Theatre, weather permitting. This is a great place for a stroll, and allows you to meet the artists and craftsmen who display and sell their unique Canadian-made art and craft work along Lakeside Drive and Front Street. Combine your visit with tickets to one of the

Festival's plays. A jazz band that drifts along the river on a boat often serenades visitors in the area.

As well, the November Craftworld Arts and Crafts Show in Stratford features Canadian handmade arts and crafts including wrought iron, fine art, candles, seasonal crafts, and country collectables at the Stratford Coliseum (519-351-8344).

St. Marys is another quaint rural-Ontario town offering dozens of picturesque craft boutiques, small art shops, tea rooms, and Upper and Lower Canadiana antique stores. The Piecemakers offer a biennial April quilt show featuring a merchants' mall at the St. Marys Community Centre (519-229-8721).

LONDON AND AREA

In London, the local Potters Guild Christmas Show and Sale is held in mid-November, featuring wheel-thrown and hand-built pottery (519-472-2223). The London Regional Art and Historic Museum hosts the Victorian Christmas Antique and Craft Show each November (519-672-4580). London also hosts the annual Christmas Craft Festival at the Western Fairgrounds in early December, featuring more than 150 craftspeople from across the province (519-679-1810).

Come spring, London hosts its annual Arts and Crafts Spring Show and sale at Western Fairgrounds (519-679-1810).

London parks are popular spots for summertime craft shows. Visitors can view original paintings by local artists on Sundays in Springbank Park (519-668-0667). The venerable Home County Folk Festival, featuring traditional and contemporary folk music performers in London, also features more than a hundred regional craft artisans, children's activities, and plenty of food. It is held for four days in mid-July in Victoria Park and attracts thousands of visitors (519-645-2845).

HOME COUNTRY FOLK FESTIVAL, LONDON

The London New Arts Festival again brings art and excitement to the downtown core in late summer, with art displays, sidewalk chalk painting, concerts, and various workshops (519-432-3926).

Lucan's Christmas Craft Show and Sale is held at the Lucan Community Centre (519-227-4442). The show is especially known for the quality of woodcrafted items shown by local artisans. The community's spring craft show runs in early May (519-227-4253).

Deck the Halls with the Ingersoll Christmas show and sale of original quality fine arts and crafts. It is held in Victoria Park, late November (519-485-4691).

LAKE ERIE SHORELINE

Chatham is a typical, small residential town in southwestern Ontario. While it isn't known for its tourist attractions, it has a surprising number of craft shows

worth visiting. The Festival of Crafts in Chatham is a show and sale of craft items including woodworking, stained glass, and dried flower arrangements (519-352-3888). Also in Chatham, the Thames Art Gallery features a variety of art shows throughout the year including silk screening, selections from their permanent collection, and works by local artists (519-354-8338). The Craftworld Arts and Crafts Show is held at the beginning of March in Chatham, featuring thousands of handmade Canadian arts and crafts (519-351-8344).

WINDSOR AND AREA

In Windsor in November, the Willistead Coach House Arts and Craft Show has been held annually for eleven years (519-254-2984). The magnificent Willistead Manor was built by the Hiram Walker Company and is well worth a tour. In early June, Willistead Park also hosts a two-day arts and craft show. This is a celebration that has grown to become one of the most successful festivals of its kind with about three hundred participants from Ontario, Quebec, and Michigan (519-253-6382). In late July, the arts council of Windsor and Region presents a juried Fine Art and Crafts Fair (519-252-6855). Also in Windsor, the Winter Art in the Park exhibition, with more than ninety exhibitors, runs in mid-November. The show features photography, Christmas decorations, glass, fine art, and wood sculptures (519-253-6382).

LAKE HURON AND GEORGIAN BAY

In the summer months, visitors will find "Art in the Park" exhibits in many communities, with artists and crafters producing and selling goods in the open air. In Goderich, the Festival of Arts and Crafts runs rain or shine on the second weekend of July in Courthouse Park. Arts, crafts, paintings, and sculptures are all on display by more than 165 exhibitors in the show that attracts, on average, ten thousand visitors each year.

TEDDY BEAR FROM THE SEAFORTH GIFT AND CRAFT SHOW

Courthouse Park is located at the centre of town. A number of art and craft shops are located on this square. Also in Goderich, the Festival of Arts and Crafts runs in early July (519-524-5333). In the same town, the Huron Tract Spinners and Weavers offer a November sale and exhibition. This unique showcase of incredible talent features handspun and handwoven items as well as hands-on demonstrations (519-482-5259).

In August, Bayfield hosts art and craft shows in the community park

(1-800-214-5855). Bayfield is worth a visit at any time of the year, however. Dozens of quaint shops are located in this town which, on the banks of Lake Huron, is easily one of the most picturesque in the province.

Continuing on to Grand Bend, the Christmas Sale and tree decorating program runs at the Pinery Provincial Park from mid-November to mid-December (519-243-2220).

In Owen Sound, the Tom Thomson Memorial Art Gallery Christmas sale is held mid-November, featuring handcrafted items by regional artisans (519-376-1932). It seems appropriate that this gallery plays host to this craft show as it features a collection of works by Thomson and his Group of Seven colleagues— local artists, some of whom actually started their careers as artisans in the graphic arts.

In Sarnia, Art at the Bay is a show and sale of visual art, pottery, and fine crafts early in November by members of the Sarnia Artists' Workshop (519-344-2787). Also in Sarnia, a November Big Sisters Show and Sale features quality crafts and goods (519-336-0940).

In Seaforth, the local Agricultural Society features annual Farm Toy, Teddy Bear, Doll, Gift, and Craft shows and sales at the beginning of December. Three individual shows are held in separate buildings with free hayrides between venues (519-527-1790).

Arts and crafts are a booming cottage industry in southwestern Ontario. The visitor will find appealing handcrafted items at a wide variety of shops and fairs across the province.

ITEMS FROM THE SEAFORTH GIFT AND CRAFT SHOW

CYCLING

PATRICIA BOW

Thanks to green planning, southwestern Ontario is becoming prime territory for recreational cycling. Many cities are taking bicycles as a form of transportation into account, which means that increasingly you'll find bike lanes alongside busy thoroughfares.

NIAGARA RIVER RECREATION TRAIL, NIAGARA FALLS

Even better from the viewpoint of cyclists, networks of trails are spreading within and around—and even between —communities, linking parks and conservation areas. Planners are factoring green space into development, and interurban trails are becoming more common. Designed for hikers and skiers as well as bicyclists, and generally off limits to motorized vehicles (snowmobiles sometimes excepted), these trails offer a more pleasant biking experience than street or highway cycling.

The real boost to bicycle power in southwestern Ontario has come, ironically, from railways—from disused rail lines. Rail travel was once king in Ontario and across Canada. Southwestern Ontario had steel lines connecting all the cities and towns (of any size). As train travel declined, many lines were abandoned. In the past few years the idea of putting these strips of wasteland back into use—recreational use, this time—has gained momentum. Now the "rail" trails are in constant use, creating an increasing number of green corridors through and between urban areas, and linking up existing community walk/cycleways.

Southwestern Ontario is blessed with thousands of square kilometres of protected green space, for the most part maintained by regional conservation authorities or the provincial government. Cycling conditions in the parks are diverse. Mountain bikers, for example, will find challenging rides in the conservation areas strung along the limestone ridge of the Niagara Escarpment. But not all parks and conservation areas permit cycling, and some allow cycling only on specific trails. Call ahead to be sure your wheels are welcome, and expect to pay a moderate entrance fee.

NIAGARA PENINSULA

The Niagara River Recreational Trail from Fort Erie to Niagara-on-the-Lake, a distance of fifty-six kilometres, takes you through vineyards, orchards, and along the spectacularly scenic Niagara Gorge, with some street riding as you pass through Niagara Falls. This popular trail was constructed beginning in the late eighties to give cyclists their own safe right-of-way beside the busy Niagara Parkway (905-356-2241).

To this date, the longest interurban trail in southern Ontario (aside from the 773-kilometre Bruce Trail, which is open only to hikers, not to cyclists) is the Waterfront Trail that borders Lake Ontario from Hamilton to Trenton, a distance of 325 kilometres. The trail is the expression of a shared dream that began to emerge in the late seventies and gathered force in the eighties; a dream of rescuing and revitalizing the lakefront that so many communities had lost to industrial development and pollution (416-314-9490).

In the past two decades, waterfront areas have been reclaimed, parks and marinas created, and walking and biking trails laid down along the shoreline. Although some stretches of this ambitious project are not yet complete, it is now possible to bike from Confederation Park in Hamilton, along the shores of Burlington and east to Oakville, Mississauga, and Etobicoke and then on to Toronto, partly on roadways but largely along hiking/biking paths. The aim is to move on-road sections off road as quickly as possible (416-314-8572).

West of Hamilton, the Dundas Valley, a tract of twelve hundred hectares of protected wildlands cupped in the escarpment, boasts a forty-kilometre trail system suitable for mountain bikes, and some of the most spectacular views in the area. The Dundas Valley Visitor Centre, a replica of a Victorian train station, has a food concession and washrooms (905-525-2181).

A well-maintained rail trail starts at Mohawk Park in Brantford, runs east to Jerseyville, rolls down the Niagara Escarpment into the Dundas Valley

NIAGARA RIVER RECREATION TRAIL, NIAGARA FALLS

and ends at Ewen Road in Hamilton—thirty-two kilometres in all. While some benches are provided, there are no water supplies or toilets except at the Dundas Valley Visitor Centre, noted above (519-621-2761; 905-525-2181).

CALEDON AND HALTON HILLS

The Caledon Rail Trail starts on Isabella Street in Terra Cotta and travels thirty-four kilometres over the Niagara Escarpment and the Oak Ridges Moraine, and across the Credit and Humber Rivers, to fetch up at Highway 9 east of Palgrave. The landscape along the way varies between farmland and forest, and you may spot one or two beaver dams. Since the trail also crosses many concession roads and the busy Highway 10, extra caution is advised when riding Caledon (905-584-2272).

CALEDON RAIL TRAIL

For a rougher ride best suited to mountain bikes, Hilton Falls Conservation Area, just north of Highway 401 near Campbellville, provides many kilometres of cycling up and down forest slopes and along cascading streams. Kelso Conservation Area south of Milton offers fifteen kilometres of hilly trails. Both offer washroom and picnic facilities (905-336-1158).

KITCHENER-WATERLOO AND AREA

The nineteen-kilometre Cambridge-Paris Rail Trail begins at Churchill Park in Cambridge and follows the curves of the Grand River through woods and meadows to East River Road in the northeast corner of Paris. There are benches along the route (519-621-2761).

Guelph's Royal Recreation Trails are stone-dust paths that meander throughout the city's extensive park system, often paralleling the Speed and Eramosa Rivers. By following linking trails, you can cycle continuously through most of Guelph's green spaces (519-837-5626).

STRATFORD AND AREA

In Wildwood Conservation Area located east of St. Marys off Highway 7/19, you'll find twenty-four kilometres of trails around Wildwood Lake, surrounded by peaceful grasslands, forest, and farms. Washrooms and picnic areas are available (519-451-2800).

LONDON AND AREA

A network of long trails runs through London's Thames-side parks, through the grounds of the University of Western Ontario, and links with twenty-five kilometres of hiking and cycling trails in Fanshawe Conservation Area, which has a beach, a food concession, and picnic areas.

LAKE ERIE SHORELINE

At Point Pelee National Park on Lake Erie, south of
Leamington, the Centennial Trail provides a four-and-a-
half kilometre ride through some of the park's best scenery,
beginning at the marsh boardwalk. Pelee is famous as a
gathering place for migrating birds and monarch
butterflies. Rondeau Provincial Park,
east along the lakeshore, offers
fourteen kilometres of marsh trail, and
the chance to perhaps glimpse a bald
eagle soaring overhead. Point Pelee
and Rondeau have visitor centres,
washrooms, and picnic areas (519-
322-2365; 519-674-1750).

WINDSOR AND AREA

Windsor has been making progress
since 1989 on a plan to connect the
city's greenways with a single
walking/cycling trail. So far six trails
are open, with a total length of more
than twenty-two kilometres. The
longest is the eight-and-a-half
kilometre Ganatchio Trail. Based in
part on an abandoned streetcar right-
of-way, this wide, paved trail begins at
Lauzon Road and Riverside Drive in
Windsor and takes you along the shore
of Lake St. Clair for five kilometres, to
the town of Tecumseh. One extension
at the Windsor end runs through the
wildflower meadows of Little River corridor, while another
follows quiet residential streets (519-253-2300).

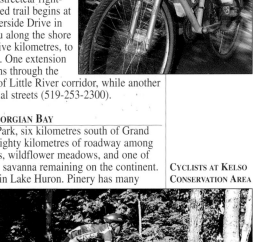

LAKE HURON AND GEORGIAN BAY

At Pinery Provincial Park, six kilometres south of Grand
Bend, you can cycle eighty kilometres of roadway among
house-high sand dunes, wildflower meadows, and one of
the final stands of oak savanna remaining on the continent.
Cool off with a swim in Lake Huron. Pinery has many

CYCLISTS AT KELSO
CONSERVATION AREA

facilities including
a visitor centre
and washrooms
(519-243-2220).

Cycling can be
one of the most
enjoyable ways to
see Southwestern
Ontario, and the
area offers
something for
every level of
cyclist from
beginner to
advanced.

FESTIVALS

MICHAEL BAGINSKI

Southwestern Ontario is "festival country." Playing on the region's distinctive history, geography, and changing seasons, special events cater to almost every interest from winter carnivals, world-famous theatres, flower shows, and wine festivals to Highland Games, arts and crafts fairs, and native powwows. Every community can offer a long list of

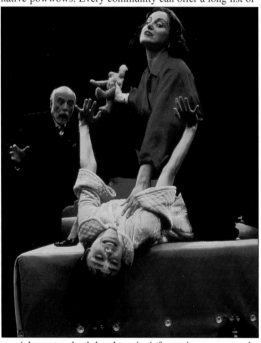

The Taming of the Shrew, Stratford Festival

special events; check local tourist information centres and brochures, because odds are very good that something special is happening near you, no matter when you visit. Whenever possible, telephone numbers have been supplied. You can also check for information about events with local Chambers of Commerce.

Many events take advantage of the area's fine summer weather, but the off-peak winter months are also busy, with activities ranging from winter carnivals to holiday season lights festivals.

The Shop at Sly Corner, Shaw Festival

THEATRE FESTIVALS

Stratford and the Shaw: those two names conjure up the magic of the very best in theatre. There are theatre festivals in many southwestern Ontario communities—Blyth, Drayton, Orangeville, and more—but Stratford and the Shaw are head and shoulders above their younger and smaller competitors. (For a detailed account of theatre throughout the region, see the theatre section in this book).

Both the renowned Stratford Festival in Stratford, and Niagara-on-the-Lake's acclaimed Shaw Festival attract world-famous players and audiences from across North America and around the globe.

As its name implies, the Stratford Shakespearean Festival, held May through November, celebrates the works of William Shakespeare, although it also features other classical dramas, modern plays, and musicals (1-800-567-1600).

The Shaw Festival in Niagara-on-the-Lake (April to October) is the only theatre company in the world devoted exclusively to the works of George Bernard Shaw and his contemporaries. It is located in perhaps the most picturesque community in southwestern Ontario, in the heart of the Niagara wine country (1-800-511-SHAW).

MUSIC FESTIVALS

Music festivals and special events abound throughout the region, all year long. Many southwestern Ontario cities are home to universities (Windsor, London, Waterloo, Guelph, Hamilton, and St. Catharines) and these schools stage ongoing cultural events, especially concerts, from classical to contemporary. As well, there are some top-notch local festivals that have put some of southwestern Ontario's communities on the musical map.

An event culminating on the July 1 weekend is London's annual Royal Canadian Big Band Music Festival, voted one of the top hundred events in North America in 1998 by the American Bus Association. Originally designed to pay tribute to big band king and local hero Guy Lombardo, the festival now encompasses dozens of free and paid concerts performed by international and local bands, and a parade of Lombardo tribute artists. Past performers have included the Tommy Dorsey Orchestra conducted by Buddy Morrow, the Lawrence Welk All Stars with Henry Cuesta, the Spitfire Band with Jackie Ross, the Nelson Riddle Orchestra, and Lombardo's Royal Canadians. (1-800-461-BAND).

Music fills the streets and halls of the small community of Elora during the last three weeks of July. Known primarily for its spectacular gorge and unique craft shops, the town comes alive with "Canadian and world premieres, competitions, symphonies, period instrumental ensembles, dancers, soloists, narrators, and some of the finest choral singing" during the Elora Festival (519-846-0331).

ELORA FESTIVAL

The Home County Folk Festival, which showcases

traditional and contemporary folk music performers in London, also welcomes more than one hundred regional craft artisans for four days in mid-July in Victoria Park (519-432-4310).

HILLSIDE FESTIVAL, GUELPH

HOME COUNTRY FOLK FESTIVAL, LONDON

In Guelph, the popular Hillside Festival is a three-day event in late July with music, crafts, exhibits, demonstrations, and kids' programs, all held at the Guelph Lake Conservation Area.

Guelph has a number of other annual music festivals as well, including the Spring Festival in late May, and the Jazz Festival in early September (519-763-6396).

Hillebrand winery at Niagara-on-the-Lake hosts a unique series of music events during the summer. The three-part Vineyard Concert Series includes a strings concert, one for jazz lovers, and one featuring blues (1-800-582-8412).

The Winter Festival of Friends is held in late November at the Hamilton Convention Centre, featuring jazz and classical concerts, all-Canadian arts and crafts, and fashion shows (1-800-263-8590).

CULTURAL FESTIVALS

HILLEBRAND WINERY, NIAGARA-ON-THE-LAKE

Most communities have some form of cultural festival. Often, they run as multicultural events like the celebration in July in Kitchener's Victoria Park.

The Mennonite Relief Sale, held the last Saturday of May in New Hamburg, is a cultural festival with a difference—handmade quilts are auctioned, thousands of delectable edibles are sold, and crafts are available, all for one good cause—every penny spent goes to Mennonite Central Committee relief and development work around the world. Events start early (experienced Relief-ers show up at 7 a.m. or earlier) and more than thirty thousand attend the one-day event each year (519-745-8458).

In Fergus, Scots of all nationalities wear the tartan at the annual Fergus Scottish Festival and Highland Games each August. The three-day festival features massed pipe bands, "heavy" events, dancing, piping, tug-of-war, and other activities with a distinctly Celtic flare (519-787-0099).

One of the largest events is put on by the descendents of German settlers in Kitchener-Waterloo and area, who carry on the grand tradition of Oktoberfest in Germany. The Kitchener-Waterloo version, in fact, is the second-

FERGUS SCOTTISH
FESTIVAL AND
HIGHLAND GAMES

largest Oktoberfest outside Munich, but unlike the original (which carries on throughout the latter half of September), it actually takes place in October. Similarities include brassy oompah bands, sizzling bratwurst, and, of course, frothy beer, served at Festhalls ranging from the Kitchener Market to the University of Waterloo, and at all of the community's famous German clubs. Festivities are highlighted by a grand parade, Thanksgiving Day, through the two cities (519-570-4267).

Visitors to southwestern Ontario can discover the culture of the region's First Nations people through a series of local powwows, which range from traditional gatherings celebrating old songs and ceremonial dancers (with proceeds donated to charity) to modern competitions that attract dancers from across North America with the promise of lucrative prize money. One of the largest, the N'Amerind Powwow, takes place in London around the end of June each year. (For dates and information, call 519-672-0131).

The Six Nations of the Grand River in Oshweken, near Brantford, puts on a number of events year-round, including the Grand River Champion of Champions Powwow on the fourth weekend of July, the Six Nations Native Pageant, an outdoor theatre production held the first three weekends in August, and the Independent Handicrafts Bazaar the first Saturday in November. For information call 519-758-5444.

FOOD FESTIVALS

The approach of spring brings a host of maple sugar festivals, when tree sap is collected and boiled into maple syrup in an age-old tradition. Visitors can witness, and taste, "sugaring off"—when fresh maple syrup is tossed in the snow to freeze into candy. One of the best festivals takes place in Elmira in early April. Visitors can tour the sugar bush, browse along the main street, which is turned into a pedestrian mall for the weekend, and, of course, fill up on pancakes and maple syrup (519-669-2605).

Summer is also a time to celebrate the bounty of the land. From the blueberry festival in Kingsville to the bean festival in Zurich, the importance of agriculture in the region is celebrated.

Strawberry Festivals are a southwestern Ontario tradition: special strawberry events are held everywhere, including Bayfield in mid-June (519-565-2021), and Lucknow in late June.

FALL FESTIVALS

Fall in southwestern Ontario means more than just coloured leaves and Halloween pumpkins. Fall fairs abound in almost every community, including the Waterford Pumpkin Festival, and the famous Western Fair in London. The list in the region is almost as long as a list of every village, town, and city in southwestern Ontario. In recent years, fair season has been moved ahead, with many communities (such as Ridgetown, Tillsonburg, and Aylmer) now celebrating the harvest in August, when the weather is good even if the crops are not yet ripe. Fair season stretches into early October.

Fall fairs are flourishing in small communities across southwestern Ontario, even as they lose their impact in the big cities. Many of the larger centres have struggled to maintain their autumn spectacle, although London's Western Fair, held in the first two weeks of September, continues to provide big-time entertainment (1-800-619-4629). Smaller cities, such as Stratford (mid-September) continue to present successful fairs,

PRODUCTS FROM THE WELLESLEY APPLE BUTTER AND CHEESE FESTIVAL

while for dozens of smaller communities, from Tavistock in Oxford County to Melbourne in Middlesex, the local fall fair is the highlight of the season for residents and visitors. A complete list of Fall Fairs in Ontario is available from the Ontario Association of Agricultural Societies (905-986-0238).

Some special events with a personality all their own that still capture the harvest time atmosphere include the Wellesley Apple Butter and Cheese Festival in Waterloo Region, which focuses on exactly those products, but adds many other attractions, and draws up to forty thousand people early in the fall (519-699-4611), and the popular Niagara Region Wine Festival in the latter half of September, when communities in the Niagara Region offer

A WELLESLEY FESTIVAL BOOTH

celebrations and, of course, samplings that have been planned for months (1-888-594-6379).

It's intriguing that some of the most popular tourist centres, such as Niagara-on-the-Lake, do not host fall fairs; it's almost as though this is the one time when less-noticed centres get their day or weekend in the spotlight. An exception to this generalization is Bayfield, with a one-day fair held early, in mid-August, in the heart of tourist season. Typical small-town fairs near

BUFFALO AND
MOOSE, WINTER
FESTIVAL OF LIGHTS,
NIAGARA FALLS

major tourist centres include the Lincoln County Fair in
Beamsville (Niagara Peninsula) in early September, with
horse races and a wine tent among the unique attractions
(905-945-5688), and the New Hamburg Fall Fair, a four-day
event in mid-September with everything typical of an old-
fashioned country fair, located only a few minutes from
Stratford to the west and Kitchener-Waterloo and St. Jacobs
to the east (519-662-6628).

WINTER FESTIVALS

Communities, towns, and cities from Windsor to Owen
Sound check in with colourful displays in November,
December, and January. The town of Simcoe is especially
known for its display, while the premium event surely
belongs to Niagara Falls. With the famous falls as a
backdrop, the city hosts a renowned International Festival
of Lights each year, combined with a wide variety of
corresponding events, from concerts and carolling to
children's shows, ballet performances, car shows, and
cheerleading competitions. From late November to mid-
February, the sparkling spectacle highlights the grandeur of
one of the world's seven natural wonders and stirs the
holiday spirit among all who take it in (905-356-6061).

The resort town of Grand Bend celebrates the snow
during the first two weekends of February with motorcycle
ice races, a parade, hayrides, free children's events, and a
popular ice sculpture competition. Hotels and resorts stoke
up crackling fires and crew-warming drinks like hot
toddies and mulled wine (519-238-2001).

More and more southwestern Ontario communities are
holding outdoor New Year's Eve celebrations in the centres
of their communities. Leading the way is Kitchener, with a
massive December 31 event at the downtown City Hall and
in Victoria Park, with big-name entertainment and activities
for all ages.

Of course, it is impossible to list every festival or event in
these pages. From St. Thomas's annual Iron Horse Festival
and Fire Muster in August to the Summerfolk Music and
Craft Festival in Owen Sound, or the Waterloo County and
Area Quilt Festival in May, there is sure to be something to
suit all interests in southwestern Ontario.

FOOD AND DINING

ROSE MURRAY

With its rich, fertile soil and many rivers and lakes, southwestern Ontario is an important part of the food story in this country. And each of its regions brings its own bounty.

NIAGARA PENINSULA

Southwestern Ontario is a prime agricultural region with several microclimates that present conditions equivalent to those in a much more temperate country. The most important example of these milder conditions is in the Niagara Peninsula. It's an area filled with grape vines, fruit trees, and a wide variety of produce.

A few years ago, in the region's restaurants, diners were hard pressed to find anything but canned fruit cocktail ... in an area that grows the best peaches in the world! The situation has changed radically, in good part due to the fact

ON THE TWENTY, JORDAN

the wine of the region has become much better. In fact, it has won many awards around the world. The region's icewine in particular is second to none.

Because food and wine are so much a part of each other, it is perfectly logical that wineries should open restaurants in which to showcase their wine. The Hillebrand Vineyard Café near Niagara-on-the-Lake and On the Twenty at Cave Spring Cellars in Jordan are only two examples of this growing trend (905-468-3201; 905-562-7313).

Chef Antonio de Luca at Hillebrand hails from the Toronto area and finds the Niagara region not only more relaxing, but much more bountiful. The local produce and other ingredients which he uses almost exclusively when in season are readily available here.

Chef Michael Olson of On the Twenty also showcases the region's food and personally seeks local purveyors to provide him with fresh ingredients.

This happy marriage of food and wine started with the hosts at Vineland Estates Winery in Vineland offering trays

of cheese and paté with a glass of wine on their lovely porch (905-562-7088). The concept was expanded to a patio bistro that, in turn, has increased in size and menu. There are plans in the works for an even bigger restaurant here and at the new Strewn Winery (905-468-1229). Other wineries have followed suit. According to Peter Gamble, executive director of the Vintners Quality Alliance (a guarantee of quality for Ontario wine consumers), more will open in the next few years, attracting some of Ontario's top chefs who prefer country air and fresh produce to the glitter of city lights.

VINELAND ESTATES WINERY

KITCHENER-WATERLOO AND AREA
The fields are huge, silos high, and markets busy in this rich farm region. It's an area of fruit, corn, pigs, maple syrup, and tall, graceful black walnut trees. This area attracted hundreds of Mennonites who came in Conestoga wagons to become the first white settlers in the interior of the province. Since 1800, their influence has been great here, where sour cream salads and Dutch apple pie are symbolic of a cuisine that is based on simplicity, economy, and experience. Mennonite recipes make use of everything grown on these Waterloo County farms. Some of the food, like pies, rosettes, noodles, egg cheese, apple butter, and summer sausage, is eagerly sought by the thousands of people who flock to the St. Jacobs Farmers' Market and the Waterloo County Farmers' Market near St. Jacobs each week. You have to grow up with other Mennonite specialties like kochkase (cooked cheese) to really appreciate the flavour.

People also flock to the Stone Crock in the village of St. Jacobs for a taste of Mennonite fare, while taverns like the Heidelberg Restaurant & Brew Pub serve similarly humble, but delicious plates of well-done ribs, pig tails, sauerkraut, schnitzel, and mugs of their own beer (519-664-2286; 519-699-4413). Actually, there are a number of good breweries like Sleemans and Brick in the area.

If you're looking for something a little less homey, try the exciting

STONE CROCK, ST. JACOBS

Bhima's Warung in Kitchener-Waterloo where the owner and chef Paul Boehmer depends on his travels east and his classical French training to present some pretty eclectic flavours (519-747-0722).

Paul was a sous chef under Nigel Didcock at Langdon Hall which is the impressive Relais & Chateaux Country House Hotel just outside Cambridge (519-740-2100). Situated on 200 acres of woodland and gardens, Langdon's present Chef Louise Duhamel uses produce from the gardens along with local products like veal, asparagus, and price-winning Woolwich goat cheese to create her wonderful menus.

Right in Cambridge, a couple of restaurants worth finding are Mimosa owned by the Jacques brothers where well-experienced Larry Jacques is the chef and Deliciously Different whose chef/owner Noland Ralph haunts the Cambridge farmers' market to buy his produce and flowers (519-624-2023; 519-740-4949).

Nearby Guelph has a number of good restaurants. The Other Brother's on Yarmouth Street has been getting rave reviews; the two-storey dramatic Vase has upscale Italian fare; and Carden Street Cafe turns out food that is very fresh (519-822-4465; 519-821-9393; 519-837-2830).

DELICIOUSLY DIFFERENT, CAMBRIDGE

STRATFORD AND AREA

Another good farm area is Perth County. But it is a cooking school and theatre that have had the greatest influence on the food climate here.

Home of the famous Shakespearean festival, the small town of Stratford swells to huge proportions when the theatre season is on, presenting great problems for local restaurants. For many years, better restaurants found it difficult to get enough qualified help for their busy summer season. After relying on casual help or importing expensive European-trained apprentices, three of the city's restaurateurs developed the idea for the Stratford Chefs School.

Jim Morris of Rundles, Eleanor Kane of The Old Prune, and The Church's Joseph Mandel (who has since left the school and sold his restaurant) opened the school in 1983. Since then, they have sent forth chefs with world-class potential who have found good positions throughout Canada, the United States, and Europe (519-271-6442; 519-271-5052; 519-273-3424).

Much to the benefit of the food scene in Stratford, some have remained in the area to start various restaurants, pubs, catering businesses, and interesting spots like York Street Kitchen, The Sunroom, The Wildwood Inn, Down the Street Bar and Cafe, Bentley's, and even a place specializing in French fries to give theatre goers and locals a good choice of excellent food (519-273-7041; 519-273-0331; 519-349-2467; 519-273-5886; 519-271-1121).

RUNDLES, STRATFORD

The upscale restaurants remain the original three with the school's head cookery instructor, Neil Baxter, still showing his creative genius at Rundles.

LONDON AND AREA

There are three food memories I have from living in London twenty-seven years ago—pick-your-own farms, Covent Garden Market, and Ann McColl's Kitchen Shop (519-663-0866). I would go out picking everything from cherries to

SUN ROOM
RESTAURANT,
STRATFORD

Brussels sprouts myself, but I suspected that the Italian population of the city kept tomato growers in business when I'd see my neighbour bring home bushels of tomatoes for her delicious sauce.

No doubt the produce farms in the surrounding area were kept busy supplying the downtown Covent Garden Market as they still do. The market is open every day and offers some of the best cheese, coffee, pasta, deli, meats, and produce in the region.

Ann McColl, who has had a great influence on the food scene in London for almost thirty years, now has her exciting shop right around the corner from the market. She explains how the market has attracted a group of small, pleasant restaurants like La Casa, Tapas, and Home where you can have a tasty "job lunch" or supper before the cinema (519-434-2272; 519-679-7800; 519-4387-5122). Murano, across from the Delta Armories Hotel on Waterloo St., is a more formal place that also sells the famous Italian glass for which it's named (519-434-7565).

Indeed, London is now a vibrant restaurant city offering a broad range of eateries. East Town Pizza is consistently voted the best pizza in the world while the tiny Verandah Cafe is the best in town for its great use of fresh produce (519-455-7010). More formal restaurants like Anthony's Seafood Bistro, bars, and Sebastian's Food Shop cluster around The Grand Theatre on Richmond as part of "Richmond Row" (519-679-0960; 519-432-2684).

LAKE ERIE SHORELINE

In the Haldimand-Norfold region, hugging the northeastern shoreline of Lake Erie, farmers are always searching for crops to replace the drop in demand for tobacco. There's now a whole range of important crops—nut trees, domestic blueberries, peanuts, ginseng, and even hemp which produces a cooking oil. There's also a new-found industry springing up in the region — big birds like Ostrich and Emu.

In Port Dover, look for the Gingerbread House, a cosy restaurant where the VanWycks collect all these local products to give their customers a taste of the new and the good (519-583-0249).

One of the new products they offer is Lake Erie Whitefish Caviar produced in Kingsville by Pelee Treasures (519-322-1366). Several restaurants and dining rooms in Port Dover are also known for their perch and pickerel taken from Lake Erie.

WINDSOR AND AREA

As in the Niagara region, this area is home to a wide variety of produce and is also seeing the beneficial effects of a thriving wine industry. There are five growing wineries: tiny LeBlanc Estate Winery, producing a limited number of exquisite wines; Pelee Island Winery that grows its grapes on the island, but makes its wine on the mainland; D'Angelo Vineyards Estate Winery; the large Colio Wines; and further along Highway 3, London Winery. It's fun to stay in the area at the Tin Goose Inn on Pelee Island and to take the tours these wineries offer.

OVERTURES, TECUMSETH

Where there's good wine, good food will follow. Seek out The Vintage Goose in Kingsville, The Old Bullock in Amherstburg, Overtures, and The Bistro in Tecumseth and The Essex Courtyard in the town of Essex (519-733-6900; 519-736-5075; 519-979-0010; 519-252-0808; 519-776-7055).

Windsor itself has the bragging rights to some good Chinese and Italian food. Pizza is big here. Made with fresh dough and sauces, it is often cooked in wood ovens like those at Spago Trattoria (519-252-2233). Erie Street East boasts a whole line of good Italian restaurants like La Contessa (519-252-2167; 519-972-5699) and look for Porcino's on Howard Avenue. Go to Wyandotte Street West for Chinese, seeking out Wah Court or any of the three Empress Garden Restaurants (519-254-1388; 519-253-3332).

LAKE HURON AND GEORGIAN BAY

We're getting away from the more populated areas and getting into fiercer weather in Huron, Grey, and Bruce counties, but there is still a strong agricultural base here. In Huron, navy beans are important while Grey is known for its pork and Bruce for its beef.

MUNSHAW'S RESTAURANT, FLESHERTON

As you travel along the Lake Huron shore, The Little Inn of Bayfield is worth a stop, especially for its wonderful wine list and single malt Scotches (519-565-2611).

Inland, Pat Crocker of Riversong Herbals and Naturals near Hanover offers lunches along with her workshops and herb walks. Pat recommends The Grey Rose in Hanover, Munshaw's Restaurant in Flesherton, Grosvenor's in Southampton, and Norma Jean's in Owen Sound as some favourite spots (519-364-2600; 519-924-2814; 519-797-1226; 519-376-2232).

We particularly enjoyed fresh whitefish when we lived in Owen Sound, but it's hard to find it in restaurants, although you can still buy fresh fish from Georgian Bay at the Owen Sound Market (519-371-3433).

Closer to Collingwood, well-known chef Michael Stadtlander has moved from the big city of Toronto to take up farming near Singhampton at Eigensinn Farm. He and his wife offer what they grow in the form of creative menus for which people reserve weeks in advance.

CHRISTOPHER'S, COLLINGWOOD

The Collingwood area is another microclimate because of the escarpment and the influence of Georgian Bay. As a result, there is a huge apple industry with roadside stands selling not only many varieties of apples (including the famous Georgian Bay Northern Spy), but all manner of apple products.

Because the Collingwood region has a four-season tourist designation, there is a huge population of skiers and cottagers summer and winter and thus a number of restaurant chains in evidence, but Christoper's on Pine continues to be a good bet (705-445-7117).

Food producers and restaurateurs alike are taking advantage of this prime agricultural part of Canada. We not only find good, fresh food offered in markets, but in the area's eating establishments as better-trained chefs pass on the bounty of the regions.

GARDENS

JIM ST. MARIE

Eight out of every ten Canadians garden, and in highly populated southwestern Ontario that figure may even be higher. Visitors will see more attractive home and public gardens here than almost anywhere in Canada.

This is Ontario's "banana belt"; the southern tip of the province is more southerly than northern California. As a result, this area offers some of Canada's horticultural gems such as the Royal Botanical Gardens in Hamilton, the

IRISES, ROYAL
BOTANICAL GARDENS

beautiful civic parks of Windsor (which is actually south of Detroit), and the world-renowned Niagara parks and gardens.

If gardening is your chosen leisure activity, there is plenty to enjoy. Here are some of the best gardens in southwestern Ontario.

NIAGARA PENINSULA

Niagara Parks Botanical Gardens just north of Niagara Falls has a rose garden boasting 2,300 bushes in formal beds. It is also the site of an official All American Selections Display Garden of the newest and best annuals and vegetables.

FLORAL CLOCK,
NIAGARA FALLS

Alpine, herb, aquatic, ornamental, and natural gardens adjoin large displays of lilacs, peonies, irises, ornamental shrubs, and a large arboretum (905-356-8554).

A 12.2 metre Floral Clock also north of the Falls is planted with pansies in early spring and then replaced by carpet bedding for a total of twenty-five thousand plants. The adjacent

Centennial Lilac Gardens blooms profusely in May with more than a thousand lilac bushes of 250 varieties (905-356-2241).Queen Victoria Park on the Niagara Parkway is a large park combining both formal and natural gardens where half a million daffodils bloom in spring. Rose and rock gardens plus beds of annuals and perennials may be enjoyed here (905-356-2241).

NIAGARA PARKS GREENHOUSE

Niagara Parks Commission Greenhouses are also on the Niagara Parkway. Tropical plants, palm trees, and local flowering and foliage plants are on display with special Christmas and spring shows and a chrysanthemum show in November. The outdoor garden contains a fragrance garden labelled in Braille and a hummingbird display (905-356-2241).

LILAC DELL, ROYAL BOTANICAL GARDENS

The Niagara Parks Butterfly Conservatory is one of North America's largest collections of free-flying butterflies, set in a lush indoor rain forest in the world's largest glass-enclosed butterfly conservatory (905-356-0025).

Thousands of mostly flowering annuals plus some perennials and vegetables in large beds can be found at the Stokes Seeds Trial Gardens in St. Catharines. This is one of only five Canadian flower and judging trial gardens of the prestigious All American Selections, and the only one in southwestern Ontario (905-688-4300).

Gage Park in Hamilton features 162 rose beds, an extensive perennial garden, plus many indigenous and exotic trees. A large greenhouse with streams and waterfalls displays more than a hundred species of exotic plants. There is a chrysanthemum show in November with 75,000 blooms of 240 varieties.

LILIES, ROYAL BOTANICAL GARDENS

NIAGARA PARKS BOTANTICAL GARDENS

Sam Lawrence Park, also in Hamilton, is a unique urban park on the brow of the Niagara Escarpment. It is primarily a rock garden with walkways, and a large perennial collection including ornamental grasses. It features a panoramic view of the city and harbour (905-546-2666).

Hamilton's Royal Botanical Gardens are well known throughout the province. They contain one thousand hectares of natural areas, enormous collections of plants, and beautiful display gardens. Its highlights include the world's largest collection of lilacs, an acre of irises (more than 250,000 blooms), two acres of roses, 125,000 spring flowering bulbs in the Rock Garden, the ninety-acre Arboretum with a rhododendron and magnolia collection, and the Laking Perennial Garden with hundreds of peonies and many beds of varied perennials. Adjacent to the Rose Garden are annual trial gardens, clematis vines, lily beds, medicinal, scented, and herb plants, and home landscaping garden displays. The Mediterranean Garden is a two-storey greenhouse. Established in 1929 by Royal Charter from King George V, the RBG is also a living museum, a rare Carolinian forest, and a wilderness and wetland area with forty-eight kilometres of trails (905-527-1158).

KITCHENER-WATERLOO AND AREA

Rockway Gardens in Kitchener is an extensive, colourful rock garden with waterfalls and pools plus many island beds of thousands of spring flowering bulbs and masses of annuals. There is also a perennial bed, and a knot garden of herbs (519-745-4669).

Guelph also has a Floral Clock Garden. This sunken garden, which is a small part of Riverside Park, contains an extensive rock garden with annuals and perennials, waterfalls and pools, dominated by a seven-

LILACS AND ARBOR AT THE UNIVERSITY OF GUELPH ARBORETUM

thousand-flowering-plant floral clock (519-837-5626).

The John McRae House—Museum and Gardens in Guelph is the home of the author of the poem "In Flanders Fields." Gardens of annuals, perennials, and shrubs around the home have recently been restored to the World War I era. Appropriate to the poem, various species and colours of poppies are featured here (519-836-1221).

The University of Guelph Arboretum has 165 hectares containing 4,100 types of trees and shrubs. Eight kilometres of signed trails though the treed areas lead to a variety of gardens: Japanese, English, Rose, Lilac, and Rhododendron to name a few. Of note are the five urban-style Gosling Wildlife Gardens, the oldest and best public example of wildlife-attracting gardens in Ontario (519-824-4120).

Lorne Park in Brantford showcases the city's horticultural gardens, displaying 500,000 annual flowering plants in many large and smaller floral beds, some with manicured carpet bedding in new designs each year, also large perennial beds, rose beds, and a Victorian gazebo. The park is on both sides of Colborne Street just west of Lorne Bridge.

TWO VIEWS OF SHAKESPEAREAN GARDENS, STRATFORD

STRATFORD AND AREA

Shakespearean Gardens in Stratford is an English–style garden, opened in the 1930s. It contains beds of flowers named in Shakespeare's plays, along with rose and herb gardens, and perennial beds set amid an old mill tower. There are also benches and a gazebo (519-273-3352).

The Shakespearean Festival Gardens, also in Stratford, was developed in 1997 during extensive renovations of the Festival Theatre. A new perennial garden beside the building now contains fifteen thousand plants of 225 varieties—many new and unusual. Designed to evolve during the 26-week play season, this informal walk-through garden also has seven thousand spring flowering bulbs and a water garden of new and rare plants (519-271-4040).

LONDON AND AREA

Civic Garden Complex in London features four different gardens and a garden centre adjacent to Springbank Park. It includes a perennial garden of 160 varieties of a thousand plants all named and tagged, two thousand rose bushes of thirty varieties in a beautiful, open setting, a woodland garden of Carolinian trees and native plants amid trails and bridges, one hundred different shrubs, and a tropical display house (519-661-4757).

The Sifton Bog, also in London, is the most southerly acidic bog in Canada—an important study area containing many fragile plants, uniquely located in a large city. Because it is surrounded by a Carolinian woods, visitors can see in a ten-minute walk what would require a trek of several hundred kilometres in the north. Signed trails lead to a boardwalk onto the floating bog. Watch for five species of carnivorous plants and nine species of orchids, plus rare trees and shrubs (519-451-2800).

Fanshawe Pioneer Village Gardens in London features a pioneer apple orchard of forty varieties, a large herb garden plus a pioneer kitchen garden, and a Victorian flower garden all grown from heritage seeds in this village of twenty reconstructed buildings of the late 1800s (519-457-1296).

LAKE ERIE SHORELINE

Swain Greenhouse near West Lorne is 1.8 hectares of tropical plants. The greenhouse specializes in rare desert cacti and hosts a wide range of houseplants and a poinsettia festival, in late November and December (519-768-1116).

WINDSOR AND AREA

The Queen Elizabeth II Sunken Gardens can be found in Jackson Park in Windsor. It features twelve thousand rose bushes of 450 varieties surrounding a WWII Lancaster Bomber. Thousands of tulips bloom in May, followed by many thousands of annuals and perennials (519-255-6276).

Colasanti's Tropical Gardens in nearby Ruthven features 1.5 hectares under cover of tropical plants and cacti. The Colasantis are commercial growers of seventeen varieties of hibiscus plus banana plants, Venus flytrap, sensitive plant, and other exotics. Outdoors there is a gigantic mature maze and several butterfly and hummingbird gardens.

LAKE HURON AND GEORGIAN BAY

Keppel Croft Farm and Gardens is near Wiarton. Natural gardens include perennial borders, ponds, pebble beds, rockeries, and trough gardens along with pit greenhouses and a woodland garden. This private garden of Dawn and Bill Loney was chosen as Canadian Gardening Magazine's 1995 Garden of the Year.

From the lush Niagara region to the rocky tip of the Bruce Peninsula, southwestern Ontario is in love with gardening, and its ambitious and expert gardeners welcome visitors to share their love from spring through fall.

JACKSON PARK,
WINDSOR

GOLF

RICK CAMPBELL

Southwestern Ontario is a driving, chipping, and putting paradise—and golfers fortunate enough to play some of the finest public-access courses in the province, located right here, will attest to that.

From the border cities of Windsor and Sarnia, north to Georgian Bay tourist hotspots, and reaching south to the Festival Country area including Kitchener-Waterloo, Cambridge, and Guelph, golfers of all abilities will be warmly welcomed at an interesting mix of mature courses and newer, challenging layouts.

ROSELAND GOLF AND CURLING CLUB, WINDSOR

The golf boom of the 1990s has spawned an explosion of new facilities, some of which are private and accessible to visitors only under special conditions. This chapter, however, focuses on courses that are public or semi-private and offer top-flight experiences. Before heading out to a specific course, it is customary to check ahead for available tee times, reservations, tournament play, and so on.

While most courses with outstanding facilities and reputations are eighteen-hole championship length, visitors should not overlook some of the quaint executive or par-three layouts that can offer a quick round in the midst of a busy schedule, and also can be combined with other side trips to make for an enjoyable day.

NIAGARA PARKS GOLF COURSE

NIAGARA PENINSULA

Visitors to the Niagara Region have a number of golfing opportunities, from King's Forest south of Ancaster to the historical Niagara-on-the-Lake (1875), the oldest golf course in North America, to the immaculate Niagara Parks Whirlpool, consistently listed in the top ten public courses in Canada (905-547-9042; 905-468-3271; 905-356-1140). An added bonus—Niagara–area courses boast a much longer season than others because of the region's moderate climate.

KITCHENER-WATERLOO AND AREA

In Kitchener, both the city-owned traditional Rockway and the more open Doon Valley layout along the 401 are superbly maintained, especially given the incredible traffic each faces on a daily basis (519-741-2585; 519-741-2711).

The public and semi-private courses in the Golden

Triangle of Kitchener-Waterloo, Cambridge, and Guelph rarely take a back seat in terms of conditioning. West of Waterloo, the twenty-seven-hole Foxwood course has a strong mix of member- and green-fee players and is investing in many on-course changes to enhance conditions (519-634-8895). Elmira, just north of Kitchener-

DOON VALLEY GOLF CLUB, KITCHENER

Waterloo and near tourist favourites St. Jacobs and Elora, is very well maintained and easily accessible, especially for weekday play (519-669-1651).

Listowel is also gaining in reputation and the recently revised twenty-seven-hole Merry-Hill executive course near Breslau, although shorter, is very challenging and boasts some of the finest greens in the area (519-291-2500; 519-648-2804).

Three courses in Guelph—Victoria Park East and its counterpart West, plus Springfield—draw golfers from a wide area (519-821-2211; 519-821-1441; 519-821-4653). Vic Park weathers early spring well and is traditionally one of the first courses to open in the area, while Springfield is

SPRINGFIELD GOLF AND COUNTRY CLUB, GUELPH

held in high regard for its unique layout and quality clubhouse amenities. Further east of Guelph, in Acton, visit the Blue Springs Golf Club, nestled in the awe-inspiring Halton Hills, and home to the Canadian Professional Golf Association (519-853-0904).

In Cambridge, the Cambridge Golf and Country Club prides itself on its "hub" location in southwestern Ontario, and has excellent practice facilities in

addition to a well laid out, undulating design (519-621-5491).

Further south, the Oaks of St. George, Brantford North Ridge, Carlisle (off Highway 6), and the short but scenic Pine Valley south of Simcoe should also be on your list (519-448-3673; 519-753-6112; 905-689-8820; 519-426-0683).

THE OAKS OF ST. GEORGE GOLF CLUB, PARIS

LONDON AND AREA

The major centres of London and area have many outstanding courses. Notably, from a municipal standpoint, London's trio of Fanshawe, Thames Valley, and River Road offer the public golfer three of the finest, most diverse layouts in the province (519-455-2790; 519-471-5036; 519-452-1822).

WINDSOR AND AREA

Canada's southernmost golf course is Oxley Beach (519-738-2672). It is half an hour's drive from Windsor, near Harrow, on the northern shore of Lake Erie. While a modest 2,380-yard par-three layout, the course has been lovingly designed to highlight the scenic beauty (and wildlife) indigenous to the area. A summertime trip to Oxley takes you past several fresh-fruit-and-vegetable stands and a venerated local institution, Klassen's Blueberry Farm.

Home base for one of Canada's finest professionals (and now senior golfer) Bob Panasik, Windsor-area courses offer a number of challenges, from Hydeaway's tricky doglegs to Roseland's Donald Rose-designed layout with lightning-fast greens and no fewer than sixty-eight sand traps (519-727-5444; 519-969-3810). Blast away!

OXLEY BEACH GOLF COURSE, HARROW

Moving along the 401 corridor, Chatham's Indian Creek, which celebrated its fortieth anniversary in 1997, is renowned for its immaculate greens and beautiful conditioning (519-354-7666).

LAKE HURON AND GEORGIAN BAY

Heading north, border travellers at Sarnia/Port Huron will be challenged by the tough plateau greens at Sarnia Greenwood

(519-542-2770). The par-three layout at the Holiday Inn course by the Bluewater Bridge is also a fun and picturesque diversion (519-336-4111).

The shores of Lake Huron are dotted with many courses, from south of Grand Bend right to Tobermory. Two of the top layouts at "the Bend" are the Oakwood Inn Resort, with many amenities on-site or nearby, including their layout that makes golfers use every club in that bag (519-238-8060). Just up the road in Exeter, the Ironwood course, carved out of dense hardwood, is also a popular and exacting test (519-235-1521).

MONTERRA GOLF CLUB, COLLINGWOOD

Other "shouldn't miss" layouts in the Lake Huron/Georgian Bay area include the immaculately conditioned twenty-seven holes at Saugeen; the tough, well-bunkered Chippewa Club at Southhampton; and the scenic Owen Sound Country Club overlooking Owen Sound Bay (519-389-4031; 519-797-3684; 519-376-1961). Many "nine-holers" in this area have also been kept in remarkable shape and are ideal spots for a "two-hour tour."

Collingwood, with its unique shopping opportunities, is also a popular destination for golfers. Two of the most acclaimed layouts are the curvy Monterra Club at the base of Blue Mountain, and Cranberry Resort, which in 1995

CRANBERRY RESORT GOLF CLUB,

received an award from the Audubon Society for its conservation efforts in preserving wildlife and natural environment elements (705-445-0231; 705-444-2699).

Most avid golfers in southwestern Ontario have visited at least once the Pike Lake Golf Centre near Harriston on Highway 89 (519-338-3010). This is a terrifically entertaining course cut out amongst a vast trailer park and recreational area. Popular for its great conditions and tournament amenities, a memorable day on the links is guaranteed at Pike Lake.

There is no question that southwestern Ontario is a golfers' paradise, with public access to a wide range of challenging and well-conditioned courses to suit golfers of every skill level.

HIKING

JANA MILLER

Southwestern Ontario is a hiker's dream. There is no better way to experience Ontario's outdoor beauty than on foot. As a recreational activity, hiking continues to grow in popularity for many reasons: it's cost effective, it can easily involve the entire family, and it's just plain good for you. As well, communities across southern Ontario are meeting the demand for walking and hiking trails, giving recreational users a wide variety of starting and ending points to choose from.

HIKING IN SOUTHWESTERN ONTARIO

With the many trail links that currently exist in Ontario, it is already possible to walk from the beginning of the Elgin Trail on Lake Erie, to either Tobermory or Niagara Falls. Many of the smaller trails have links with Ontario's largest single hiking trail facility—the Bruce Trail.

No matter what kind of hiking adventure you are looking for—a scenic stroll, a romp with the kids, or a high-endurance climb in one of southern Ontario's most difficult but equally breathtaking areas—southwestern Ontario can match you step for step and thrill for thrill.

There are countless outdoor hiking adventures just waiting to be experienced. Your habitat on the hiking trail system in southern Ontario can range from Carolinian forest to muskeg, to a wall of limestone cliffs along the Bruce Trail. Not only is the natural scenery an exhilarating sight, but hikers will encounter abundant flora including rare ferns, countless varieties of wild mushrooms and orchids, hundreds of varieties of wildflowers and trees; and fauna such as skunks, turtles, opossum, moose, deer, beaver, and wolves.

At Point Pelee National Park, in the southernmost area of Ontario, watch thousands of monarch butterflies prepare for their September migration to Mexico, or view the interesting bird migrations in May, September, and October.

All you really need to get comfortable with Ontario's nature habitat are your hiking boots, your binoculars, some field guides, and lots of energy to enjoy Ontario's hundreds of marked trails. Bring your camera or your sketch book to capture some of Ontario's beauty to take home with you.

BRUCE TRAIL

If you are a hiking enthusiast, you cannot miss a visit to the Bruce Trail system. For more information about the trails below, see the listings section. No matter where you begin or end, the hiking and the scenery are unparalleled.

The Bruce Trail is the oldest and longest of all of Ontario's trail systems, covering about 440 miles along the Niagara Escarpment from Queenston to Tobermory, and featuring limestone cliffs dating back 430 million years. There are a significant number of southwestern Ontario hikers whose life's goal is to hike the entire Bruce Trail.

The Niagara Escarpment is Ontario's predominant topographical feature, at some points rising to heights of 325 feet, providing breathtaking scenery in a geologically fascinating area.

So important is the habitat to the flora and fauna that reside there—some of which can't be found anywhere else in Ontario—that the Bruce Peninsula National Park and Trail system has been designated a World Biosphere Reserve by the United Nations.

The Bruce Trail system is a preserve of limestone cliffs, mixed woodland, marsh, and

OLD BALDY, BEAVER VALLEY

beaches and is home to a variety of wildlife, including forty-three different species of wild orchid and the odd rattlesnake.

The trail itself links more than a hundred parks in southern Ontario, from Niagara to Tobermory, and provides some of the most spectacular hiking in Ontario. Its scenic finale near Tobermory juts out eighty kilometres into Lake Huron. There are wonderful views from trails atop the cliffs as well as ancient pathways that traverse the rocky shoreline and beaches below. The forest ecosystem along the edge of

WELLAND CANAL

the cliffs is probably the oldest, most undisturbed place in North America—some of the twisted white cedars there are more than a thousand years old.

A stone cairn marks the southern terminus of the Bruce Trail in Queenston Heights, near Niagara Falls. From there, starting along the trail towards Hamilton, hikers will encounter plenty of reminders of the War of 1812. Through St. Catharines and Thorold, you will pass all four Welland Canals, built during the past 150 years. There, on one of the major waterways of the world, hikers can watch as ships from around the world pass by. A number of side trails branch off on this stretch, including the General Brock Side Trail and the Upper Canada Heritage Trail.

The Bruce Trail continues on to the Dundas Valley Conservation area where hikers can view the Hermitage Ruin and Gatehouse Lodge Museum. The Hermitage Ruin is all that remains of an estate built in 1855 and gutted by fire in 1924. The Gatehouse Lodge Museum is a small interpretive centre near the Hermitage Ruin where visitors can learn the history of the former estate, and view a photographic exhibit. Both the ruins and the museum are open to visitors, but are closed in winter.

On the Arboretum Side Trail in the same area, on property owned by the Royal Botanical Gardens of Hamilton, the walking is easy in a pleasant atmosphere.

Also in this area and connected to the Bruce is the Spencer Gorge Wilderness Area, a Y-shaped bedrock gorge featuring two very scenic waterfalls. Created by Spencer Creek, Webster's Falls was the site of a huge stone flour mill built in 1856. When the mill was destroyed by fire, one of the first hydroelectric generators in Ontario was built at the base of the falls. From the falls, you continue on the Bruce Trail along the edge of the escarpment to Tew's Falls. Formed by East Spencer Creek, these falls flow over a bowl-shaped rock formation. From there, the trail continues to the mouth of Spencer Gorge. At the tip, Dundas peak offers a spectacular view of the Dundas Valley. In the distance you can see Hamilton Harbour.

The Crawford Lake Conservation area, along the Bruce, is perched high atop the Niagara Escarpment and is surrounded by extensive woodlands, wetlands, and limestone cliffs. Hikers can branch off on several interesting side trails including the Devil's Punch Bowl Side Trail, the Albion Falls Side Trail, which is suitable for year-round hiking, and the Rattlesnake Point Side Trail which leads to the Rattlesnake Point Conservation Area overlooking Highway 401.

HIKERS IN THE DUNDAS VALLEY

BOARDWALK, ROYAL BOTANICAL GARDENS

The Guelph area meets the Bruce Trail via the Guelph Radial Trail, running from Guelph to Limehouse through meadows, bush, and the steep, rough areas in-between.

Also connected to the Bruce is the Grand Valley Trail, which follows the Grand River Valley from Rock Point to Alton, passing near Brantford, Paris, Cambridge, Kitchener, Elora, and Fergus. The terrain along the Grand Valley Trail is mostly river ridge, rural meadows, and woodlands.

The Bruce has connections to southern Ontario through a myriad of winding paths and side trails, many of which forge through meadows and small forests, and then through wilder habitat towards the northern end of the trail.

GRAND RIVER

Along the limestone cliffs surrounding the Scenic City (Owen Sound), the Bruce Trail meets up with Jones Falls and a small but popular side trail referred to as the Glen. Heading towards Wiarton, hikers will encounter more cliffs and more spectacular scenery. A popular pathway in this area, the Bruce Caves Side Trail offers some more challenging hiking conditions and a few caves as stop-off points.

The northernmost end of the Bruce Trail—where another stone cairn marks the north terminus—is in Tobermory. Many experienced hikers say that the northern end is the most spectacular part of the trail. Travelling inland from the cairn for a short distance, hikers will arrive at the top of the Niagara Escarpment and Overhanging Point, a dolomite cap, beneath which the layers of limestone have been eroded away.

If you are planning a hiking tour of southwestern

BRUCE TRAIL

Ontario, the Bruce Trail includes some of the best scenery this province has to offer. For more information, see the listings section.

The Bruce Trail is clearly the pre-eminent hiking trail in Ontario. But the expanse of southwestern Ontario, the high proportion of rural area, and the attention that urban communities have given to walking trails have resulted in a multitude of other hiking opportunities. The following outlines a few of the best.

NIAGARA TRAIL

A recreational trail stretches along the Niagara Parkway, a picturesque path ideal for a brisk walk or a slow stroll. The views are wonderful from the many lookouts and picnic areas along the way.

The Niagara Parkway stretches fifty-six kilometres from Fort Erie to Niagara-on-the-Lake. These were some of the first protected parklands in the province. They were created in 1885 in response to alarm at commercial development crowding the falls. The parks include some of the most scenic and historic sites in the province (1-800-422-0552).

GUELPH TRAILS

In addition to the connection of the Guelph Radial Trail to the Bruce Trail, this area has several interesting systems of pathways in and around the city. The Ivey Trail is a simple, one-kilometre stretch that runs through the Guelph Arboretum, providing access to a spider web of other trail systems leading to the arboretum. The Trillium Trail also exists there and is a two-kilometre loop that passes through various plant collections.

Starkey Hill is one of Guelph's best-kept secrets. This is a three-and-a-half-kilometre trail that can be handled easily by even beginner hikers. The trail is located just outside Guelph near the village of Arkell and is marked only by a Guelph Off Road Bicycling sign (519-837-5626).

NIAGARA RIVER RECREATION TRAIL

CAMBRIDGE TRAILS

In 1994, the Grand River became the first urban waterway to be named a Canadian Heritage River. This distinction is due to the rich diversity of natural and human heritage found along the valley lands.

The Cambridge Heritage River Trail offers some unique glimpses of the river area combined with stunning and unexpected wilderness beauty. Hike the rugged Mill Run Trail; discover ancient fossils on the Living Levee Trail; or catch a glimpse of the great blue heron along the Linear Trail.

Throughout the year, hikers are welcome to take advantage of guided hikes, or explore the trail on their own. Access points to the trail are clearly identified. Guide books are also available.

In this area, there is also the Cambridge-to-Paris Rail Trail. It takes about four hours to walk—longer if you plan to dawdle or stop and study the natural history. It's a quiet, scenic trail, beginning on Highway 24 in south Cambridge at Churchill Park.

THAMES VALLEY TRAIL

For natural and rail history buffs, there are many lookouts over the Grand River, as well as railway bridge ruins, railway artifacts, and varied wildlife (519-621-2761).

THE AVON TRAIL

The Avon Trail is a hiking trail linking the Thames Valley Trail and the Grand Valley Trail.

Starting where the Thames Valley Trail terminates in St. Marys, it continues on to Wildwood Lake and then in an easterly direction towards Harrington. It travels northeast to Stratford as well. Following the banks of the Avon River and Silver Creek, the trail reaches the hamlets of Amulree and Bamberg and then skirts the city limits of Waterloo before heading towards the village of Conestogo, where it ends at the start of the Grand Valley Trail.

THAMES VALLEY TRAIL

The Thames Valley Trail is a growing network of one hundred kilometres of public trails along the Thames River between Kilworth and St. Marys. The trail offers a number of routes of varying difficulty, from a one-hour stroll to a demanding three-day hike. The trail is operated by the Thames Valley Trail Association based in London (519-645-2845).

POINT PELEE NATIONAL PARK

Point Pelee National Park entertains more than a half million visitors annually who come to enjoy the 347 species of birds and the monarch butterflies. There are plenty of pathways throughout the area and hikers and nature enthusiasts are asked to stick to them to help preserve the fragile wildlife environment of the area. Hiking and picnicking are permitted year-round but the best times to visit are September, October, and May when the birds are preparing for/returning from their migration south. In September millions of monarch butterflies are also getting ready to head for the warmer temperatures of Mexico (519-322-2365).

From the trails along the scenic Niagara Parkway to the challenging rocky pathways of the Bruce system, southwestern Ontario has something for every type of hiker from novice to expert.

KIDS' STUFF

JANA MILLER

Southwestern Ontario has a wide variety of attractions to entertain children. Reconstructed forts and living museums bring the history of the region alive. Small nature lovers can visit a bird sanctuary, a butterfly conservatory, reptile exhibits, zoos—even a lion safari. When something more imaginative is required, there are storybook gardens, lighthouses, cliffs, and beaches to explore. And, of course, when all else fails—there are the ubiquitous water and amusement parks.

JOURNEY BEHIND THE FALLS, NIAGARA FALLS

It might be wise to call ahead to some of the locations you wish to visit to confirm hours of operation and any special events that may be planned.

NIAGARA PENINSULA

The Falls Incline Railway is transportation with a scenic view—travel down the Niagara Escarpment in twin cable rail cars and get a great view of the falls. The railway runs between the Minolta Tower parking lot and the Table Rock area (905-354-1221).

Descend by elevator and follow a tunnel to the edge of the waters of the whirlpool rapids on the Great Gorge

Adventure (905-354-1221).

Take a journey behind the falls. Elevators carry visitors 125 feet down through solid rock to tunnels that pass behind and in front of the falls. An outdoor observation deck

MARINELAND, NIAGARA FALLS

just above river level allows a close-up view of Horseshoe Falls. Journey Behind the Falls is in the Table Rock Complex at the brink of Horseshoe Falls (905-354-1551).

The world-famous Maid of the Mist takes passengers right in front of the American Falls, Rock of Ages, and Cave of Winds. Raincoats and hoods are provided for this beathtaking thirty-minute cruise. Cruises start in May depending on ice conditions in the river (905-358-8571).

Its famous killer whale presentations are Marineland's biggest drawing card. Visitors to the park will also see lovable sea lions and talented dolphins in a variety of shows. Rides include Dragon Mountain, the world's largest steel roller coaster. Kids will enjoy the deer petting park. You'll also see elk, buffalo, bears, and more (905-356-8250).

Niagara Parks Butterfly Conservatory is housed in a $15-million, eleven-thousand square foot conservatory in the Niagara Botanical Gardens. North America's largest collection of free-flying butterflies enjoy a lush rain forest setting. This is a new attraction but already fantastically

popular—visitors are now admitted by timed tickets (905-356-8119).

One of the most popular attractions in Hamilton is the Royal Botanical Gardens. Located in the northern part of the city, the famous gardens cover over one thousand hectares of land and fifty kilometres of walking trails (905-527-1158).

The Canadian Warplane Heritage Museum is a delight for the whole

NIAGARA PARKS BUTTERFLY CONSERVATORY

family. As you approach the museum, note the CF-104 Fighter Jet climbing at a seventy-five degree angle. The museum has many interactive displays. View the more than twenty-five aircraft on display (905-679-4183).

CALEDON AND HALTON HILLS

The excellent and varied conservation areas of the Halton Region are ideal for a day out with the kids. Dotted along the Niagara Escarpment area on both sides of Highway 401, the six parks offer lovely woodlands and unique topography. Kelso/Glen Eden features recreational activities ranging from summertime swimming and windsurfing to fine wintertime downhill skiing.

Crawford Lake, in addition to the boardwalk surrounding it, features an Iroquoian village built on the

site of a fifteenth-century longhouse village.

Mountsberg Conservation Area operates a raptor rescue centre, and offers frequent live shows starring bald eagles, owls, and turkey vultures. Along with Rattlesnake Point, Hilton Falls, and Mount Nemo, these conservation areas are great places to hike, picnic, and experience nature from incredible vantage points (905-336-1158).

CRAWFORD LAKE CONSERVATION AREA, MILTON (TOP); AFRICAN LION SAFARI, CAMBRIDGE (CENTRE); DOON HERITAGE CROSSROADS, KITCHENER

KITCHENER-WATERLOO AND AREA

Go wild at the African Lion Safari! Visitors to the safari, near Cambridge, will enjoy face-to-face encounters with more than a thousand exotic animals and birds. There are a range of diversions to keep you and the kids enthralled, such as the white tiger display, two nature rides, the giant pachyderms at the Elephant Swim, and you may even witness the births of baby animals if you visit early in the spring (1-800-461-WILD).

Woodside National Historic Site in Kitchener is the boyhood home of Canada's tenth and longest-serving prime minister, William Lyon Mackenzie King. It has been beautifully restored to represent the 1880s. The house brings the Victorian era of kerosene lamps, mangles, corsets, and wood stoves to life. Enjoy guided tours by costumed staff members (519-571-5684).

Discover the early twentieth century at Doon Heritage Crossroads, a sixty-acre living history museum in Kitchener that re-creates the sights and sounds of bygone times (519-748-1914).

The height of extravagance in the heart of the country, Castle Kilbride in Baden is the 1877 Italianate home of James Livingston, a one-time flax king. It boasts a unique trompe l'oeil ceiling and wall paintings throughout. This is a fun way to absorb a history lesson (519-634-8444).

Step aboard the Fifties Streamliner at the Waterloo-St. Jacobs Railway and it's the 1950s again. As your train rolls into the heart of southwestern Ontario's Mennonite country, catch a glimpse of the world of Old Order Mennonites from the window of your climate-controlled car. Along the route, explore the

Canadian Clay and Glass Gallery, Waterloo Park, the St. Jacob's Farmers' Market, and the St. Jacobs' Factory Outlet Mall. You may disembark the train at any of the three stops, spend time exploring, and then resume your tour on a later train (519-746-1950).

Sportsworld is a twelve-hectare amusement park featuring a heated wave pool, a five-flume water-slide, a hot-rock spa, bumper boats, bumper cars, go-karts, two eighteen-hole mini-golf courses, a full video arcade, batting cages, amusement rides, an indoor driving range, an ice cream parlour, and a deep dive tube slide (519-653-4442).

SKA NAH DOHT VILLAGE, MT. BRYDGES

STRATFORD AND AREA

The Beachville District Historical Society Museum provides a history lesson for the whole family. This museum features a two-storey home built in 1851 and reveals the history of the area from 1789. A highlight is the history of the first recorded baseball game in North America, which took place in the area on June 4, 1828. Two large, newer buildings hold agricultural exhibits (519-423-6497).

LONDON AND AREA

Ska Nah Doht Indian Village is a re-creation of a prehistoric Iroquoian village with sixteen native structures that include longhouses and a palisade. The village is located in Longwoods Road Conservation Area, with trails, picnic areas, and wetland boardwalks nearby (519-264-2420).

Experience the living history of London at Fanshaw Pioneer Village. Weavers, printmakers, blacksmiths, and farmers demonstrate the trades of the past. View farm animals, more than twenty restored buildings, and the many artifacts of yesteryear (519-661-5770).

Storybook Gardens is just that. This famous park, in Springbank Park in the heart of London, brings well-loved childrens' stories to life. Storybook Gardens has enchanted children with its animals, displays, and playgrounds since 1958. The gardens feature the Island Stage Theatre, jugglers, mimes, and clowns. Shows are included in the admission price (519-661-5770).

STORYBOOK GARDENS, LONDON

London's East Park Golf Gardens is a summer-fun place for kids of all ages. It features more than ninety-five acres of parkland, waterslides, go-karts, batting cages, and picnic grounds. There is an eighteen-hole golf course, and miniature golf, as well as a driving range (519-451-2950).

The London Regional Children's Museum is a unique museum that offers kids a hands-on approach to learning. The signs read Please Touch and Try Me. Children can participate in as many activities as they wish during their visit. Special themes include dinosaurs, caves, space, and the Inuit (519-434-5726).

Each Saturday during the summer, weather permitting, the Hume Cronyn Memorial Observatory at the University of Western Ontario invites the public to view the stars, planets, and moons through the observatory's main telescope. There is a slide show before dark. The observatory is named in memory of one of Canada's best-known actors, who was a native of London (519-661-3183).

Take the kids to the London Museum of Archaeology to encounter the archaeology, art, and history of a First Nations people. In this partially reconstructed five-hundred-year-old Iroquoian village you'll find travelling and permanent displays (519-473-1360).

LAKE ERIE SHORELINE

The Port Burwell Marine Museum and Lighthouse stands across the street from Canada's oldest wooden lighthouse. Learn the history of the Great Lakes. Adventuresome visitors—including the kids—can climb to the top of the lighthouse (519-874-4343).

The Port Stanley Terminal Railway is a year-round train connecting Port Stanley and St. Thomas. The standard gauge, diesel-powered trains use specially built cars for comfort and open coaches for a great view of the Kettle Creek Valley. Your family can picnic in the 1921 box car (519-782-4385).

WINDSOR AND AREA

Birds, butterflies, plants, and reptiles draw more than half a million visitors each year to Point Pelee National Park, near Kingsville. Kids and parents alike will enjoy viewing the 700 different types of plants and 347 different species of birds that have been recorded there (519-322-2365).

JACK MINER BIRD SANCTUARY, KINGSVILLE

North of Kingsville is the world-renowned Jack Miner Bird Sanctuary. Miner established the sanctuary in 1904 to protect the Canada Goose, which had come close to extinction. His work led to the enactment of laws to protect migratory birds in Canada.

His sanctuary, home, and community park are open year-round, except on Sundays (519-733-4034).

Windsor Reptile World is Canada's largest live display of reptiles and amphibians. Housing over a hundred exhibits and displaying more than four hundred creatures, Windsor's Reptile World offers a rare glimpse into the fascinating realm of reptiles, and provides an opportunity for supervised hands-on fun.

The John Freeman Walls Historic Site and Underground Railroad preserves an almost forgotten period of Canadian and American history. The twenty-acre site is owned and operated by descendants of fugitive slaves from the United States. Conductors make history come alive for the whole family (519-258-6253).

Near Chatham, to the east of Windsor, is Uncle Tom's Cabin Historic Site. This building was the home of Reverend Josiah Henson, whose early life in slavery influenced Harriet Beecher Stowe, the author of the novel *Uncle Tom's Cabin*. The museum tells the story of the underground railway and contains nineteenth-century artifacts and literature. The tour is self-guided.

Fort Malden National Historic Park is an eleven-acre site located on the banks of the Detroit River in Amherstburg. It was constructed in 1796 and was a strategic military post during the War of 1812 and the Rebellion of 1837. Children experience the life of a soldier through exhibits and demonstrations, and by examining living quarters and artifacts (519-736-5416).

FORT MALDEN NATIONAL HISTORICAL PARK, AMHERSTBURG

Taking a Wreck Exploration Tours is like being on the Discovery channel, but live! Enjoy a shoreline cruise while listening to a historical narration of the Great Lakes shipping industry in the 1800s. Then, anchored above a 130-year-old shipwreck, explore the wreck site while sitting high and dry on the boat. A high-tech underwater camera and a diver submerge to provide an unbelievable fish-eyed perspective viewed on deck via television monitors. This tour runs from Colchester Harbour.

LAKE HURON AND GEORGIAN BAY

The shores of Lake Huron provide southwestern Ontario with some of the best beaches anywhere. Pack a picnic lunch for the family and head to almost any shore community in Ontario and you're sure to find great swimming—and great fun. Three of Lake Huron's most famous beaches—Grand Bend, Sauble Beach, and Wasaga Beach—offer miles of warm, sandy beaches, eateries,

BEACH, GODERICH

arcades, souvenir shops, and small theme parks.

The Huron County Gaol and Museum is a Goderich National Historic Site featuring the community's first jail. It's a three-storey octagonal structure with surrounding walls, built in 1839 to1842. Send the kids into the cell block to experience life behind bars in the nineteenth century, and visit the beautifully restored Governor's House (519-524-2686).

GRIST MILL STONES, INGLIS FALLS

In Wroxeter you can visit a working sheep farm with more than five hundred sheep. Indoor presentations at Lismore Sheep Farm include information about fifteen breeds of sheep and a sheep-shearing demonstration. Small fry can watch a working sheep dog gather the flock and they can also feed the lambs (519-335-3374).

Farther north is the City of Owen Sound—the Scenic City—flanked on both sides by the impressive limestone cliffs of the Niagara Escarpment. Take the kids on a nature hike or picnic to any of the three Owen Sound area waterfalls—Inglis Falls, Jones Falls, or Indian Falls. All are part of the popular hiking- and walking-trails system.

If you happen to be visiting the city during the winter, you can't miss the Chi Chi Maun, the large passenger ship that sails between Tobermory and Manitoulin Island each summer. She sits in dry dock each winter and is an awesome spectacle that the kids are sure to enjoy.

Whether your children are interested in the lastest, state-of-the-art, high-tech attractions, real-life adventures, or old-fashioned fun on the beach, southwestern Ontario has just about everything a kid could want!

MUSEUMS AND HISTORIC SITES

PAUL KNOWLES

Southwestern Ontario historic sites range from Indian longhouses reconstructed in their original locales, to well-preserved pioneer log cabins, to beautifully furnished grand Victorian mansions, built only a few decades after the first settlers arrived in the region. Along the frontiers, there are also military museums, reconstructed forts from the days of conflict between England and France and then, in 1812–1814, the last battles between the United States and the British colony then known as Upper Canada.

FORT GEORGE,
NIAGARA-ON-THE-
LAKE

Dozens of communities, from villages to cities, have museums and historic sites at which visitors can learn about life at every point in the history of the region. Although many of the communities in this part of the province have existed for less than two centuries, today's citizens have invested much energy and creativity in ensuring that the region's history is preserved and honoured.

NIAGARA PENINSULA

We'll start our historical exploration on one of Upper Canada's frontiers; the Niagara Region has settlement history predating most of the rest of the area by several

HISTORIC FORT ERIE

decades. On the Niagara Peninsula, two forts—Fort George in Niagara-on-the-Lake and Fort Erie in the city of the same name—are open to visitors during the warmer months, from May through October. Both feature costumed interpreters and offer military and domestic demonstrations. The often unhappy life of the soldier circa–1812 is well presented.

Fort George is actually a Parks Canada reconstruction of the fort that stood on the Niagara-on-the-Lake site two centuries ago, although the Navy Hall, closer to the river bank, is an original building. Across the river and slightly downstream on the American side is Old Fort Niagara in Youngstown. Today the only battle between these two ancient forts is the fight to attract visiting tourists (Fort George 905-468-4257; Fort Erie 905-871-1332).

Of course, the Niagara district is home to dozens of museums, some historic and others, especially in Niagara Falls, entertainment-based; contact local tourist information centres for specific information. The museum in Niagara-on-the-Lake is especially recommended, while the Mackenzie Printery, in Queenston, is a unique museum of newspapers and publishing located in the building (at the foot of Queenston Heights) which once housed the newspaper published by Ontario (then Upper Canada) radical William Lyon Mackenzie, ancestor of the prime minister raised at Woodside. Also in Queenston is the Laura Secord Homestead where the heroine of the War of 1812 once lived.

DUNDURN CASTLE, HAMILTON

Today the museum is owned and operated by the candy company of the same name (905-357-4020).

Visitors with an interest in war-time history will want to visit the Canadian Warplane Heritage Museum, located at Hamilton International Airport. In addition to the chance to see a world-class collection of vintage aircraft, visitors can also watch the heritage planes in flight, every day, weather permitting, or even purchase a flight in a vintage aircraft (1-800-386-5888).

Also in Hamilton is one of the great homes of southwestern Ontario, Dundurn Castle, the mid-nineteenth century home of Sir Allan McNab. Dundurn is not truly a castle, but a Regency period Tuscan villa. Finished in 1835, it was the first European-style mansion built in Ontario and the largest building ever constructed in Upper Canada. It has seventy-two rooms and seventeen fireplaces. Dundurn Park is also home to buildings and exhibits associated with the castle, including a coach house and gardener's cottage as well as military pieces located on the grounds (905-546-2872).

CALEDON AND HALTON HILLS

Native Canadian history is explored at Crawford Lake Conservation Area in Halton Hills, where a longhouse and other features have been reconstructed on an authentic settlement site. The longhouse, which contains reproduction artifacts, is open to visitors who can experience the life of native Canadians prior to European settlement. Crawford Lake's interpretive program also focuses on life in those early days (905-336-1158).

KITCHENER-WATERLOO AND AREA

Kitchener-Waterloo and area was settled relatively late (mostly after 1820), but the number of heritage sites open today is unparalleled in southwestern Ontario.

A good first stop is Kitchener's Joseph Schneider Haus, a museum and gallery located in the house built by one of Kitchener's first residents. Well staffed with costumed interpreters, and offering a busy schedule of special activities (from sheepshearing to apple schnitzing), Schneider Haus offers a comprehensive look at the life of the early Mennonite settlers in this area (519-742-7752) .

JOSEPH SCHNEIDER HAUS, KITCHENER

A second Waterloo Region site dealing with Mennonite history is the Meetingplace, in St. Jacobs. This clever, creative museum is of interest to anyone intrigued by the faith and culture of the Mennonite pioneers. It is housed in a modern building outfitted with audio-visual features (including a fine movie) and historic tableaux and displays (including an Old Order Mennonite Meeting House and Old Order Kitchen) (519-664-3518).

CASTLE KILBRIDE, BADEN

While Schneider Haus focuses on life in the early part of the nineteenth century, Doon Heritage Crossroads takes visitors ahead to 1914 in Waterloo County. The village includes businesses, homes, and farms from that era. Costumed interpreters staff many of the stores and homes in the village, and Doon is frequently host to special events (519-748-1914).

If Doon primarily demonstrates the life of the middle class in 1914, Castle

Kilbride, in Baden, just west of Kitchener, offers a glimpse into the life of one wealthy family, in the heart of the Victorian era. Kilbride, a National Historic Site, was built by Scottish immigrant James Livingston in the 1870s. It is beautifully furnished to that era (with some exceptional artifacts from later in the life of the castle). As a prosperous farmer and industrialist—as well as a prominent national politician—Livingston was able to build the Italianate mansion of his dreams, complete with unique and spectacular trompe l'oeil (three-dimensional) and geometric paintings on the ceilings of every room. The libraries at Castle Kilbride and at Woodside (see below) are two of the most beautiful Victorian rooms to be found anywhere in the province. Castle Kilbride also includes a Canadian Legion military museum room, and a Wilmot Township museum (519-634-8444).

A more celebrated politician with roots in Kitchener was William Lyon Mackenzie King, Canada's longest-serving prime minister. His boyhood home, Woodside, is now a museum decorated in full Victorian elegance, in the midst of the beautiful Woodside National Historic Park. Costumed interpreters staff the house and offer presentations on Victorian clothing and other domestic details (519-571-5684).

A southwestern Ontario historic site that has attracted much attention of late is the McCrae House in Guelph, the birthplace of Col. John McCrae, author of the poem "In Flanders Fields." The house and heritage garden has been open for years, but the 1997 donation of McCrae's military medals, purchased by a private citizen at auction for about $400,000, has been a public relations triumph for the home. A combined admission ticket is available and includes the Guelph Civic Museum (519-836-1482).

LONDON AND AREA

In London, Fanshawe Pioneer Village features more than twenty-four restored homes and businesses, staffed by costumed interpreters. The city is also home to a number of other museums and historic sites, including Eldon House, London's oldest surviving private dwelling, where visitors step back in time more than a century and a half. To travel back even further, visit London's Museum of Indian Archaeology, tracing the eleven-thousand-year history of the native peoples of southwestern Ontario (Fanshawe, 519-451-2800; Eldon House, 519-661-5169; Museum of Indian Archaeology, 519-473-1360).

FANSHAWE PIONEER VILLAGE, LONDON

LAKE ERIE SHORELINE

Intriguing homes and historic buildings abound in the smaller centres of southwestern Ontario as well. One of the

ANNANDALE HOUSE, TILLSONBURG

best is Annandale House. Annandale, built by E.D. Tillson in 1880, is a fine example of the Aesthetic Movement, and there is evidence that the Tillsons were influenced in design and ornamentation by Oscar Wilde. The Aesthetic Movement, which began in England in the 1860s, was a reaction among designers and decorators against highly carved, heavy wooden ornamentation typical of the early Victorian era. The Aesthetic Movement stressed line detail in furniture, elaborate upholstery, marquetry, and oriental influences. The influence soon spread beyond furniture to entire room sets—draperies, wallpapers, cornices, door frames, and so

on. At Annandale, painted ceilings, stained glass, and intriguing furnishings make this a must-see for lovers of Victoriana (519-842-2294).

South of Tillsonburg, on the Lake Erie shore, is the fishing port of Port Burwell, where Canada's oldest wooden

BACKUS MILLS CONSERVATION AREA, PORT ROWAN

lighthouse (built in 1840) can be visited, still open to the public because it also now serves as the community's tourist information centre.

Pioneer villages or historic settlements have been reconstructed at a number of sites. One of the best is at the Backus Mills Conservation Area, north of Port Rowan. The highlight there is the mill itself, an eighteenth-century masterpiece of huge timbers and machinery worthy of Rube Goldberg. But Backus also has a number of other pioneer buildings, including an intriguing octagonal schoolhouse, a farmhouse, and farm buildings housing an enormous collection of farm implements (519-428-4623).

WINDSOR AND AREA

Windsor is home to Willistead Manor, an elaborate home built in 1904–1906 in the Tudor-Jacobean style of English manor homes. Willistead is the pride of the unique community of Walkerville—unique in that the entire town (homes, church, civic facilities, and all) was constructed and governed by the Hiram Walker company to provide homes for its executives and workers. Willistead itself was built some years after the rest of the privately owned community by Edward Walker, son of Hiram, to emulate English country mansions. It has been restored and, although the house is sparely furnished, Willistead's key features such as the great hall, the Elizabethan fireplace, and the elaborately carved grand staircase have been beautifully refurbished. Willistead hosts several major events during the year, including a two-day Art in the Park in the spring, and the Classic and Antique Car Show in August (519-253-2365).

LAKE HURON AND GEORGIAN BAY

Just south of Grand Bend, across from the Pinery Provincial Park, is Lambton Heritage Museum, another site with galleries and restored buildings, including a school and a slaughterhouse (519-243-2600).

A short drive north along the Lake Huron shoreline, the community of Goderich is home to a number of museums. Two of them are of special interest. The Huron Historic Gaol, a National Historic Site, is the best such museum in southwestern Ontario. This jail, which functioned as the county jail from 1842 to 1972, captures the realities of penal servitude very well, and admission also includes a tour of the well-restored and furnished Governor's House. Nearby is the Huron County Museum, which should be awarded a quality-per-capita community museum prize. This excellent facility, founded on one man's passion for history, features a variety of galleries filled with historic treasures, including the incredible History Hall, with full-scale store fronts that once stood on the main street of the village of Wroxeter (519-524-6600).

In Owen Sound, the County of Grey-Owen Sound Museum has display galleries and five restored period buildings, including a blacksmith shop (common to most heritage villages) and an automotive garage from the first half of this century—not nearly so common (519-376-3690).

There are dozens of other small museums and historic sites, open by chance or on limited schedules. Visitors planning to stop at the larger sites in cities or towns should always check for other historic points nearby; little-known and publicized treasures are common, despite inconsistent scheduling. The only limit to a fascinating exploration of history and heritage in southwestern Ontario is the time a visitor can allot to his or her personal quest.

WILLISTEAD MANOR, WINDSOR

HURON COUNTY MUSEUM, GODERICH

SHOPPING

JOYCE SPRING

Shopping opportunities abound in southwestern Ontario. Every city, town, or village offers a selection of shops, and a surprising number feature that special something that transforms shopping from a duty to a pleasure. For more information about the stores below, see the listings section.

THE WEE SCOTTISH LOFT, NIAGARA-ON-THE-LAKE

NIAGARA PENINSULA

Niagara-on-the-Lake is a favourite destination for those seeking a leisurely shopping experience. To stroll its charming streets, admiring the carefully preserved buildings, is to return to a more gracious era.

Many of the dozens and dozens of stores in Niagara-on-the-Lake are theme shops. The Wee Scottish Loft offers quality imports from Scotland (905-468-0965). Angie Straus features all her own work—her delicate paintings decorate T-shirts, sweatshirts, and other clothing as well as notepaper, china, and home and garden accessories. The Silly Old Bear Shop specializes in Winnie the Pooh (905-468-5411).

THE SILLY OLD BEAR SHOP, NIAGARA-ON-THE-LAKE

Part of the Niagara-on-the-Lake experience is visiting Maple Leaf Fudge to watch the candy being made (905-468-2211). As well as fudge, few visitors leave without

buying an ice-
cream cone.
Strolling along
pretty streets
eating an ice-
cream cone seems
a very old-
fashioned thing to

do, perfectly in keeping with the town's ambience.

There are wonderful restaurants and tea rooms, a number of first-class hotels, and the new wine bar is worth a visit.

CALEDON AND HALTON HILLS

Erin is situated at the western end of the Halton Hills and is involved with "Art in the Hills." It has also sponsored the "Hills of Erin Studio Tour" and the "Hills of Erin Arts Festival."

With so much emphasis on the arts, Erin is the perfect place to shop for unique, locally handcrafted artifacts, displayed in its boutiques and specialty shops. Tintagel has distinctive clothing and jewellery, and a small cafe (519-833-0019). Most of the shops have panache. An upholstery business calls itself "Recovering Nicely" (519-833-0225).

This area offers an unusual number of businesses involved in home renovation or restoration such as the wooden Victorian fretwork and gingerbread for older homes. Snow Shake and Shingle supplies and installs cedar shakes and shingles (519-941-1221).

An added attraction is that Erin is close to Terra Cotta, a pretty little village on the Credit River, with its interesting shops and galleries, and is also close to Ballinafad with its General Store and Tack Shop.

KITCHENER-WATERLOO AND AREA

The Kitchener-Waterloo area abounds in fine galleries, offering unusual pleasures and treasures. The Canadian Clay and Glass Gallery is an exhibition gallery; its gift shop sells Canadian ceramics, glass, and enamel (519-746-1882). The Cobblestone Gallery features jewellery as well as crafts (519-746-5829). For book lovers, or people who buy gifts for book lovers, there are several excellent stores. Words Worth, opposite Waterloo Square, manages with limited space to provide a surprising variety (519-884-2665). A Small Bookshop in the Frederick

Street Mall offers the kind of personal service that is increasingly rare (519-743-8741).

Kitchener-Waterloo has many speciality shops and boutiques. Household China and Gifts is renowned for quality china at tremendous savings (519-884-2792).

"The Royal City"—Guelph—has a rich architectural heritage with many century-old limestone buildings. Quebec Street, in downtown Guelph, is a great place to shop. Duncan-McPhee is an old, established Guelph business with an exceptional gift collection (519-821-1260). Nearby, Baba Yaga has fashions, crafts, and exquisite jewellery (519-767-2001). The Bookshelf, also on Quebec Street, is more than a bookstore (519-821-3311). With its promotion of the Eden Mills Festival and art movies and concerts, it's an important part of the cultural life of the city. Across the street, La Maison de Madelaine provides full-service interior design (519-763-5023).

Of course, Quebec Street isn't the only good place to shop in Guelph. The Barber Gallery on Suffolk West has two floors of paintings, prints, and gifts (519-824-0310). For an off-beat shopping experience, how about the Sleeman Brewery? They have a retail store and no, they don't just sell beer (519-822-1834).

The village of Elora owes its existence to the Grand River Falls, where in the early 1800s a five-storey grist mill was built. This stone building is one of many excellently restored heritage buildings and is now a country inn, the Elora Mill (519-846-5356). Many of the peaceful, tree-lined streets still have their old settler homes of stone, brick, and timber.

On Mill Street, the heart of the village, most of the attractive boutiques and gift shops still have their original limestone facades. The Mill Street Mews houses, Maggie's for quilts, Cobwebs Gourmet Kitchen Shop, Steve's Sheepskin & Leather Shop and a MacLeods

SHOPS IN ELORA

Scottish Shop. Einhorn's boasts "the best chocolate this side of Belgium" (514-846-9160).

This little town continues to attract artists and artisans and is well known as an artists' colony. It's fascinating to watch an artist or a craftsperson at work. In the old church, the potter doesn't mind an audience, and the finished pottery is displayed for sale.

There are cozy little tea rooms and cafes and, of course, fine dining at the Elora Mill.

St. Jacobs, in the heart of Mennonite country, has the added advantage of being just a few kilometres from the hugely popular St. Jacobs Farmers' Market, and from Kitchener-Waterloo, world-famous home of the largest Oktoberfest celebration outside Munich, Germany (519-747-1830; 519-570-0552).

This Waterloo County village offers hearty Mennonite food, both in its restaurants and its food speciality shops. More than a million and a half people are drawn to St. Jacobs annually to browse through craft studios and workshops, galleries, and gift and specialty shops. At the

EINHORN FINE CHOCOLATE, CALEDON EAST

Forge & Anvil visitors can watch the blacksmith at work (519-664-3622). The Village Silos houses many excellent gift, clothing, and specialty shops (519-664-2421). Sip a delicious cafe latte while enjoying the cream-and-gold ambience of La Creme and

FARMERS' MARKET, ST. JACOBS

checking out its selection of elegant clothing, jewellery, and gifts (519-664-3275). There are weavers, wheat weaving, glass blowing, stained glass, leather work, and many other arts and crafts. One of the places handcrafted Mennonite quilts can be admired or purchased is St. Jacobs Mennonite Quilts (519-664-1817).

Cambridge, also on the Grand River, is a place that keeps getting better. Some of its heritage buildings have been preserved, and the Southworks is one of these. This cream-coloured brick factory complex is 150 years old, and has been converted into an outlet mall that is attracting more than a million shoppers a year.

SHOPS IN ST. JACOBS

Cambridge Towel, Florsheim, Biltmore, Kodiak, Reebok, London Fog, and Gore-Tex are some of the brand names at the Southworks (519-740-0110). Travellers Warehouse Ltd. sells luggage, handbags, wallets, and more (519-622-5232). The Paderno Cookware Factory Store has cookware, cooking tools, and gadgets (519-623-8652). Jack Rabbits Clothing Co. sells quality children's wear (519-622-6111). There is a good mix of outlets, and merchandise sells for 70 per cent off retail. As well, they advertise twenty-six thousand square feet of antiques.

An added attraction is Tiger Brand (519-624-9407). This well known and very popular manufacturer of casual wear has an outlet next door to the Southworks.

During good weather, street vendors sell hot dogs, sausage-on-a-bun and soft drinks from carts in the parking lot. The Cafe Grand, located in the antique section of the Southworks, serves an English Cream Tea, as well as soups, sandwiches, and homemade desserts.

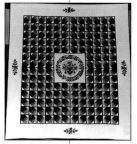

QUILT BY RENSKE HELMUTH, ST. JACOBS MENNONITE QUILTS

Paris is a delightful little town situated on the scenic Grand River. It's rather disappointing to be told that it wasn't named after Paris, France—it was really named for a former plaster-of-Paris mine. Regardless, it's a great place to shop, with numerous craft and gift boutiques. The biggest attraction here is the Mary Maxim outlet, at 75

Scott Avenue—*the* place to go if you're interested in crafts (519-442-6342). But Paris has so much to offer that even if Mary Maxim is your objective, leave yourself time to savour some of the other treats to be found here.

PBR Custom Cabinetry offers classic designs in traditional woods (519-442-2415). Two Rivers rents canoes, kayaks, or bicycles (519-442-4220). For and From the Garden is a garden shop offering old, new, unique and unusual items (519-442-5129). John M. Hall "The House of Quality Linens" is a wonderful old-fashioned dry goods store that has been doing business in the same store on the Paris main street for more than a century (519-442-4242).

As well as boasting a beautiful setting, with its treed hills and lovely old homes, Paris has several interesting cobblestone buildings. This type of cobblestone is quite unusual in this area. And, of course, there are charming tea rooms and cafes.

STRATFORD AND AREA

Stratford is a little city that has everything, beginning with its beautiful setting on the Avon River. The Stratford Festival attracts hundreds of thousands of visitors each year and although theatre is the main drawing card, Stratford offers much more: boating on the river, picnicking in the riverfront park, many good restaurants, and best of all, great shopping.

A good place to start is the recently expanded Theatre Store in the Festival Theatre lobby, with a superb collection of theatre gifts, costume sketches, books, music, and clothing. The Shakespearean Gift Shop is on George Street West, across from the Avon Theatre, with Shakespeare's works, theatrical references, posters, and so on (519-271-9491).

BUST FROM THE SHAKESPEAREAN GIFT SHOP, STRATFORD

It's not surprising that many of Stratford's shops are theatrically named—the Dressing Room has women's fashions and Poor Yorick is a CD and video emporium on Downie Street next to the Avon Theatre (519-273-2392; 519-272-1999). Anything Grows is a garden shop where whimsy is one of their best crops (519-272-1100). At Family and Company toy and games store, shopping can include a magic show or rocket demonstrations, and gift wrappers may ask, "Will that be with bugs or without?" (519-273-7060). Aunt Louise's

SHOPS IN STRATFORD

Apartment, on Ontario Street, is a treasure trove of rare finds (519-273-6617). Look there for distinctive prints and original artwork and pottery. No visit to Stratford is complete without spending some time at Bradshaws to browse through the unequalled selection of gifts, tableware, and crystal and their housewares department, Kitchen Detail (519-271-6283).

LONDON AND AREA

White Oaks Mall in London, with more than two hundred stores is, if not the biggest, probably the busiest mall in southwestern Ontario (and there is a fine selection of malls in this region). Even before you enter, you will realize that this mall is distinctive. Landscaping has been used very effectively and the lawns and gardens give it a parklike setting (519-681-0434).

In the mall, the use of skylights to provide natural light, and the abundance of foliage and trees, encourage the feeling of a streetscape instead of the usual mall corridor of stores.

The businesses are chosen to ensure diversity. There are the stores shoppers expect to find in a mall (Wal-Mart, the Bay, and so on), but 20 per cent of the shops here are independents. This mix of stores enhances the unique atmosphere of White Oaks, and it will appeal to all shoppers, from those who are looking for competitive prices to those who seek upscale shopping.

White Oaks is located on Wellington Road just north of Highway 401, which makes it readily accessible.

WINDSOR AND AREA

If you're looking for a family shopping getaway, try Colasanti's, a wonderland of exotic birds and gardens near Ruthven (519-326-3287). Step into a tropical paradise where, year-round, you can wander among beautiful flowering plants and shrubs, bougainvillea, hibiscus, and orchids. In the restaurant, which seats five hundred, sit under a real lemon or orange tree, or a weeping fig, while you enjoy coffee or a meal.

Everything you could possibly need for indoor and outdoor gardens, including expert advice, is available there. Also available is a complete line of accessories for home decorating. Shoppers can bring photos of their rooms and consult with professional interior decorators. Special orders are made up on-site. There is a full line of crafts and craft supplies, as well as a number of small shops like Bounty of the Country that sell honey, jam, and other Canadian-produced foodstuffs.

Meanwhile, for the children, there are animals to pet and animals not to pet. The reptile exhibit includes boa constrictors, pythons, alligators, and more. There is an eighteen-hole mini-golf course and a new carnival area.

Kingsville, with sandy beaches, interesting historic buildings, and craft and gift shops, is just five kilometres west. A ferry service connects Kingsville with Pelee Island and Sandusky, Ohio.

Sombra is a picturesque village in a beautiful location on the St. Clair Parkway. The drive along the St. Clair River is pretty and the parks are open year-round.

Sombra's turn-of-the-century Victorian buildings have been restored and house boutiques and charming little restaurants. The Hummingbird Gift Shop sells a variety of decorative accessories and gifts, original carvings, and

ITEMS FROM WINDSOR SHOPS

other creations of Canadian artists and artisans (519-892-3245). The Old Bank has an interesting selection of distinctive crafts and collectables. The Sombra Bed and Breakfast is Victorian-era and furnished with antiques.

Its unusual name was given to the village by Peregrine Maitland, lieutenant-governor of Upper Canada from 1818 to 1828. He was a veteran of the Peninsular War, and upon viewing the heavily wooded riverbank, he called it Sombra—Spanish for "shade."

Although it has a fine museum, with a Marine Room and a pioneer log cabin, Sombra's present claim to fame is the Bluewater Ferry, which runs year-round between Sombra and Marine City, Michigan. There is a duty free shop on the American side (519-892-3879).

LAKE HURON AND GEORGIAN BAY

Bayfield, on the shore of Lake Huron, was, by the 1840s, a busy shipping port for the export of grain. Today, Bayfield Harbour is one of the prettiest on Lake Huron, and has excellent marina facilities.

During the 1800s, the community prospered and hotels, stores, and many fine residences were built. Fortunately, this heritage has been lovingly preserved. The village has retained its old-fashioned charm, with its clapboard homes and spreading chestnut trees. The wide main street is lined with old buildings, restored to their former elegance, and now housing a variety of craft and specialty shops. These boutiques offer handcrafted jewellery, one-of-a-kind gifts, china, linens—everything for the discerning shopper, and are a browser's paradise. Shop Dizzi Designs for creative, hand-painted fashions for the family, the Wardrobe for its extensive Linda Lundstrom collection, including the famous LaParkas, and the elegant Times & Places for antiques and collectables (519-565-2332; 519-565-2996;

THE VILLAGE GUILD, BAYFIELD

519-565-2700). Penhale's, just north of town, makes horse-drawn carriages (519-565-2107).

There are attractive restaurants and outdoor cafes. The Little Inn of Bayfield is a perennial favourite (519-565-2611). It's hard to believe that it has been catering to diners and overnight guests for the past 162 years.

Shopping in southwestern Ontario encompasses everything from superstores and malls to specialty establishments and funky boutiques. Whatever the desired item—vintage clothing, Victoriana, pine furniture, or fine china—shoppers will find it in this part of the province.

SNOW SPORTS

MICHAEL BAGINSKI

Ten thousand years ago, southwestern Ontario was shaped by receding ice. Glaciers gouged huge holes in the earth, leaving the landscape pitted and scratched, and creating an abundance of lakes, rivers, waterfalls, and ski terrain. Southwestern Ontario boasts dozens of hills that will appeal to all ages and levels of talent, including Blue Mountain, the most popular ski resort in the province.

BLUE MOUNTAIN RESORT, COLLINGWOOD

CROSS-COUNTRY SKIING

Nordic enthusiasts will find thousands of kilometres of trails suitable for cross-country skiing and will be happy to note that crowds on the hills and trails of southwestern Ontario rarely reach the high levels common to other eastern seaboard resorts.

HARRISON PARK, OWEN SOUND

A good place to start is Owen Sound, which has been measured as the "seventh snowiest city in North America." On average, 340 centimetres of the white stuff drops annually on the town, which is located in the Georgian Bay snowbelt.

Top cross-country areas near Owen Sound include forty-acre Harrison Park in the heart of the city, and Inglis Falls (follow Second Avenue East south—really!—to signs for Inglis Falls), which features an eighteen-metre waterfall and a deep gorge carved by the sheer force of running water. Combined, the two offer more than eight kilometres of trails. Another popular ski area near Owen Sound is Hepworth.

Virtually every community in

INGLIS FALLS, OWEN SOUND

southwestern Ontario boasts a network of groomed and patrolled ski trails for the Sunday afternoon skier.

Goderich, which claims to be the prettiest town in Canada, devotes a great deal of attention to grooming and buffing trails, as well as promoting routes that are yet to be discovered. As with most of the Lake Huron communities, the town benefits from "lake-effect" snow that ensures suitable ground cover all winter long, often starting as early as November and lasting through to the end of April. Early or late-season skiing can often prove to be the most idyllic, as slightly warmer weather takes the edge off a frosty winter sport. Ski trails exist right within the town, and in the surrounding Huron County countryside, including at the beautiful Benmiller Inn a few miles inland. For information on skiing in Goderich and area, call Tourism Goderich (519-524-6600).

Another option is to combine a ski excursion with one of the region's many winter carnivals. The resort town of Grand Bend, for example, celebrates the snow during the first two weekends of February with motorcycle ice races, a parade, hayrides, free children's events, and a popular ice-sculpture competition. Hotels and resorts stoke up crackling fires and brew warming drinks such as hot toddies and mulled wine.

Provincial parks and conservation areas are another excellent venue for recreational cross-country enthusiasts, with limits set only by the number of trees that might stand in the way. Pinery Provincial Park near Grand Bend, for example, is noted primarily as a summer getaway; however, in the winter it offers excellent routes through forested dunes and oak savanna. The young-at-heart will also find thrills on the park's toboggan hill.

BLUE MOUNTAIN RESORT, COLLINGWOOD

Many communities offer cross-country skiing within city limits. Kitchener, for example, offers many kilometres of groomed tracks throughout city parks and along the Grand River. The Laurel Creek Conservation Area in Waterloo has twelve kilometres of professionally groomed trails, while the Pinehurst Lake Conservation Area, ten kilometres north of Paris, has thirteen kilometres of zigzagging routes. The scenic Elora Gorge is the backdrop to twelve kilometres of winding trails at the Elora Gorge Conservation Area in Elora.

DOWNHILL SKIING

Downhillers, meanwhile, have a number of choices in southwestern Ontario.

The most popular is Blue Mountain, near Collingwood, which is Ontario's largest ski resort. Blue Mountain, with thirty-six downhill trails, attracts as many skiers as the rest of southwestern Ontario's downhill resorts combined. Blue Mountain has the top snow-making system in North America, which in 1997 converted millions of litres of water into snow on the slopes. The system of runs is 1.5 km wide, and offers the highest vertical in southwestern Ontario. The longest run is the .5 km "Big Baby." Blue Mountain can accommodate up to a thousand overnight visitors in a ninety-seven-room, five-star hotel, and one hundred condominium units (705-445-0231).

The Beaver Valley Ski Club is located south of Kimberley near Owen Sound. Friday through Sunday, skiers may use three surface lifts and a 152 m drop. The longest run is 1,463 m.

One resort caters to both downhill and cross-country skiers. Talisman, located north of Kimberley, has ten kilometres of cross-country trails, plus eight surface lifts, a vertical drop of 183 m and longest run of 1, 220 m for downhillers. The mega resort also offers snowboarding, snowmobiling, snowshoeing, skating, dog sledding, tubing, and snow-blade skiing, as well as Kids Klub and Power Pac children's programs, and slopeside accommodation.

Further south, in Orangeville, the Cedar Highlands Ski Club operates weekends with a 91 m drop and top run of 990 m, while Hockley Valley checks in on a daily basis at 100 m and 533 m respectively.

HOCKLEY VALLEY, ORANGEVILLE

Toronto-area visitors may hit the slopes at Glen Eden, about thirty minutes west of the city, in Milton. The vertical drop is 73 m, with a longest run of 610 m. The resort also boasts three chairlifts including a quad, a snowboarders' park, and one of Ontario's largest professional ski schools. Runs operate seven days and six nights a week.

Alpiners can check in at the Chicopee Ski Club in Kitchener, with a 60 m drop and 610 m longest run.

The London Ski Club operates at Boler Mountain in London. It too welcomes snowboarders. Vertical drop is 38 m and the longest run is 305 m.

So stop making excuses. Get out there and enjoy the snow!

SWIMMING

MICHAEL BAGINSKI

Many rivers of great length and beauty crisscross southwestern Ontario, and with a little luck and research, bathers might discover the perfect waterfall in which to shower, or a secluded water hole suitable for belly flops and diving.

WATERFRONT, LION'S HEAD

LAKE ERIE

The north shore of Lake Erie offers dozens of warm, sandy beaches, usually in proximity to small fishing or resort villages. One of the most noteworthy is Port Stanley, south of London. A popular day-trip destination for Ontarians, the town offers an old-time pier, shops, boutiques, galleries, and a tourist train linked to St. Thomas, as well as three beaches and a deep-water harbour, ideal for both sailboats and Great Lakes vessels.

Other Erie ports that cater to the beach crowds include Port Dover, Port Glasgow, Port Bruce, Port Rowan, and Port Burwell. Each town is distinct in its own fashion, and all coordinate a wide range of activities to attract and suit visitors, particularly families.

Many of these port communities have provincial parks, with beautiful beaches, close to hand. Port Dover has Turkey Point; Port Rowan is near the world-famous Long

BEACH, PORT STANLEY

Point; Port Burwell has one of the best beaches in Canada at Port Burwell Provincial Park. Very wide and two thousand metres long, the beach offers wide open spaces and ideal swimming.

Not far east of Port Burwell is the privately run Sand Hill Park, which features a naturally occurring, 135-metre high sand hill, which can be hiked to the top for a scenic view of

Lake Erie and the beach below (519-586-3891).

Another venue with beach and swimming possibilities is Point Pelee National Park, Canada's southernmost point (519-322-2365). Although noted primarily for its wildlife and bird migration habitat, the 1,618-hectare park, which juts out into Lake Erie south of Leamington, has numerous beaches for summer swimming.

LAKE HURON

First port of call for many Lake Huron fans is Grand Bend, well known to Ontario residents as a summer playground and gateway to the sand beaches of Pinery Provincial Park, just south of town (519-243-2220).

BEACH, PORT DOVER

The town itself has all the characteristics of a classic resort town, with up to fifty thousand weekend visitors in the summer. Sunbathers can bask on the beach and then boogie at clubs in town.

For peace and quiet and a natural beach experience, visitors head to Pinery. The park has 2,500 hectares of forest and marsh, but is best known for its long, white, sandy beach and magnificent dunes. With sand stretching for nearly ten kilometres, it's easy to stake out a spot away from the crowds, which don't reach overwhelming numbers.

Midway along the Huron "sun coast," which is generally regarded as the stretch from Grand Bend in the south to Sauble in the north, is Goderich, a pretty, Victorian town known for its shady, tree-lined streets and Great Lakes marine heritage. However, the town also boasts two sandy beaches, the Town Beach and St. Christopher Beach, linked by an old-fashioned boardwalk. Either beach is a must-visit at sundown, when Goderich stakes claim to being "the best sunset viewing spot in North America," as declared in *National Geographic* magazine.

Further north, Southampton is one of the only urban centres in Ontario with a natural dune system. Located at the southern end of the town's waterfront area, the Chantry Dunes are a protected zone, featuring trails designed to allow visitors to view the unique ecosystem, while

BEACH, SOUTHAMPTON

preventing unnecessary erosion. For those who can't keep their toes out of the sand, wide beaches beyond the dunes beckon.

The sun coast ends at nearby Sauble, at the foot of the Bruce Peninsula, which checks in with twelve kilometres

of clean, sandy beach and a full range of resort activities, from an amusement park to mini golf and water slides.

GEORGIAN BAY

Not all beaches are necessarily made for sunbathing and swimming. The east coast of the Bruce Peninsula, which sticks out like a finger between Lake Huron and Georgian Bay, for example, offers more stone than sand, more boulders than bikinis—although loyal, long-time cottage owners and vacationers in this district would undoubtedly dispute this.

The rocky shoreline is amongst the province's most scenic and presents ideal opportunities for beachcombers, fossil hunters, history buffs, and those with just a passing interest in geology, for it is here that southwestern Ontario's defining geological formation, the Niagara Escarpment, dwindles to a rocky end in the northern Great Lakes. But not before creating a coastline of scenic limestone cliffs that tower, at times, fifty metres above the turquoise blue waters of the bay and cobblestone beach outcrops below.

The one exception to the rocky rule for Georgian Bay beaches in this area is the spectacular Wasaga Beach, east of Collingwood. With little exception, the shoreline from Owen Sound to Collingwood is largely shale, such as that found at Craigleith Provincial Park. But then comes Wasaga Beach, the longest freshwater beach in the world. This has been a well-known sun and swim place for the past hundred years, and visitors will find all of the resort amenities they would expect at such a popular vacation destination.

In the summer months, southwestern Ontario offers visitors some of the finest beaches in Canada. Lake Erie, Lake Huron, and Georgian Bay offer countless opportunities to enjoy warm water and spectacular scenery.

FLOWERPOT ISLAND

THEATRE

ROBERT REID

Southwestern Ontario is justly famous for two renowned drama festivals—Stratford and Shaw. These festivals draw famous actors and large crowds to well-known plays by Shakespeare, Shaw, and other classical and contemporary dramatists. What many visitors don't know is that this part of the province is also home to many interesting small companies. A visit to any one of the dozens of small theatres in this area can be an enjoyable experience as well.

MAJOR BARBARA, SHAW FESTIVAL

STRATFORD FESTIVAL

At its best, the Stratford Festival affirms its reputation as North America's leading classical repertory theatre (1-800-567-1600). Founded in 1953 in the small city that provides its name, the Stratford Festival made believers out of early skeptics who dismissed as lunacy the idea of an annual drama festival devoted primarily to the works of William Shakespeare.

However, few theatregoers are not familiar with the festival's colourful history, beginning with its first artistic director, Tyrone Guthrie—who at the time was one of Britain's leading directors—and the legendary designer Tanya Moiseiwitsch, who designed the Festival Theatre's celebrated thrust stage, based on Elizabethan-era stages. Sir Alec Guiness starred in the title role of Richard III when the festival opened in a tent in 1953.

The festival has expanded from a six-week summer season with two productions to a six-month season featuring 576 performances of a dozen plays and musicals presented at the Festival Theatre, Avon Theatre, and Tom Patterson Theatre.

THE TAMING OF THE SHREW, STRATFORD FESTIVAL

The festival celebrated its forty-fifth season in 1997 with historic box office revenue exceeding $21 million, and attendance numbers topping half a million.

The Festival offers a varied theatrical program of Shakespearean plays, classical and modern plays, and musicals ranging from Gilbert and Sullivan operettas to Broadway classics; its celebrated writers' series also remains popular.

Although heavily influenced by British theatre in its formative years, the festival has nurtured many accomplished Canadian classical actors including William Hutt, Douglas Rain, Christopher Plummer, Martha Henry, and the late Kate Reid. Richard Monette is the festival's eighth—and first Canadian-born—artistic director.

SHAW FESTIVAL

Located in the historically picturesque town of Niagara-on-the-Lake, the Shaw Festival is newer and smaller than the Stratford Festival, but its artistic achievement is comparable (1-800-511-SHAW). Founded in 1962, the festival is the only one of its kind devoted to the plays of George Bernard Shaw and his contemporaries.

MAJOR BARBARA, SHAW FESTIVAL

THE FESTIVAL THEATRE, NIAGARA-ON-THE-LAKE

After an initial season of eight amateur performances, the festival turned professional. In 1966, Barry Morse—known to television fans of the mid-1960s as the detective who pursued David Janssen in *The Fugitive*—transformed the festival from a tourist attraction into a major theatrical event. However, it was Paxton Whitehead who consolidated its international reputation in the decade spanning 1967 through 1977.

Beginning in the historic Court House Theatre, the festival expanded to take in the Festival Theatre, designed by Canadian architect Ron Thom, and the more recently renovated Royal George Theatre. In a recent season the festival presented 758 performances of 12 productions over a six-month season. It generated more than $11 million in box office receipts and enjoyed attendance of 308,000.

Christopher Newton has been artistic director since 1980; it would be difficult to name another Canadian theatre program that bears the stamp of its artistic head more than the Shaw. Luckily for a theatre dedicated to the work of a single playwright and his contemporaries, Bernard Shaw lived a long life, which enables the festival to comb the plays and musicals from the latter part of the nineteenth century through the mid-20th century for its repertoire. Although the festival has mounted many acclaimed productions, from *Cyrano de Bergerac* to *Peter Pan*, its reputation rests on the brilliance with which Newton and his guest directors have blown the dust off a playwright once dismissed as a period relic. Indeed, Newton has gone a long way to securing Shaw's stature as one of the century's greatest playwrights.

Although the Stratford and Shaw Festivals are supported by the Canada Council and Ontario government, most of their income is generated through box-office receipts and private contributions. Because of this, both festivals walk a tightrope, balancing creative adventure with commercial popularity. Nonetheless, they have combined to put a distinctly Canadian brand on some of the world's greatest drama and musical theatre.

BLYTH FESTIVAL

The Blyth Festival is small potatoes compared to southwestern Ontario's two major festivals, but it has been a staple of Canadian theatre since it was co-founded in 1975 by Keith Roulston, local newspaper editor, and James Roy, a young director raised in the area (519-523-9300). A

BLYTH MEMORIAL
COMMUNITY HALL

main impetus for the summer theatre was the slated demolition of the Blyth Memorial Hall, which subsequently became home to the festival, situated in the quaint village nestled in the countryside of Huron County.

The fact that the festival developed through the commitment of a group of local citizens is significant. Although it has gained national prominence as a producer of original Canadian plays—it has premiered more than eighty Canadian works—the festival's survival depends on the support of its core audience from the immediate area. True to its roots, many of its plays deal with historical themes and local concerns, or with rural issues of local relevance. This is not to imply that the festival is restrictively parochial. Many plays premiered at Blyth, such as Peter Colley's rural gothic thriller *I'll Be Back*

Before Midnight, have been produced elsewhere, thereby solidifying the festival's reputation for new play development.

In addition to the four plays usually mounted each season at the Blyth Memorial Hall, the festival has established an alternative space, known as The Garage, and a young company (which is a smaller and younger version of Stratford Festival's Young Company). Blyth Festival attracts between thirty and forty thousand visitors annually during a season running from mid-June through early September.

REGIONAL THEATRE

The remaining theatre in southwestern Ontario can conveniently be divided into summer theatre and regional theatre (with a season extending from the fall through to the spring). In the latter category are two significant theatres—Hamilton's Theatre Aquarius and London's Grand Theatre (905-522-7815; 519-672-8800).

The Grand has been in operation in one way or another since 1899, occupying its current site since 1901. London Little Theatre was formed in 1934 and became the Grand's resident amateur company.

London Little Theatre was transformed into the professional Theatre London over a three-year period in the early 1970s and soon emerged as one of the leading professional theatres in the country under artistic director William Hutt. In more recent times, the Grand Theatre has been guided by such accomplished

THE GRAND THEATRE, LONDON

artistic directors as Robin Phillips and Martha Henry. On a good night, the Grand Theatre can be considered one of the country's most vital regional theatres with an annual mainstage playbill of six or seven productions from September through May. Alternative productions and theatre for young audiences are offered at the McManus Theatre.

GUNMETAL BLUES, THEATRE AQUARIUS, HAMILTON

After mounting productions in various locations for eighteen years, founding artistic director Peter Mandia oversaw the move of Theatre Aquarius to its new

permanent home at the du Maurier Ltd. Centre. Recently celebrating the theatre's twenty-fifth anniversary, managing artistic director Max Reimer presented a diverse playbill of eight productions from September through

May, in addition to three productions as part of its acclaimed Stage Wright Series in the Studio Theatre at Hamilton Place.

Theatre Aquarius is capable of presenting first-rate productions of the classics, modern plays (including a respectable number of Canadian works), and musicals, featuring Canada's best actors. The proximity of Theatre Aquarius and the Grand Theatre to Stratford has meant that many festival veterans who reside in southwestern Ontario work during the winter months at these two fine regional theatres.

SMALLER COMPANIES

On a much reduced scale, Kitchener-Waterloo and Windsor both have small professional companies trying to carve out niches in predominantly local markets. Kitchener's Theatre and Company has presented four or five productions annually since 1990, while Waterloo Stage Theatre, which opened in 1997, presents a year-round repertoire of Broadway musical theatre (519-571-0928; 519-888-0000).

WAITING FOR GODOT, **THEATRE AND COMPANY, KITCHENER**

Similarly, Windsor Feminist Theatre has been producing plays with socio-political thrusts that are not restrictively doctrinaire (519-254-8393). Windsor's proximity to Detroit has thwarted professional theatre although energetic theatres such as Theatre Alive and Windsor Light Opera try to fill an obvious void (519-969-0660; 519-974-6593).

In addition to professional theatre, a number of areas, including Hamilton and Niagara, Kitchener-Waterloo and Windsor, have long traditions of amateur and semi-professional theatre of consistently high quality. Kitchener-Waterloo Musical Productions has mounted at least one annual musical with combined professional and amateur personnel since 1949. Similarly, St. Catharines has Garden City Productions, while Hamilton has Hamilton Theatre Inc., as well as Hamilton Players Guild, reputed to be the oldest continuously operating community theatre in North America.

SUMMER THEATRE

For convenience sake, summer theatre can be subdivided into those areas that serve predominantly resort audiences and those that serve local and tourist audiences, the latter facilitated primarily through bus tours. The former category includes Lighthouse Festival Theatre, located in Port Dover on the north shore of Lake Erie, and Huron Country Playhouse, located in Grand Bend on Lake Huron.

The Lighthouse Festival Theatre has offered a staple of light summer entertainment—comedies, romantic

STAGE THEATRE, WATERLOO (CENTRE); CAST MEMBERS, WINDSOR LIGHT OPERA THEATRE

161

comedies, farces, murder mysteries, and pocket musicals—since 1980 (519-583-2221). Over the years it has premiered several original Canadian plays. Huron Country Playhouse has offered much the same in summer fare; however, its Broadway–style musicals are bigger and more ambitious, accommodated in its spacious mainstage theatre.

The two most significant theatres in the latter category are Theatre Orangeville, in the bustling Halton Hills community of Orangeville, and Drayton Festival Theatre, located somewhat unexpectedly in the Wellington County farming crossroads of Drayton (519-942-3423; 519-638-5555). Theatre Orangeville and Drayton Festival Theatre offer the same kind of repertoire, laced heavily with comedies, romances, farces, pocket musicals, and murder mysteries.

However, Theatre Orangeville has presented a higher percentage of original Canadian works, some written by the theatre's founding artistic director Jim Betts. Established in 1994 in the beautifully restored Orangeville Town Hall Opera House, Theatre Orangeville has quickly developed into one of southwestern Ontario's premium summer theatres.

Artistic director Alex Mustakas and Drayton Festival together represent one of the most remarkable theatrical success stories in Canada. After renovating the village's historic vaudeville house, the festival held its inaugural season in 1991. Expanding over the years from a nine-week to a twenty-week season, the festival has gone on to enjoy incredible increases in ticket sales.

The remaining theatres in the latter category include Bluewater Summer Playhouse in Kincardine, Georgian Theatre Festival in Meaford, Summer at the Roxy in Owen Sound, Theatre on the Grand in Fergus, Tottenham Summer Theatre in Tottenham, and Victoria Playhouse in Petrolia. Although the Victoria Playhouse has been around for some time, Theatre on the Grand was founded in 1993, while Bluewater Summer Playhouse and Tottenham Summer Theatre shared an inaugural season in 1994.

The season for these theatres runs from six to eleven weeks, usually starting sometime in June, and features anywhere from two to nine productions. With rare exceptions, the playbills consist of standard light summer fare. Some theatres augment their play production with modest musical programs featuring mostly Canadian performers.

Fine theatre can be found year-round in southwestern Ontario, and some of the best theatre anywhere in the world during the Stratford and Shaw Festival seasons.

THEATRE ON THE GRAND, FERGUS

WINE TASTING

HENRY MOORE AND PAUL KNOWLES

Wine making, wine tasting, wine tours—the wine industry is one of the most dramatic success stories in southwestern Ontario.

Wine making in Ontario dates back to the Jesuits, who made the beverage for sacramental purposes. The accepted date for the start of more conventional wine making in the province is 1811, when a retired corporal of the German Army settled in Cooksville and established a vineyard and a small winery.

Most of the wine made in those early days had the rather unpleasant taste of the native Lambrusca grape which imparts a "foxy" flavour to the wine. This is why so much of the wine made then was fortified, such as ports and sherries. Sweetening the wines with sugar helped overcome its shortcomings in flavour to some degree.

The situation was improved with the importation of vines from Europe, including the classical Cabernet, Merlot, and Chardonnay. From these, hybrids were developed, resulting in vines that adapted to the Ontario climate and soil. This process produced varieties such as Seyval Blanc and Vidal in the whites, and Baco Noir and Marechal Foch in the reds. Some of these are producing excellent wines and many have outclassed the European varieties from which they were born. The Vidal produces the internationally renowned Icewines for which Ontario has become justifiably famous.

The Vintners Quality Alliance (VQA) was established in the 1980s to set and safeguard high standards for Ontario's fine wines. The VQA mark guarantees that the wine is made from a specific grape type and that the grapes are indeed grown in the Ontario region. It is a guarantee of provenance, as well as a promise of quality. The VQA has

VINELAND ESTATES WINE

163

ensured that southwestern Ontario winemakers have concentrated on improving the quality of locally grown vines, instead of blending grapes imported from other countries. A VQA wine is indeed a unique Ontario wine.

Ontario winemaking is concentrated in three viticultural areas—the Niagara Peninsula, Pelee Island, and the Lake Erie north shore, especially along the western end. Although there are similarities in climate and soil types, the variances in these districts create differences in viticulture. For example, the "Beamsville Bench" is a microenvironment on a plateau halfway up the Niagara Escarpment, a great asset to the wineries in this unique climatic mini-zone that is especially conducive to wine production.

NURSERY WEST OF NIAGARA-ON-THE-LAKE

ICEWINE FROM HILLEBRAND ESTATES WINERY, NIAGARA-ON-THE-LAKE

WINE TOURS AND TASTING

Many wineries offer wine tastings free of charge (usually featuring three or four of their wines, with a charge levied for other wines); in other wine boutiques, a fee is charged for all tastings (usually $.50 for a tasting; $3 for icewine) although the fee may be waived informally (ignoring government regulations) if you buy bottles or cases of the wines you have tasted.

Touring southwestern Ontario's vineyards can involve much more than tasting and purchasing wine. Almost all the vineyards offer full tours on a regular basis. Most wineries have excellent gift boutiques. Several also have restaurants or lunchrooms; and some offer picnic facilities to visitors. Many are located in picturesque settings close to parkland or shoreline, perfect for picnicking. Some of the vineyards also offer special events, concerts, and exhibitions. Wineries may on occasion hold special tastings, where wines are matched with food or cheese.

Visitors should not miss the other attractions that go hand-in-hand with wineries—lovely scenery, farm markets

and road-side produce stands, antique stores, and bed and breakfasts.

Visitors to Ontario's wine regions usually follow the well-signed Winte Route. The Wine Route includes thirty-one wineries, the first twenty-seven on the Niagara Peninsula, and the remainder along the west end of the Lake Erie shoreline, and on Pelee Island. For more information call 1-888-594-6379.

NIAGARA PENINSULA

Andrés Wines in Grimsby is first on the Wine Route and is one of southwestern Ontario's largest and most established wineries. Tours and tastings are offered year-round, and special events are scheduled frequently. Stoney Ridge Cellars is in Winona. This premium boutique winery is considered a leading producer of quality wines. Because of the success it has found, Stoney Ridge is planning to move to new, larger facilities in Jordan. Also in Winona, but not on the official Wine Route because facilities for visitors are not yet completed, is Peller Estates. Try the Peller Chardonnay French Oak Aged, which has a distinctive, under-ripe apple flavour and a hint of oak from the cask. Kittling Ridge Estate is in Grimsby. Their Cabernet Sauvignon is a full-bodied red wine with lots of fruit; this is the famous grape of Europe. Kittling Ridge Estates, a beautiful site where the Niagara Escarpment rises very sharply, and where hawks and migratory birds may actually outnumber the crowds of visiting wine lovers, is also home to a distillery and a gift shop.

THE WINE SHOP, KITTLING RIDGE, GRIMSBY (BELOW)

Taking full advantage of the microenvironment of the Beamsville Bench, Thirty Bench Winery in Beamsville is producing some of the finest wines in southwestern Ontario. They specialize in Rieslings. Tours are available by appointment. Walters Estates, also in Beamsville, is set in one of the prettiest locations on the Wine Route. On a clear day, you can see across the sweep of Lake Ontario to Toronto, with its soaring CN Tower. The new winery building has been constructed from wood harvested from the Walters woodlots. Visitors are welcome to enjoy the deck and brunch or a barbecue on weekends. One of several wineries that now has facilities in the Toronto area as well, Magnotta

VINELAND ESTATES WINE

HERNDER ESTATES WINERY, ST. CATHARINES

Cellars in Beamsville is one of the most popular locations for visitors. Self-directed tours are always available; guided tours by appointment. Another Beamsville winery with a Toronto cousin, Maplegrove Vinoteca Estate Winery is a small winery specializing in 100 per cent Ontario wines. DeSousa Wine Cellars, Beamsville, is a taste of Portugal, with a pink winery building surrounded by beautiful flower beds and featuring picnic facilities. The winery is operated by the DeSousas, grape growers and winemakers for four generations in the Azores. Unlike most of their winemaking neighbours, 95 per cent of the production here is red wine.

Known for excellent wines, Willow Heights in Vineland operates a premium wine boutique. Eddie and Lorraine Gurinskas have built Lakeview Cellars Estate Winery—and their reputation for quality 100 per cent VQA wines—on a favoured location on the Beamsville Bench. At Vineland Estates on one of the most beautiful sites in the Niagara Peninsula, try the Semi-Dry Riesling, slightly spicy with a good bouquet, like the Rieslings of old. Almost equally enjoyable is the view from the wine deck and patio at this 150-year-old homestead located at the base of the Niagara Escarpment. Tours and tastings run regularly, and there are a gift shop and dining facilities.

Cave Spring Cellars in nearby Jordan is housed in a historic building built in 1871. The winery building is also home to gift and antique boutiques, and On the Twenty, a highly acclaimed restaurant. Their Gamay is recommended, the full-bodied red wine famous in Beaujolais and meant to be enjoyed while still young and fresh. Old world charm and a deck and picnic area that overlook the vineyards can be found at V.P. Cellars Estate Winery, also in Jordan.

Hernder Estate Wines in St. Catharines is home to fine wines, and more—the beautiful, expansive setting, complete with covered wooden bridge, is also perfect for events like craft shows. Take a tour of the winery, browse in the gift shop in the 127-year-old stone barn, and enjoy a tasting offered by friendly and entertaining staff members. Henry of Pelham Family Estate Winery in St. Catharines is a good vineyard at which to sample the Vidal, one of the new hybrid white grapes now popular in Ontario;

Icewine is made from Vidal. The winery, operated by the Speck family, is on land that has been in the family since 1794. The gift shop is located in a historic inn; picnic sites are available.

Château des Charmes Wines in St. Davids is owned by the Bosc family and housed in an amazing new $6-million French chateau. A Château des Charmes Chardonnay was the only North American first-place winner at a recent prestigious wine competition in Europe. Also try the southwestern Ontario wine made from Cabernet Franc, one of the famous red wine grapes of France.

HILLEBRAND ESTATES WINERY, NIAGARA-ON-THE-LAKE

Hillebrand Estates Winery in Niagara-on-the-Lake is more than a winery; it is an entertainment complex, with regular tours year-round, the Vineyard Café restaurant (where chef Tony de Luca creates dishes to match the wines of winemaker J.J. Groux), a gift shop, and frequent special events including the Vineyard String, Vineyard Jazz, and Vineyard Blues music festivals.

COUNTRYSIDE WEST OF NIAGARA-ON-THE-LAKE

Stonechurch Vineyards, also in Niagara-on-the-Lake, is new but thriving; it has been open since 1990. Distinctive touches include a patio and a hospitality room with a fireplace. Konzelmann Estate Winery in Niagara-on-the-Lake is known for innovation; this was the first vineyard in Canada to introduce vertical vine training. The friendly folks at Konzelmann are happy to share their Johannisberg Riesling, a spicy white wine famed in Europe. At Strewn, Niagara-on-the-Lake, the visitors find the innovative combination of a winery producing premium wines, and the Wine Country Cooking School, operating in a large and busy facility. Strewn is brand new, open only since June 1997, although the wines offered are from three vintages, 1994–1996. Distinctive touches at Pellitteri Estates, Niagara-on-the-Lake, like the fresh bread you can buy to go with your VQA premium wines, tells you that this is a winery owned and operated by a family in love with their business. Pillitteri has a banquet room and gift shop.

Joseph's Estate Wines, Niagara-on-the-Lake, is a new facility. It is another small, cottage winery specializing in premium wines produced primarily from estate-grown grapes. Sunnybrook Farm Estate in Niagara-on-the-Lake specializes in fruit wines from tree fruits and berries,

ICEWINE FROM REIF
ESTATE WINERY,
NIAGARA-ON-THE-
LAKE

offering choices such as Winter Peach, Iced Apple, or cherry wines.

Reif Estate Winery is an accessible winery located right on the beautiful Niagara Parkway just south of the town of Niagara-on-the-Lake. Try the Seyval Blanc, made from a hybrid vine that has flourished in Ontario. On the Reif Estate is the beautiful Grand Victorian Bed and Breakfast, where evenings before the fire or on the enormous porch include complimentary Reif wines. Inniskillen Wines in Niagara-on-the-Lake was founded in the 1970s by two of the heroes of Niagara winemaking—founder Donald Ziraldo (in 1998 named to the Order of Canada) and legendary winemaker Karl Kaiser. Inniskillen's beautiful shop in a restored barn features wine, wine tasting, and more—a second-floor area serves as display area and gallery (often featuring items from the Shaw Festival). Tours, both guided and self-guided, are offered. Sample the Pinot Noir Reserve, the famous red wine of Burgundy fame, with lots of body and flavour. Marynissen Estates in Niagara-on-the-Lake is a smaller winery with a large reputation. John Marynissen was the first grape grower in Canada to plant Cabernet Sauvignon grapes, and the wine of that name is considered among the best in the country. As with many of the smaller wineries, visitors to Marynissen are very likely to find themselves in conversation with members of the family or even the winemaker—perhaps over a tasting of the best from the winery.

At Vincor-Niagara Cellars, in Niagara Falls, no public tours are offered, but there is a wine store on-site.

LAKE ERIE SHORELINE

At Pelee Island Winery, a tour involves the added pleasure of a boat ride; while the winery is in Kingsville, the vineyard and wine pavilion are on Pelee Island, reached via the Pelee Island ferry. The island, which is slightly nearer the equator than Rome, enjoys the longest growing season of any wine region in Canada. During a tour of the island, be sure to sample the award-winning Pinot Noir, with the characteristics of the full-bodied red wine of Burgundy. This winery has a toll-free number for information about tours (1-800-597-3533).

At Colio Estate Wines, Harrow, tours are offered daily year-round, with a twenty-minute walking visit concluding in the hospitality room for a wine tasting. Try the Cabernet Franc, an excellent red wine from a famous grape of Bordeaux.

At D'Angelo Estate Winery, near Amherstburg, tours and tastings are offered daily, featuring estate-grown wines.

The wine region of Ontario includes some of the most beautiful countryside that visitors to the province are likely to encounter. A wine-tasting tour of establishments in the Niagara Peninsula, on Pelee Island, or along the north shore of Lake Erie can easily be combined with other activities—theatre, cycling, hiking, historic explorations—and spun out to take anywhere from a weekend to a week. The trip is almost guaranteed to be pleasant and palatable.

CONTENTS

Getting There   170

170 By Road
170 By Air
170 By Rail

Travel Essentials   170

170 Money
170 Passports
171 Customs
171 Taxes
171 Ontario Travel Information
    Centres

Getting Acquainted 172

172 Time Zone
172 Climate

Getting Around   172

172 By Car
172 By Rail
172 By Bus
173 By Boat

Accommodation   173

173 Accommodation and Travel
    Associations
173 Niagara Peninsula
174 Caledon and Halton Hills
174 Kitchener-Waterloo and Area
174 Stratford and Area
175 London and Area
175 Lake Erie Shoreline
176 Windsor and Area
176 Lake Huron and Georgian Bay

Antiquing   176

**Art Galleries
and Studios**   177

Birding   177

Boating   178

Camping   178

Craft Shows   179

Cycling   180

Dining   180

180 Niagara Peninsula
181 Caledon and Halton Hills
182 Kitchener-Waterloo and Area
183 Stratford and Area
183 London and Area
184 Lake Erie Shoreline
184 Windsor and Area
185 Lake Huron and Georgian Bay

Farmers' Markets   185

Festivals   185

Gardens   186

Golf   187

Hiking   187

Kids' Stuff   188

**Museums and
Historic Sites**   188

Shopping   189

189 Niagara Peninsula
189 Caledon and Halton Hills
189 Kitchener-Waterloo and Area
189 Stratford and Area
189 Windsor and Area
190 Lake Huron and Georgian Bay

Snow Sports   190

Swimming   190

Theatre   190

Wine Tasting   191

Index   192

Photo Credits   205

Contributors   207

GETTING THERE

Southwestern Ontraio is usually described as the part of the province west of Toronto, bounded by Georgian Bay in the north, Lake Huron in the west, and Lake Erie in the south. See the map on pages 4 and 5 for an overview of the area.

BY ROAD

If you're coming to southwestern Ontario from the Toronto region, the 401 is your quickest route. The 403 also leads out of the Burlington and Hamilton area to Brantford and meets up with the 401 at Woodstock.

For visitors from New York State, the points of entry on the Canadian side are Queenston, Niagara Falls, and Fort Erie. All of these routes feed into the QEW (or Queen Elizabeth Way), which then proceeds to Hamilton. From here, via Highway 8, you can get onto the 403.

Visitors from Michigan can cross over to Highway 402 at Sarnia or the 401 at Windsor.

Greyhound Canada is the most comprehensive bus line serving southwestern Ontario. Greyhound can be contacted for fares and information at 1-800-361-1235.

BY RAIL

Southwestern Ontario is served by VIA Rail. For general information and reservations call 1-800-361-1235. In the Windsor area call 519-256-5511. In the London area call 519-672-5722.

BY AIR

The largest airport close to southwestern Ontario is the Lester B. Pearson International Airport in Toronto. The airport is accessible from highways 401, 427, and 409. For general information, including information on Terminals 1, 2, and 3 (Trillium Terminal), call 416-247-7678.

There are also smaller, international airports in Hamilton, London, and Windsor:

Hamilton International Airport: 905-679-8359.

London International Airport: 519-452-4015.

Windsor Airport, Transport Canada: 519-969-2430.

TRAVEL ESSENTIALS

MONEY

Currency can be exchanged at any Canadian bank at the prevailing rate. If you use a small local branch, we recommend you call ahead to confirm its capacity to exchange, on the spot, any currency other than American funds. The Ontario Travel Information Centres listed below can exchange most major international currencies for Canadian dollars, and vice versa. If you wish to exchange a large amount, or to exchange a less common currency, telephone ahead (1-800-ONTARIO). Units of currency are similar to those of the United States, excepting the Canadian one-dollar (loonie) and two-dollar (twoonie) coins.

Many stores and services will accept U.S. currency, but the exchange rate they offer may vary greatly. Since there are no laws enforcing currency rates of exchange, we strongly recommend that you convert to Canadian funds before you make your purchases.

Visitors may also use bank or credit cards to make cash withdrawals from automated teller machines that are tied into international networks. Before you leave home, check with your bank to find out what range of services its cards will allow you to use.

PASSPORTS

American visitors may be asked to verify their citizenship with a document such as a passport, or a birth or baptismal certificate. Naturalized U.S. citizens should carry a naturalization certificate. Permanent U.S. residents who are not citizens are advised to bring their Alien Registration Receipt Card. Citizens of all other countries, except Greenland and residents of St. Pierre et Miquelon, must bring a valid passport. Some may be required to obtain a visitor's visa. For details, please consult the Canadian embassy or consulate serving your home country.

CUSTOMS

Arriving

As a nonresident of Canada, you may bring in any reasonable amount of personal effects and food, and a full tank of gas. Special restrictions or quotas apply to certain specialty goods, and especially to plant-, agriculture-, and animal-related materials. All items must be declared to Customs upon arrival and may include up to 200 cigarettes, 50 cigars, 400 grams of manufactured tobacco, and 400 tobacco sticks. Visitors are also permitted 1.1 litres (40 oz.) Of liquor or wine, or 8.2 litres (24 x 12 oz. bottles or cans) of beer.

You may bring in gifts for Canadian residents duty-free, up to a value of $60 (Canadian) each, provided they do not consist of alcohol, tobacco, or advertising material.

For more detailed information, please see our federal Customs (Revenue Canada) website (www.rc.gc.ca), the Customs information booklet "I DECLARE," or contact Revenue Canada, Customs/Border Services Office, #604, 6725 Airport Rd., PO Box 6000, Mississauga ON L4V 1V2, 905-676-3574.

Departing

For detailed customs rules for entering or re-entering the U.S., please contact a U.S. Customs office before visiting southwestern Ontario. Copies of the U.S. Customs information brochure "Know Before You Go" are available from U.S. Customs offices or by mail.

Travellers from other countries should also check on customs regulations before leaving home.

TAXES

Goods and Services Tax (GST)

The federal Goods and Services Tax is 7%. This is a value-added consumption tax that applies to most goods, purchased gifts, food/beverages, and services, including most hotel and motel accommodation.

Provincial Sales Tax (PST)

The Ontario provincial sales tax is 8% on any goods you buy, but not on services or accommodation.

Room Tax

A 5% provincial tax (in place of PST) is added to most tourist accommodation charges, as well as the 7% GST.

Food Service

In restaurants, 7% GST and 8% PST will be added to the food portion of your final bill, as well as a 10% provincial tax on alcoholic beverages (in addition to the 7% GST).

ONTARIO TRAVEL INFORMATION CENTRES

Ontario Travel Information Centres are operated by the Ministry of Economic Development, Trade and Tourism; they provide tourist information on every aspect of Ontario, and are open daily. Call 1-800-ONTARIO to check for extended hours in summer.

Fort Erie
- 100 Goderich St. (near the Peace Bridge), 905-871-3505, Fax: 905-871-6461.

Niagara Falls
- 5355 Stanley Ave. (West on Hwy. 420 from the Rainbow Bridge), 905-358-3221, Fax: 358-6441.

St. Catharines
- QEW at Glendale Ave., 905-684-6354, Fax: 905-684-3634.

Sarnia
- Bluewater Bridge, 1415 Venetian Blvd., 519-344-7403, Fax: 519-332-4576.

Windsor
- 110 Park St. East (Windsor-Detroit tunnel), 519-973-1338, Fax: 519-973-1341.
- 1235 Huron Church Rd. (East of the Ambassador Bridge), 519-973-1310, Fax: 519-973-1313.

GETTING ACQUAINTED

TIME ZONE

Southwestern Ontario falls within the Eastern Standard Time Zone.

CLIMATE

The following are Daily Maximum, Minimum, and Mean temperatures for London, centrally located within southwestern Ontario:

January	-2.8 °C
	-10.7 °C
	-6.7 °C
February	-2.0 °C
	-10.5 °C
	-6.2 °C
March	3.8 °C
	-5.0 °C
	-0.5 °C
April	11.7 °C
	0.7 °C
	6.2 °C
May	18.7 °C
	6.4 °C
	12.6 °C
June	23.8 °C
	11.6 °C
	17.7 °C
July	26.4 °C
	14.2 °C
	20.3 °C
August	25.2 °C
	13.3 °C
	19.3 °C
September	20.9 °C
	9.6 °C
	15.3 °C
October	14.2 °C
	3.9 °C
	9.1 °C
November	7.1 °C
	-0.6 °C
	3.3 °C
December	-7.1 °C
	-3.4 °C

Average annual rainfall
77.78 cm
Average annual snowfall
212.3 cm

GETTING AROUND

BY CAR

A valid driver's license from any country is good in Ontario for three months. Evidence of a car's registration is required (a car-rental contract will also serve). If you are driving into Ontario or importing a vehicle, bring with you its registration documents, and either a Canadian Non-Resident Motor Vehicle Liability Insurance Card (obtained from your insurance agent), or else the insurance policy itself. If you're driving a rented car, bring a copy of the rental contract.

Speed limits are measured in kilometres per hour and vary depending on the type of road, with 400-level controlled-access highways having the highest limit. Speed limits on most highways are 80 to 90 kph, and 100 kph on freeways. On city streets the normal speed is 50 kph unless otherwise posted. Seat belt use by passengers and drivers is mandatory in Ontario.

One kilometre equals about 5/8 of a mile. To convert from kilometres to miles, multiply kilometres by 0.6. To convert from miles to kilometres, multiply miles by 1.6. We use metric measurements for motor fuel. One litre equals about 1/4 of a U.S. gallon, or about 1/5 of an Imperial gallon. For car rentals, check the Yellow Pages.

BY RAIL

Southwestern Ontario is served by VIA Rail. For general information and reservations call 1-800-361-1235. In the Windsor area call 519-256-5511. In the London area call 519-672-5722.

BY BUS

Greyhound Canada is the most comprehensive bus line serving southwestern Ontario. They can be contacted for fares and information at 1-800-361-1235.

By Boat

There is a ferry service for visitors who want to travel between Niagara Falls or Niagara-on-the-Lake and Toronto. Call Hydrofoil Lake Jet Lines at 1-800-313-3237 for more information.

ACCOMMODATION

What follows is a good cross-section of the accommodation options in southwestern Ontario. We have given preference to fine, independently run inns, where they exist. Failing these, we have found the best in chain hotels and motels for value and service.

Price alone has never been a factor in making our selections. Approximate prices are indicated, based on the average cost, at time of publishing, for two persons staying in a double room (excluding taxes): $ = $50-$90; $$ = $90-$180; $$$ = above $180.

The accommodation and travel associations listed below also provide guides to their respective regions, either in print format or on the internet. The Ontario South Central Trip Planner, available from any Ontario Travel Information Centre (1-800-ONTARIO), also has accommodation listings for each town or city of note.

Accommodation and Travel Associations

- Ontario Accommodation Association, #2, 347 Pido Rd., RR#6, Peterborough ON K9J 6X7; 705-745-4982, Toll Free: 1-800-461-1972, Fax: 705-745-4983, Email: info@ontarioaccommodation.com, Website: www.motelsontario.on.ca
- Niagara and Mid-Western Ontario Travel Association, 180 Greenwich St., Brantford ON N3S 2X6; 519-756-3230, Toll Free: 1-800-267-3399, Fax: 519-756-3231; Website: www.niagara-midwest-ont.com
- Simcoe Georgian Bay Marketing, Simcoe County Bldg., Midhurst

ON L0L 1X0; 705-726-9300, ext. 220, Toll Free: 1-800-487-6642, Fax: 705-726-3991
- Southwestern Ontario Travel Association, #112, 4023 Meadowbrook Dr., London ON N6L 1E7; 519-652-1391, Toll Free: 1-800-661-6804, Fax: 519-652-0533
- General Information: Ontario Tourism: 1-800-668-2746

Niagara Peninsula

Jordan
- The Vintner's Inn, 3845 Main St., Jordan ON L0R 1S0; 905-562-5336, Toll Free: 1-800-701-8074, Fax: 905-562-3232. Home of the elegant On the Twenty restaurant, and across the street from Cave Spring Cellars. $$ - $$$.

Niagara Falls, *see also Niagara-on-the-Lake*
- Michael's Inn-By the Falls, 5599 River Rd., Niagara Falls ON L2E 3H3; 905-354-2727, Toll Free: 1-800-263-9390, Fax: 905-374-7706. 130 room motor inn overlooking the falls, just north of the Rainbow Bridge. $ - $$.
- The Skyline Brock Hotel, 5685 Falls Ave., Niagara Falls ON L2E 6W7; 905-374-4444, Fax: 905-358-0443. Grand old 1929 hotel overlooking the falls with fitness facilities and good public areas. $$ - $$$.

Niagara-on-the-Lake
- The Kiely Inn, 209 Queen St., Niagara-on-the-Lake ON L0S 1J0; 905-468-4588. 1832 Georgian-style home within walking distance of the Shaw festival, with eleven guest rooms. $$.
- Lakewinds Country Manor, 328 Queen St., PO Box 1483, Niagara-on-the-Lake ON L0S 1J0; 905-468-1888, Fax: 905-468-1061. 1881 summer mansion situated on an acre of flower gardens; all guest rooms are uniquely decorated with period furniture.
- Moffat Inn, 60 Picton St., Niagara-on-the-Lake ON L0S 1J0; 905-468-4116. Historic country inn with dining facilities. $$.
- The Pillar & Post Inn, 48 John St.,

PO Box 1011, Niagara-on-the-Lake ON L0S 1J0; 905-468-2123, Toll Free: 1-800-361-6788, Fax: 905-468-3551. 123 well-furnished rooms, spa facilities, and Vintages Wine Bar and Lounge. $$ - $$$.

- The Prince of Wales Hotel, 6 Picton St., Niagara-on-the-Lake ON L0S 1J0; 905-468-3246, Toll Free: 1-800-263-2452. Distinguished 1864 hotel with well-appointed rooms, Prince of Wales Dining Room, and saunas. $$ - $$$.

- Queen's Landing Inn, 155 Byron St., PO Box 1180, Niagara-on-the-Lake ON L0S 1J0; 905-468-2195, Toll Free: 1-800-361-6645, Fax: 905-468-2227. Spacious rooms, saunas, whirlpool, a marina go towards earning this Inn a Four Diamond Award from the CAA. $$$.

- White Oaks Inn and Racquet Club, 4 Taylor Rd., RR#4, Niagara-on-the-Lake ON L0S 1J0; 905-688-2550, Toll Free: 1-800-263-5766. $$.

CALEDON AND HALTON HILLS

Alton
- The Millcroft Inn, 55 John St., Alton ON L0N 1A0; 519-941-8111, Toll Free: 1-800-383-3976, Fax: 519-941-9192. CAA Four Diamond Award winner; fine dining and 100 acres of outdoor trails. $$$.

KITCHENER-WATERLOO AND AREA

Brantford
•Best Western Brant Park Inn, 19 Holiday Dr., PO Box 1900, Brantford ON N3T 5W5; 519-753-8651, Toll Free: 1-800-528-1234, Fax: 519-753-2619. 115 large rooms; wading pool, whirlpool, sauna, and playground. $.

Cambridge
- Langdon Hall, RR#33, Cambridge ON N3H 4R8; 519-740-2100, Toll Free: 1-800-268-1898, Fax: 519-740-8161. 200 acre rural estate with excellent dining and full spa services. $$$.

Elora
- Elora Mill Inn, 77 Mill St. West, Elora ON N0B 1S0; 519-846-5356, Fax: 519-846-9180. 19th century grist mill, with a dining room overlooking the the Grand River falls. $$ - $$$.

Fergus
- Breadalbane Inn, 486 St. Andrews St. West, Fergus ON N1M 1P2; 519-843-4770, Fax: 519-843-7600. $ - $$.

Guelph
- Holiday Inn, 601 Scottsdale Dr., Guelph ON N1G 3E7; 519-836-0231, Fax: 519-836-5329. Putting green, sauna, and whirlpool plus restaurant with entertainment. $$.

St. Jacobs
- Jakobstettel Guest House, 16 Isabella St., St. Jacobs ON N0B 2N0; 519-664-2208, Fax: 519-664-1326. Twelve Victorian guest rooms, a pool and a tennis court in the heart of Mennonite country. $$.

Kitchener
- Four Points Hotel Kitchener, 105 King St. East, Kitchener ON N2G 2K8; 519-744-4141, Fax: 519-578-6889. 199-room hotel with fitness and children's facilities. $$.

- Travelodge Hotel Kitchener, 2960 King St. East, Kitchener ON N2A 1A9; 519-894-9500, Fax: 519-894-9144. Includes two dining rooms (steakhouse and Italian). $.

Waterloo
- Destination Inn, 547 King St. North, Waterloo ON N2L 5Z7; 519-884-0100, Fax: 519- 746-8638. Small and comfortable motel. $.

- Waterloo Inn, 475 King St. North, Waterloo ON N2J 2Z5; 519-884-0220, Toll-Free: 1-800-361-4708. Mid-size motor inn with wading pool, whirlpools, and saunas. $$.

STRATFORD AND AREA

- Stratford and Area Bed & Breakfast Association, PO Box 21016, Stratford ON N5A 7V4; 519-271-5644, Fax: 519-272-0156, Email: amcroft@orc.ca oravonview@cyg.net

- Tourism Stratford, PO Box 818, Stratford ON N5A 6W1; 519-271-5140, Toll Free: 1-800-561-6926, Fax: 519-273-1818

St. Marys

- Westover Inn, 300 Thomas St., PO Box 280, St. Marys ON N4X 1B1; 519-284-2977, Toll Free: 1-800-368-8243, Fax: 519-284-4043. Limestone Victorian mansion offers 22 guest rooms, swimming, tennis, and patio dining. $$ - $$$.

Stratford

- Stratford Festival Inn, 1144 Ontario St., PO Box 811, Stratford ON N5A 6W1; 519-273-1150, Toll Free: 1-800-463-3581, Fax: 519-273-2111. Luxurious rooms, fitness equipment, and restaurant. $$.
- Queen's Inn at Stratford, 161 Ontario St., Stratford ON N5A 3H3; 519-271-1400, Toll Free: 1-800-461-6450, Fax: 519-271-7373. $$.
- Stone Maiden Inn, 123 Church St., Stratford ON N5A 2R3; 519-271-7129, Fax: 519-271-4615. 1872 inn with 14 rooms, some with canopy beds, whirlpools, and fireplaces. $$.
- Swan Motel, 959 Downie St., Stratford ON N5A 6S3; 519-271-6376, Fax: 519-271-0682. Pleasantly situated. $.
- Twenty-Three Albert Place Hotel, 23 Albert St., Stratford ON N5A 3K2; 519-273-5800, Fax: 519-273-5008. $ - $$.
- The Victorian Inn on the Park, 10 Romeo St., Stratford ON N5A 5M7; 519-271-4650, Toll Free: 1-800-741-2135, Fax: 519-271-2030. Five minutes from the festival, with fitness facilities and restaurant. $$.
- Woods Villa, 62 John St. North, Stratford ON N5A 6K7; 519-271-4576, Fax: 519-271-7173. 1870s home restored as a bed & breakfast, with six rooms and shared bathrooms. $$.

Woodstock

- Quality Inn, 580 Bruin Blvd., Woodstock ON N4V 1E5; 519-537-5586, Fax: 519-421-1304. 75 spacious rooms, plus sauna and aerobics facilities. $.

LONDON AND AREA

Ingersoll

- Elm Hurst Inn, Junction of Hwy. 401 & 19, PO Box 123, Ingersoll ON N5C 3K1; 519-485-5321, Toll-Free: 1-800-561-5321, Fax: 519-485-6579. Well-decorated Victorian gothic mansion, close to London and Stratford. $$.

London

- Delta London Armouries Hotel, 325 Dundas St., London ON N6B 1T9; 519-679-6111, Toll Free: 1-800-668-9999, Fax: 519-679-3957. An inspiringly innovative re-use of the old London armouries, with all the amenities. $$.
- Idlewyld Inn, 36 Grand Ave., London ON N6C 1K8; 519-433-2891, Toll Free: 1-800-267-0525, Fax: 519-433-2891. Large bed & breakfast in Victorian mansion furnished with antiques. $$.
- Radisson Hotel London Centre, 300 King St., London ON N6B 1S2; 519-439-1661, Toll Free: 1-800-333-3333, Fax: 519-439-9672. Part of the London Convention Centre; health club and children's facilities. $.
- Station Park Inn, 242 Pall Mall St., London ON N6A 5P6; 519-642-4444, Toll Free: 1-800-561-4574, Fax: 519-642-2551. Located in Richmond Row, London's shopping and dining district. $$.

St. Thomas

- Cardinal Court Motel, RR#7, St. Thomas ON N5P 3T2; 519-633-0740, Fax: 519-633-9616. 15 room motel in a park setting with a playground. $.

LAKE ERIE SHORELINE

Kingsville

- Adams Golden Acres Motel, 438 Hwy 18 West, Kingsville ON N9Y 2K2; 519-733-6531. $.
- Kingswood Inn, 101 Mill St. West, Kingsville ON N9Y 1W4; 519-733-3248, Fax: 519-733-8734. Bed & breakfast in 1859 octagonal home; five elegantly furnished rooms.

Pelee Island
- The Tin Goose Inn, 1060 East-West Rd., Pelee Island ON N0R 1M0; 519-724-2223. Victorian Inn set on 6 wooded acres has 6 rooms and 2 suites. $$.

Port Stanley
- Kettle Creek Inn, 216 Joseph St., Port Stanley ON N5L 1C4; 519-782-3388, Fax: 519-782-4747. 1849 Inn with pub, gazebo, and gardens; whirlpools in some suites. $$.

WINDSOR AND AREA

Chatham
- Best Western Wheels Inn Resort & Conference Centre, 615 Richmond St. at Keil Dr., 519-351-1100, Fax: 519-436-5541. Full spa and sports facilities, dining and entertainment. $$.
- Comfort Inn, 1100 Richmond St., Chatham ON N7M 5J5; 519-352-5500, Fax: 519-352-2520. 81 room motel with interior corridors. $.

Windsor
- Best Western Continental Motor Inn, 3345 Huron Church Rd., Windsor ON N9E 4H5; 519-966-5541, Fax: 519-972-3384. 71 spacious rooms. $.
- Cadillac Motel, 2498 Dougall Rd., Windsor ON N8X 1T2; 519-969-9340, Fax: 519-969-9342. Whirlpool, laundry, and breakfast. $
- Comfort Inn, 2765 Huron Church Rd., Windsor ON N9E 5K4; 519-972-1331, Fax: 519- 972-5574. 100 rooms with morning coffee and restaurant. $
- Windsor Hilton, 277 Riverside Dr. West, Windsor ON N9A 5K4;519-973-5555, Fax: 519-973-1600. Overlooks Detroit skyline and the waterway, and features the Park Terrace restaurant. $$.

LAKE HURON AND GEORGIAN BAY

Bayfield
- Bayfield Village Inn, PO Box 2039, Bayfield ON N0M 1G0; 519-565-2443. $$.
- The Little Inn of Bayfield, PO Box 100, Bayfield ON N0M 1G0; 519-565-2611, Toll Free: 1-800-565-5474, Fax: 519-565-5474. Historic 1832 Inn with ensuite whirlpools, fireplaces, and private verandahs. $$.

Goderich
- Bedford Hotel, 92 The Square, Goderich ON N7A 1M7; 519-524-7337, Fax: 519-524-2913. 100-year-old hotel, renovated, with restaurant and bar. $$.
- Benmiller Inn, RR#4, Goderich ON N7A 3Y1; 519-524-2191, Toll Free: 1-800-265-1711, Fax: 519-524-5150. CAA Four Diamond Award winner; five old mills and mill owners' homes overlooking a river. $$.

Grand Bend
- Bonnie Doone Manor, 16 Government Rd., PO Box 550, Grand Bend ON N0M 1T0; 519-238-2236, Fax: 519-238-5252. $$.

Owen Sound
- Comfort Inn, 955 - 9th Ave. East, Owen Sound ON N4K 6N4; 519-371-5500, Fax: 519-371-6438. $.

Sarnia
- The Drawbridge Inn, 283 North Christina St., Sarnia ON N7T 5V4; 519-337-7571, Fax: 519-332-8181. Tudor accented, 97 room motor inn with sauna. $.

Strathroy
- Countryside Motel & Restaurant, RR#5, Strathroy ON N7G 3H6; 519-245-0115, Fax: 519-245-0199. $.

ANTIQUING

Antiquing opportunities in southwestern Ontario are so extensive it would be impossible to list them all. Below are some of the better-known shops, as well as contact numbers for regional representatives of the Canadian Antique Dealers Association. Antique afficionadoes are encouraged to contact CADA for an informed picture of antiquing in the Niagara and western Ontario regions.

General Information
- Canadian Antique Dealers Association (CADA), 250 Eglinton Ave. East, Toronto ON M4P 3C1, 416-483-1481; Niagara Information: 905-687-8770; Western Ontario Information: 519-625-8307

Stores
- The Antique Emporium, 765 Exeter Rd., London ON N6E 3T1; 519-668-8838
- Antique Warehouse, 805 King St. North, RR#15, PO Box 280, St. Jacobs ON N0B 2N0; 519-725-2644
- The Antiquities Shoppe, 129 Wellington St., London ON N6B 2K7; 519-663-9400
- C.J.'s Antiques and Refinishing, RR#4, Waterford ON N0E 1Y0; 519-443-4197
- Glen Manor Galleries, 21 Huron St., Shakespeare ON N0B 2P0; 519-625-8920
- Jonny's Antiques, 10 Shakespeare St., Shakespeare ON N0B 2P0; 519-625-8307
- Jordan Antique Centre, 3836 Main St., Jordan ON L0R 1S0; 905-562-7723
- Old London South Antiques, 169 Wortley Rd., London ON N6C 3P6; 519-432-4041
- Red Barn Antique Mall, 2017 Niagara Stone Rd., RR#3, Niagara-on-the-Lake ON L0S 1J0; 905-468-0900
- Regency House Antique Galleries, 87 Main St. North, Campbellville ON L0P 1B0; 905- 854-2727
- St. Jacobs Antique Market, 8 Spring St., St. Jacobs ON N0B 2N0; 519-664-1243

ART GALLERIES AND STUDIOS

Though not so thickly clustered as in the major urban centre of Toronto, art galleries in southwestern Ontario are varied and unique, sometimes centering on a single, celebrated artist.

The ten galleries below are all worth a visit.

General Information
- Ontario Association of Art Galleries (OAAG), #306, 489 King St. West, Toronto ON M5V 1K4; 416-598-0714, Fax: 416-598-4128; Email: oaag@interlog.com, Website: www.culturenet.ca/oaag/

Galleries
- Art Gallery of Hamilton, 123 King St. West, Hamilton ON L8P 4S8; 905-521-0110, Fax: 905-577-6940; Email: agh@netaccess.on.ca, Website: www.culturenet.ca/agh
- Art Gallery of Windsor, 3100 Howard Ave., Windsor ON N8X 3Y8; 519-969-4494, Fax: 519-969-3732
- Canadian Clay and Glass Gallery, 25 Caroline St. North, Waterloo ON N2L 2Y5; 519-746-1882, Fax: 519-746-6396
- Gallery/Stratford, 54 Romeo St., Stratford ON N5A 4S9; 519-271-5271, Fax: 519/271-1642
- Homer Watson House and Gallery, 1754 Old Mill Rd., Kitchener ON N2P 1H7; 519-748-4377, Fax: 519-748-6808
- Kitchener-Waterloo Art Gallery (KWAG), 101 Queen St. North, Kitchener ON N2H 6P7; 519/579-5860, Fax: 519-578-0740
- Macdonald Stewart Art Centre, 358 Gordon St., Guelph ON N1G 1Y1; 519-837-0010, Fax: 519-767-2661
- McMaster Museum of Art, 1280 Main St. West, Hamilton, ON L8S 4M2; 905-525-9140, ext. 2308, Fax: 905-527-4548; Email:museum@mcmail.cis.mcmaster.ca
- Preservation Fine Art Gallery, 177 King St., Niagara-on-the-Lake ON; 1-800-667-8525
- Tom Thompson Memorial Art Gallery, #840, 1 Ave. West, Owen Sound ON N4K 4K4; 519-376-1932, Fax: 519-376-3037; Website: www.tomthomson.org

BIRDING

Southwestern Ontario is a birders' paradise. Some of the best areas for viewing birds are listed below.

General Information

- Federation of Ontario Naturalists (FON), 355 Lesmill Rd., Toronto ON M3B 2W8; 416-444-8419, Fax: 416-444-9866, Toll Free: 1-800-440-2366.
- Ontario Field Ornithologists (OFO), PO Box 62014, RPO Burlington Mall, Burlington ON L7R 4K2; Email: ofo@interlog.com, Website: www.interlog.com/~ofo/

Sites

- Essex Region Conservation Authority, 360 Fairview Ave. West, Essex ON N8M 1Y6; 519-776-5209, Fax: 519-776-8688; Website: www.wincom.net/~erca/
- Grand River Conservation Authority, 400 Clyde Rd., PO Box 729, Cambridge ON N1R 5W6; 519-621-2761, Fax: 519-621-4844; Website: www.grandriver.on.ca
- Halton Region Conservation Authority, 2596 Britannia Rd. West, RR#2, Milton ON L9T 2X6; 905-336-1158, Fax: 905-336-7014; Email: admin@hrca.on.ca; Website: hrca.on.ca; Crawford Lake Conservation Area forms part of the HRCA.
- Long Point Provincial Park, PO Box 99, Port Rowan ON N0E 1M0; 519-586-2133
- MacGregor Point Provincial Park, RR#1, Port Elgin ON N0H 2C5; 519-389-9056
- Niagara Peninsula Conservation Authority, 2358 Centre St., Allanburg ON L0S 1A0; 905-227-1010, Fax: 905-227-2998
- Point Pelee National Park; RR#1, Leamington ON N8H 3V4; 519-322-2365
- Rondeau Provincial Park, RR#1, Morpeth ON N0P 1X0; 519-674-1750

BOATING

The Ontario Marina Operators Association issues a free, detailed annual directory to the over 370 marinas in Ontario. Pick up a copy at an Ontario Travel Information Centre, or a marina, or contact the OMOA directly. Listed below are a sampling of stops that can take you along the Niagara Peninsula, along Lake Erie and up the shores of Lake Huron and into Georgian Bay.

General Information

- Ontario Marina Operators Association (OMOA), #211, 4 Cataraqui St., Kingston ON K7K 1Z7; 613-547-6662, Fax: 613-547-6813; Email: omoa@marinasontario.com, Website: www.marinasontario.com

Marinas

- Fifty Point Marina, 1479 Baseline, Winona ON L8E 5G4; 905-643-2013, Fax: 905-643-1668; Email: lakeontario@marineontario.com
- Maitland Valley Marina, 100 North Harbour West, PO Box 175, Goderich ON N7A 3Z2; 519-524-9895
- Newport Marina, 226 South Service Rd. East, Oakville ON L6J 2X5; 905-643-0195
- Niagara Parks Marina, 200 Niagara Pkwy., Fort Erie ON; 905-356-2241, Fax: 905-356-7262
- Owen Sound Marina, #195, 24 St. West, PO Box 934, Owen Sound ON N4K 6H6; 519-371-3999, Fax: 519-371-3024
- Port Dalhousie Pier Inc., 124 Welland Ave., PO Box 23067, St. Catharines ON L2R 4M9; 905-646-5515
- Riverside Marina of Dunnville (Grand River), 101 Maple St., Dunnville ON N1A 2G1; 905-774-3199, Fax: 905-774-6611
- Royal Hamilton Yacht Club, Foot of McNab St. North, Hamilton ON L8L 1H1; 905-528-8464, Fax: 905-528-2622; Email: sailrhyc@nas.net, Website: www.nas.net/~leslie/sailrhyc.htm
- Stan's Marina Inc., 246 Colborne St., Port Stanley N5L 1B9; 519-782-3553
- Sugarloaf Harbour Marina Centre, 3 Marina Rd., Port Colborne ON L3K 6C6; 905-835-6644, Fax: 905-835-6910

CAMPING

Ten of southwestern Ontario's stellar camp sites are listed below. For a comprehensive picture of camping in the region, pick up a copy of the *Ontario Parks Guide*, or *Gray's*

Ontario Camping and Recreation Guide, at any Ontario Travel Information Centre (1-800-ONTARIO), or contact one of the organizations listed below.

General Information
- Canadian Heritage (for National Parks), #500, 5160 Yonge St., Toronto ON M2N 6L9; 416-954-9243, Toll Free: 1-800-839-8221, Website: parkscanada.pch.gc.ca
- Conservation Ontario (for Conservation Areas), 120 Bayview Pkwy., Box 11, Newmarket ON L3Y 4W3; 905-895-0716, Fax: 905-895-0751
- Ontario Camping Association (OCA), #302, 1810 Avenue Rd., Toronto ON M5M 3Z2; 416-781-0525, Fax: 416-781-7875; Email: oca@ontcamp.on.ca, Website: www.ontcamp.on.ca
- Ontario Parks Head Office, 300 Water St., PO Box 7000, Peterborough ON K9J 8M5; 705-755-7275; Website: nrserv.mnr.gov.on.ca/MNR/parks/index.html
- Ontario Private Campground Association (OPCA), RR#5, Owen Sound ON N4K 5N7; Fax: 519-371-5315; Website: www.camping.in.ontario.com. The OPCA also issues Camping in Ontario, available at any Ontario Travel Information Centre. To reserve at an OPCA campground, call 1-800-353-4313.

Parks
- Earl Rowe Provincial Park, PO Box 872, Alliston ON L9R 1W1; 705-435-4331
- Long Point Provincial Park, PO Box 99, Port Rowan ON N0E 1M0; 519-586-2133
- MacGregor Point Provincial Park, RR#1, Port Elgin ON N0H 2C5; 519-389-9056
- Pinery Provincial Park, RR#2, Grand Bend ON N0M 1T0; 519-243-2220
- Rock Point Provincial Park, PO Box 158, Dunnville ON N1A 2X5; 905-774-6642
- Rondeau Provincial Park, RR#1, Morpeth ON N0P 1X0; 519-674-1750
- Sauble Falls Provincial Park,

RR#3, Wiarton ON N0H 2T0; 519-422-1952
- Sherkston Shores, RR#1, Empire Rd., Sherkston ON L0S 1R0; 905-894-0972, Toll Free: 1-800-263-8121, Fax: 905-894-5352
- Turkey Point Provincial Park, PO Box 5, Turkey Point ON N0E 1T0; 519-426-3239
- Wheatley Provincial Park, PO Box 640, Wheatley ON N0P 2P0; 519-825-4659

CRAFT SHOWS

Southwestern Ontario's foremost craft shows are listed here. Attendance at any one will bring suggestions for others from exhibitioners, who will have their favourites. The Ontario Crafts Council also issues *The Craft Directory*, which gives comprehensive listings to all individual craftspersons and their studios, by region, in the province.

General Information
- Ontario Crafts Council, Chalmers Bldg., 35 McCaul St., Toronto ON M5T 1V7; 416-977-3551, Fax: 416-977-3552; Email: occ@astral.magic.ca, Website: www.craft.on.ca

Shows
- Bayfield Premier Art & Craft Show, c/o Norton Group, PO Box 592, Owen Sound ON N4K 5R1; 1-800-214-5855, Fax: 519-371-9545
- Chatham Festival of Crafts, c/o Chatham-Kent Recreation Dept., 25 Creek Rd., Chatham ON N7M 5J3; 519-352-3888, Fax: 519-352-4241
- Craftworld Arts & Crafts Show, 136 Thames St., Chatham ON N7L 2Y8; 519-351-8344
- Goderich Festival of Arts & Crafts, c/o Claire Tompkins, RR#1, Wingham ON N0G 2W0, 519-357-3155; or call 519-524-5333
- Independent Indian Handcrafters Bazaar, c/o The Woodland Cultural Centre, 184 Mohawk St., PO Box 1506, Brantford ON N3T 5V6; 519-758-5444
- London Arts & Crafts Spring Show, 120 Wharncliffe Rd. South, London ON N6J 2K3; 519-679-1810
- London New Arts Festival, Galleria

London, Box 78, 355 Wellington St., London ON N6A 3N7; 519-432-3926
- Mennonite Relief Sale and Quilt Auction, c/o Mennonite Central Committee Ontario, 50 Kent Ave., Kitchener ON N2G 3R1; 519-745-8458, Toll Free: 1-800-3131-6226; Email: info@imagitek.com, Website: www.imagitek.com/reliefsale/index. html
- Willistead Coach House Arts & Crafts Show, c/o Angie Casella, 1545 Victoria Ave., Windsor ON N8X 1P4; 519-254-2984
- Winter Festival of Friends, c/o Creative Arts Inc., 401 Main St. West, Hamilton ON L8P 1K5; 905-525-6644; Website: www.creativearts.on.ca

CYCLING

You can cycle wherever the spirit takes you in southwestern Ontario; down the banks of the Grand River, along the Lake Erie shoreline, or deep into the Niagara Peninsula, hedged with vineyards and studded with bed & breakfasts. Some more formal trails are listed below, as well as the association that ties it all together for cyclists in the province.

General Information
- Ontario Cycling Association, #408, 1185 Eglinton Ave. East, Toronto ON M3C 3C6; 416-426-7242, Fax: 416-426-7349; Email: ocycling@istar.ca, Website: www.ontariocycling.org

Trails
- Caledon Rail Trail, Town of Caledon, 200 Church St., PO Box 1000, Caledon East ON L0N 1E0; 905-584-2272
- Cambridge-Paris Rail Trail, c/o Grand River Conservation Authority, 400 Clyde Rd., PO Box 729, Cambridge ON N1R 5W6; 519-621-2761, Fax: 519-621-4844
- Ganatchio Trail, c/o Parks and Recreation Dept., City of Windsor, 2450 McDougall St., Windsor ON N8X 3N6; 519-253-2300
- Hamilton to Brantford Rail Trail, c/o Grand River Conservation Authority, 400 Clyde Rd., PO Box

729, Cambridge ON N1R 5W6; 519-621-2761, Fax: 519-621-4844
- Niagara River Recreational Trail, c/o Niagara Parks Commission, PO Box 150, Niagara Falls ON L2E 6T2; 905-356-224, Fax: 905-356-5488; Email: npinfo@niagaraparks.com, Website: www.tourismniagara.com/npc/
- Pinery Provincial Park, RR#2, Grand Bend ON N0M 1T0; 519-243-2220
- Point Pelee National Park; RR#1, Leamington ON N8H 3V4; 519-322-2365
- Rondeau Provincial Park, RR#1, Morpeth ON N0P 1X0; 519-674-1750
- Waterfront Trail, c/o The Waterfront Trust, #580, 207 Queen's Quay West, PO Box 129, Toronto ON M5J 1A7; 416-314-9490, Fax: 416-314-9497; Email: webmaster@wrtrust.com, Website: www.waterfronttrail.org

DINING

Southwestern Ontario boasts some of the finest restaurants in Canada. We have tried to give as broad a sampling of these as possible, concentrating on establishments that reflect the individual flair of the presiding chef.

The listings below are broken into the regions outlined in the "Food and Dining" chapter in the main body of the colourguide. Within each region, individual restaurants are then listed alphabetically by city. We advise calling ahead to make reservations for most of them.

Approximate prices are indicated, based on the average cost, at time of publication, of dinner for two, including wine (where available), taxes, and gratuity: $ = under $45; $$ = $45-$80; $$$ = $80-$120; $$$$ = over $180. Meals served are indicated as B = breakfast; L = lunch; D = dinner.

NIAGARA PENINSULA

Jordan
- On the Twenty, 3836 Main St., Jordan ON L0R 1S0; 905-562-7313. Fine regional cuisine using

local produce; the restaurant is housed in an old winery facing Twenty mile creek. L/D, $$$$.

Niagara-on-the-Lake

- Carriages & Cannery Dining Rooms, King St. at John St., PO Box 1011, Niagara-on-the-Lake ON L0S 1J0; 905-468-2123, Toll Free: 1-800-361-6788, Fax: 905-468-3551. This is the restaurant for the luxurious Pillar and Post Inn, and it offers exceptional fresh market cuisine, including full country breakfasts and buffets. B/L/D, $$$$.
- The Epicurean, 84 Queen St., Niagara-on-the-Lake ON L0S 1J0; 905-468-3408. This café features provençal decor and Mediterranean influences. Chef Ruth Aspinall's specialties include wild mushroom lasagne and a variety of focaccia made on the premises. Live jazz can be heard Thursday through Saturday evenings. L/D, $$.
- Giardino, The Gate House, 142 Queen St., Niagara-on-the-Lake ON L0S 1J0; 905-468-3263. Especially good for lunch, where fish or veal are favorites. L/D, $$$.
- Hillebrand Vineyard Café, Hwy. 55, Niagara-on-the-Lake ON L0S 1J0; 905-468-2444, Toll Free: 1-800-582-8412, Fax: 905-468-4789. Offers a wide range of wine country cuisine using local ingredients. L/D, $$$.
- Royals Dining Room, The Prince of Wales Hotel, 6 Picton St., Niagara-on-the-Lake ON L0S 1J0; Classic fresh market cuisine with a French influence, and an extensive array of local and imported wines. B/L/D, $$$$.
- Tapestries Restaurant, 209 Queen St., Niagara-on-the-Lake ON L0S 1J0; 905-468- 4588, Fax: 468-2194. Continental cuisine with a mediterranean flair. Tapestries forms part of the Kiely Inn, housed in an elegant, late Georgian, post and beam family home. B/L/D, $$$.
- Tiara Restaurant at the Queen's Landing Inn, 155 Byron St., PO Box 1180, Niagara-on-the-Lake ON L0S 1J0; 905-468-2195, Toll Free: 1-800-361-6645, Fax: 905-468-2227. A team of

award-winning chefs serve up an eclectic and well-presented cuisine. Try the foie gras with Niagara peach preserve. B/L/D, $$$$.

St. Catharines

- Bansaree, 342 St. Paul St., St. Catharines ON L2R 3N2; 905-684-3411. Great Indian food from a clay oven. L/D, $$.
- da Caruso Ristorante, 26 Church St., St. Catharines ON L2R 3B6; 905-641-0279; Diana Caruso has brought the best from Italy and blended it well with local produce, and her daughter painted the frescoes in the Tudor-style town house that the restaurant occupies. L/D, $$ - $$$.
- Wellington Court Restaurant, 11 Wellington St., St. Catharines ON L2R 5P5; 905-682-5518. Fine dining, well presented using local ingrediants; the restaurant is Edwardian on the outside and jazzy on the inside. L/D, $$ - $$$.

Vineland

- Vineland Estates Winery Restaurant; 3620 Moyer Rd., Vineland ON L0R 2C0; 905-562-7088, Fax: 905-562-3071, Website: www.vineland.com. The region's first wine restaurant; Mediterranean cuisine changes seasonally to reflect local harvests and the pasta is made fresh on the premises daily. L/D (2 seatings), $$$$.

Welland

- Rinderlin's Dining Rooms, 24 Burgar St., Welland ON L3B 2S7; 905-735-4411. Generous servings of a wide variety of European fare, located in the Fortner House, an 1806 Queen Anne Revivial building. L/D, $$$.

CALEDON AND HALTON HILLS

Alton

- The Cataract Inn, 1498 Cataract St., RR#2, Alton ON L0N 1A0; 519-927-3033, Toll Free: 1-800-928-3033. Cheerful and inexpensive; open for lunch Fridays, Saturdays, and Sundays. L/D, $$.

- Millcroft Inn Restaurant, 55 John St., Alton ON L0N 1A0; 519-941-8111, Toll Free: 1-800-383-3976, Fax: 519-941-9121. Located in the Caledon Hills; sports four diamond cuisine. L/D, $$$.

Orangeville
- Bluebird Café, 102 Broadway, Orangeville ON L9W 1J9; 519-941-3101. Unpretentious streetfront restaurant with great baking and good pasta dishes. L/D, $$.

Terra Cotta
- Terra Cotta Inn, King Rd., Terra Cotta ON L0P 1N0; 1-800-520-0920. Don't let the name fool you, this is no longer an inn, but maintains its restaurant with a good wine list. L/D, $$ - $$$.

KITCHENER-WATERLOO AND AREA

Cambridge
- Blackshop Restaurant & Lounge, 20 Hobson St., Cambridge ON N1S 2M6; 519-621-4180, Fax: 519-621-9128. Casual, continental cuisine, served by friendly staff in an elegant stone building facing the Grand River. L/D, $$.
- Deliciously Different Creative Cuisine, 49 Main St., Cambridge ON N1R 1V6; 519-740-4949. Chef Noland Ralph transforms fresh produce from the local farmers' market. The bistro-style menu changes monthly and includes dishes from many nationalities. Catering demands close the restaurant on Saturdays during the summer. D, $$.
- Langdon Hall, RR#33, Cambridge ON N3H 4R8; 519-740-2100, Toll Free: 1-800-268-1898, Fax: 519-740-8161. Regional and classical cuisine augmented by produce grown on the estate. Try the twice-cooked duck or the sea bass. Also open for Sunday Brunch and afternoon tea. Diners sit in a glassed-in terrace tastefully built as an extension to the main house. The wine list is extensive and varies considerably in price. B/L/D, $$$$$.

- Mimosa Restaurant, 121 Ainslie St. North, Cambridge ON N1R 3P2; 519-624-2023. Veteran Chef Larry Jacques presents innovative cuisine with a West Coast flair, in a charming home setting. L/D, $$$.

Elora
- Elora Mill Inn, 77 Mill St. West, Elora ON N0B 1S0; 519-846-5356, Fax: 519-846-9180. The fireside dining room overlooks the headwater falls of the Grand River. An diverse menu based on locally-grown foods is complimented by an excellent wine list. L/D, $$.
- La Cachette, 13 Mill St. E., Elora ON N0B 1S0. Seasonal menus feature light Provençal cuisine in an intimate setting. L/D $$$.

Guelph
- Carden Street Café, 40 Carden St., Guelph ON N1H 3A2; 519-837-2830. A "turtle's-eye view" wall mural decorates this small, inventive restaurant. Lunch is served Thursdays to Saturdays. L/D, $$.
- Other Brother's Restaurant & Lounge, 37 Yarmouth St., Guelph ON N1H 4G2; 519-822-4465. New Californian cooking and friendly service, located in Guelph's Raymond Sewing Machine factory. Winner of the "Best Fine Food Restaurant in North America" by Elan International Brands in 1997. L/D, $$$.
- Vase, 9 Wyndham St. North, Guelph ON N1H 4E2; 519-821-9393. Upscale Italian fare, with dancing in the evenings. $$$.

Heidelberg
- Heidelberg Restaurant & Brew Pub, Main St., PO Box 116, Heidelberg ON N0B 1Y0; 519-699-4413. Humble but delicious plates of ribs, pig tails, sauerkraut, and schnitzel, served with Heidelberg's own beer. Two dinner specials per evening and live entertainment (piano, acoustic, some sing-along) on Fridays and Saturdays. There's an adjoining motel if you want to stay and explore. L/D, $.

Kitchener
- Twenty King St, 20 King St. E., Kitchener ON N2G 2K6; 519-745-8939. Excellent soups; delicious lamb. $$$

St. Jacobs
- Stone Crock, 41 King St., St. Jacobs ON N0B 2N0; 519-664-2286. Hearty Mennonite fare served on platters and bowls in a family setting. Order à la carte or as a group. B/L/D, $.

Waterloo
- Bhima's Warung, 262 King St. North, Waterloo ON N2J 2Y9; 519-747-0722. Exotic recipes from South East Asia, married with French techniques and Canadian ingredients. D, $$$.
- Janet Lynn's Bistro, 92 King St. South, Waterloo ON N2J 1P5; 519-725-3440, Fax: 519-725-5580. Fresh market cuisine with French and Italian influences. The menu changes seasonally; the setting is casually elegant. L/D, $$$.

STRATFORD AND AREA

St. Marys
- The Westover Inn, 300 Thomas St., St. Marys ON N4X 1B1; 519-284-2977, Toll Free: 1-800-268-8243, Fax: 519-284-4043. An intimate limestone Victorian mansion is the setting for exceptional regional cuisine. L/D, $$$ - $$$$.
- The Wildwood Inn Restaurant, RR#2, St. Marys ON N4X 1C5; 519-349-2467. Chef Chris Woolf's innovative menu changes daily, offering both modern and traditional dishes. L/D, $$.

Stratford
- Bentley's Inn, Bar and Restaurant, 99 Ontario St., Stratford ON N5A 3H1; 519-271-1121. Fisherman's Stew highlights a wide range of entrees and beer on tap. L/D, $.
- The Church, 70 Brunswick St., Stratford ON N5A 6V6; 519-273-3424, Fax: 519-272-0061, Email: churchrest@orc.ca. An innovative French menu complimented by an extensive wine list. Lunch is served in the belfry, and dinner in the main body of the church. L/D, $$$.
- Down the Street Bar and Café, 30 Ontario St., Stratford ON N5A 3G8; 519-273-5886. Modern cuisine with something for everyone, including particularly excellent vegetarian dishes. B/L/D, $$$.
- Keystone Alley Café, 34 Brunswick St., Stratford ON N5A 3L8; 519-271-5645. A favorite with both locals and visitors, great for either a quick lunch or lengthy dinner, with an open kitchen and attentive service. L/D, $$.
- The Old Prune, 151 Albert St., Stratford ON N5A 3K5; 519-271-5052, Fax: 519-271-4157, Email: oldprune@cyg.net. Chef Bryan Steele creates a natural cuisine abundant in flavour, with fish as his strong suit. Dinner price is fixed at $52 per person, but you may want to supplement this. L/D, $$$$.
- Rundles, 9 Cobourg St., Stratford ON N5A 3E4; 519-271-6442, Fax: 519-271-3279. Chef Neil Baxter has made headlines with duck, shellfish, and salmon dishes, served in a superbly decorated setting. Open Wednesdays, Saturdays and Sundays for lunch; closed Mondays. L/D, $$$$.
- York Street Kitchen, 41 York St., Stratford ON; 519-273-7041. If you're looking for lunch, this is the place. L/D, $$.

LONDON AND AREA

- Anthony's Seafood Bistro, 434 Richmond St., London ON N6A 3C9; 519-679-0960. Try the Trust Me, a four-course dinner for $38: each person receives a different appetizer, entree and dessert – all of which are surprises, hence the name. L/D, $$ - $$$.
- East Town Pizza; 519-455-7010. Best pizza in town. L/D, $.
- Home, 113 King St., London ON N6A 1C3; 519-438-5122. Traditional French and Italian cooking featuring a wide variety of game, including ostrich. L/D, $$.
- La Casa Ristorante, 117 King St., London ON N6A 1C3; 519-434-2272. L/D, $$.

- Murano, 394 Waterloo St., London ON N6B 2N8; 519-434-7565. Northern Italian restaurant with a great selection of seafood, including swordfish. The Grilled Romaine is also delcious. Only ten tables means you should call in advance, but there is a terrace open in summer. L/D, $$$.
- Tapas, 119 King St., London ON N6A 1C3; 519-679-7800. Mediterranean cuisine leaning toward the Spanish. L/D, $$$.
- Sebastian's, 539 Richmond St., London ON N6A 3E9; 519-432-2684. Sebastian's is a food shop as well as a cafeteria-style restaurant. There's no alcohol or smoking; the accent is on hearty fare, and includes a grill. L/D, $.
- The Verandah, 546 Dundas St., London ON N6B 1W8; 519-434-6790. Prices are low and the lamb is fabulous. L/D, $$.

LAKE ERIE SHORELINE

Port Dover
- Gingerbread House, 19 St. Andrew St., Port Dover ON; 519-583-0249. A varied menu including ostrich, buffalo, and venison is highlighted by Cedar Plank Salmon. The restaurant takes its name from the variety of gingerbread baking available. Call in advance about the salmon: They have to pre-soak the planks. Unlicensed, closed Tuesdays. L/D, $.

Port Stanley
- Kettle Creek Inn, 216 Joseph St., Port Stanley ON N5L 1C4; 519-782-3388, Fax: 519-782-4747. Locally-raised rhea and fresh perch, trout, and pickerel highlight the menu at the Inn, which welcomes off-site visitors. L/D, $$$.

WINDSOR AND AREA

Amherstburg
- The Old Bullock Tavern, 269 Dalhousie St., Amherstburg ON N9V 1W8; 519-736-5075.

Essex
- The Essex Courtyard, 19 Laird Ave., Essex ON N8M 1R5; 519-776-7055. Known for its chicken and ribs. L/D, $.

Kingsville
- The Vintage Goose, 24 Main St. West, Kingsville ON N9Y 1H1; 519-733-6900.

Tecumseh
- Overtures, 1107 Lesperance Rd., Tecumseh ON N8N 1X1; 519-979-0010. An eclectic dinner menu, from Thai to Italian. D, $$.

Windsor
- Chatham Street Grill, 149 Chatham St. West, Windsor ON N9A 5M7; 519-256-2555. An old steak house which still does great beef, but now also features California-style cooking. L/D, $$$.
- Empress Garden Restaurant(s): 675 Goyeau St., Windsor ON N9A 1H3, 519-253-3332; 3032 Dougall Ave., Windsor ON N9E 1S4, 519-969-9723; 13420 Tecumseh Rd. East, St. Clair Beach ON N8N 3N7, 519-735-7512. Any one of these locations are a good bet for Chinese food fans. L/D, $.
- La Contessa, 780 Erie St. East, Windsor ON N9A 3Y2; 519-252-2167. Italian cooking in the broad sense of the term, including over 20 pasta dishes. L/D, $$$.
- Porcino's, 3847 Howard Ave., Windsor ON N9G 1N6; 519-972-5699. A small, select California-Italian menu. L/D, $$.
- Spago Trattoria, 614 Erie St. East, Windsor ON N9A 3X9; 519-252-2233. Northern Italian cooking with a smattering of central Italy and the south. Call to reserve on weekends. L/D, $ - $$.
- Wah Court, 2037 Wyandotte St. West, Windsor ON N9G 1N6; 519-254-1388. Another Chinese favorite. L/D, $.

LAKE HURON AND GEORGIAN BAY

Bayfield
- The Little Inn of Bayfield, Main St., Bayfield ON N0M 1G0; 519-565-2611. Fresh fish and mussels are recommended, as is the great wine list and fine selection of single malt Scotches. B/L/D, $$$.

Collingwood
- Beild House Country Inn, 64 Third St., Collingwood ON L9Y 1K5; 1-705-444-1522, Toll Free: 1-888-322-3453, Fax: 705-444-2394. Five-course dinners and breakfasts for off-site diners are part of the charm of the Inn's restaurant, situated in a grand century home. B/L/D, $$$.
- Christopher's, 167 Pine St., Collingwood ON L9Y 2P1; 705-445-7117. A small, local treasure housed in a turn-of-the century doctor's residence, featuring private rooms and a verandah. Also open for afternoon tea. Dinner reservations are advised. L/D, $$.

Flesherton
- Munshaw's Bistro, 1 Toronto, Flesherton ON N0C 1E0; 519-924-2814. Open Thursday through Sunday. L/D.

Goderich
- Bailey's Restaurant, 120 The Courthouse Square, Goderich ON N7A 1M8; 519-524-5166. Ben Merritt presents an eclectic cuisine which changes daily. L/D, $$.
- The Ivy Room at the Benmiller Inn, RR#4, Benmiller ON 524-2191, Toll Free: 1-800-265-1711, Fax: 519-524-5150. Innovative continental cuisine reflecting seasonal changes. L/D, $$$.

Hanover
- The Grey Rose, 394 - 10th St., Hanover ON N4N 1P6; 519-364-2600. A good stop for a weekend buffet. L/D, $ - $$.

Owen Sound
- Norma Jean's, 243 - 8th St. East, Owen Sound ON N4K 1L2; 519-376-2232. A small establishment with a strong, simple menu (crepes, pastas, steaks, or lamb), complemented by daily lunch and dinner specials. L/D, $$.

Southampton
- Grosvenor's, 124 Grosvenor South, Southampton ON; 519-797-1226. Local Chef Paul Johnston's servings are generous and the staff, courteous. D, $$$.

FARMERS' MARKETS

Going to market early on a Satruday morning is a tradition in southwestern Ontario. Three of the best markets are listed below.

General Information
- Ontario Association of Agricultural Societies, PO Box 220, Blackstock ON L0B 1B0; 905-986-0238; Website for Ontario Fairs: www.RR3.com/fairs/ontario/index.html

Markets
- Kitchener-Waterloo Farmers' Market, 49 Frederick St., PO Box 1118, Kitchener ON N2G 4G7; 519-741-2287, Fax: 519-741-2767
- St. Jacobs Farmers' Market, PO Box 443, Waterloo ON N2J 4A9; 519-747-1830, Fax: 519-747-9469
- St. Marys Farmers' Market Association, PO Box 1674, St. Marys ON N4X 1C1; 519-284-2568 or 519-284-2340; Email: aslater@quadro.net, Website:www.geocities.com/NapaValley/8566/

FESTIVALS

There's something festive for everyone in southwestern Ontario. The categories of music, cultural, fall, and winter festivals are highlighted below. For theatre festivals, see the theatre listings.

General Information
- Festivals & Events Ontario, 180 Greenwich St., Brantford ON N3S 2X6; 519-756-3359, Fax: 519-756-3231

Music

- Elora Festival, 33 Henderson St., PO Box 990, Elora ON N0B 1S0; 519-846-0331; Email: elora@sentex.net, Website: www.sentex.net/elora
- Royal Canadian Big Band Music Festival, Cherry Hill Village Mall, 301 Oxford St. West, PO Box 24070, London ON N6H 5C4; 519-663-9467, Toll Free: 1-800-461-2263, Fax: 519-663-5319; Email: bigband@execulink.com, Website: www.execulink.com/~bigband/

Cultural

- Fergus Scottish Festival and Highland Games, 431 St. Andrew St. West, PO Box 25, Fergus ON N1M 2W7; 519-787-0099, Fax: 519/787-1274; Email: scottish@sentex.net, Website: www.sentex.net/fergus.scot
- Kitchener-Waterloo Oktoberfest, 17 Benton St., PO Box 1053, Kitchener ON N2G 4G1; 519-570-4267, Fax: 519-742-3072; Email: info@oktoberfest.ca, Website: www.oktoberfest.ca
- N'Amerind Powwow, c/o N'Amerind Friendship Centre, 260 Colborne St., London ON N2B 2S6; 519-672-0131, Fax: 519-672-0717; Website: schoolnet2.carleton.ca/english/ext/aboriginal/namerin/

Fall

- Niagara Region Wine Festival, 145 King St., St. Catharines ON L2R 3J2; 905- 688-0212, Toll Free: 1-888-594-6379, Fax: 905-688-2570; Email: vidal@niagarafest.on.ca, Website: www.niagarafest.on.ca
- Wellesley Apple Butter and Cheese Festival, 519-699-4611; Website: www.mgl.ca/~infobahn/apples/
- Western Fair Association, PO Box 4550, London ON NsW 5K3; 1-800-619-4629; Email: fair.info@westernfair.on.ca, Website: www.westernfair.on.ca

Winter

- Grand Bend, Village of Grand Bend, ON N0M 1T0; 519-238-2001
- Winter Festival of Lights, c/o Niagara Falls, Canada Visitor and Convention Bureau, 5515 Stanley Ave., Niagara Falls, ON L2G 3X4 905-356-6061, Toll Free: 1-800-563-2557; Email: nfcvcb@tourismniagara.com, Website: tourismniagara.com/nfcvcb/wfol/wfolmain.html

GARDENS

Greenery is everywhere you look in spring and summer in southwestern Ontario, but much of it survives over winter, too, in the greenhouses and conservatories listed below. Dedicated garden-goers may want to contact the provincial association for an informed look at the beauty that abounds here.

General Information

- Ontario Horticultural Association, PO Box 842, Sutton West ON L0E 1R0; Website: www.interlog.com/~onthort/

Gardens and Greenhouses

- Colasanti's Tropical Gardens, located near Ruthven, 5 km east of the Jack Miner Bird Sanctuary; open Monday to Thursday from 8 am to 5 pm, Fridays from 8 am to 9 pm, and Saturdays and Sundays from 10 am to 6 pm; call 519-326-3287
- Gage Park, located at Main St. East and Gage Ave.; open from 6 am to 11:30 pm daily; the tropical greenhouse is open Monday to Friday from 9 am to 2:30 pm; call 905-549-9285
- Jackson Park Queen Elizabeth II Gardens, c/o Parks & Recreation Dept., 2450 McDougall Rd., Windsor ON N8X 3N6; 519-255-6276, Fax: 519-255-7990
- London Civic Garden Complex, located at 625 Springbank Dr., London ON; 519-661-4757
- Niagara Parks Botanical Gardens, c/o Niagara Parks Commission, PO Box 150, Niagara Falls ON L2E 6T2; 905-356-2241, Fax: 905-356-5488; Email: npinfo@niagaraparks.com, Website: www.tourismniagara.com/npc/
- The Niagara Parks Commission also administers the following sites:
- The Floral Clock, located 10 km north of the Falls on the Niagara Pkwy

- Queen Victoria Park, located on the Niagara Pkwy., at the Falls
- Niagara Parks Commission Greenhouses, located on the Niagara Pkwy. Just south of the Horseshoe Falls; open daily from 9:30 am to 8:30 pm, June to Labour Day. For the rest of the year, open Sunday to Thursday 9:30 am to 5 pm, Friday and Saturday 9:30 am to 6 pm; wheelchair accessible
- Niagara Parks Butterfly Conservatory, located on the grounds of the Niagara Parks Botanical Gardens, open daily from 9 am year-round; closing times vary according to season; admission charge; call 905-356-8119
- Queen Elizabeth II Sunken Gardens, located at Tecumseh Rd. And Ouellette St.; call 519-255-6276
- Rockway Gardens, c/o Kitchener Horticultural Society, 519-745-4669
- Royal Botanical Gardens, PO Box 399, Hamilton ON L8N 3H8; 905-527-1158, Fax: 905-577-0375
- Sifton Bog, located on the south side of Oxford St., west of Hyde Park Rd. next to the Oakridge Mall; for more information contact the Upper Thames River Conservation Authority, 1424 Clarke Rd., London ON N5V 5B9; 519-451-2800, Fax: 519-451-1188; Email: infoline@thames-conservation.on.ca, Website: www.thames-conservation.on.ca
- Shakespearean Gardens, located on Huron St. at York St., Stratford ON; 519-273-3352
- Shakespearean Festival Gardens, located at New Water St. and Parkview, open dawn to midnight; call 519-271-4040
- Swain Greenhouse, located at the junction of Highways 3 and 76 at the Village of Eagle, open daily 9 am to 5:30 pm, Monday to Saturday, and from 10 am to 6 pm Sundays; for more information contact RR#2, West Lorne ON N0L 2P0, 519-768-1116
- University of Guelph Arboretum, located on Arboretum Rd., east off the University of Guelph's East Ring Rd.; 519-824-4120, ext. 2113, Fax: 519-763-9598; Website: www.uoguelph.ca/~arboretu

GOLF

Ontario Tourism (1-800-ONTARIO) produces an annual directory, *Golf Ontario Style*, that covers all the golf courses in southwestern Ontario. Below are some of the best courses.

- Blue Springs Golf Club, 13448 Dublin Line, RR#1, Acton ON L7J 2L7; 519-853-0904
- Cambridge Golf and Country Club, RR#6, Cambridge ON N1R 5S7; 519-621-5491
- Niagara Golf Club, 143 Front St., PO Box 45, Niagara-on-the-Lake ON L0S 1J0; 905-468-3271
- Greenwood Golf Club, 2212 London Rd., Sarnia ON N7T 7H2; 519-542-2770
- Oxley Beach Golf Course, County Rd. 50, Oxley ON N0R 1G0; 519-738-2672
- Pike Lake Golf Centre, RR#3, Clifford ON N0G 1M0; 519-338-3010 or 519-338-2812
- Rockway Golf Club, Kitchener ON; 519-741-2919
- Saugeen Golf Club, Port Elgin ON; 519-389-4031, Fax: 519-389-5530; Email: golf@saugeengolf.com, Website: www.saugeengolf.com
- Thames Valley Golf Club, 850 Sunning Hill Ave., London ON; 519-471-5036
- Victoria Park East Golf Club, Victoria Rd., RR#2, Guelph ON N1H 6H8; 519-821-2211

HIKING

Either Hike Ontario or the Bruce Trail Association are the best places to start when looking for information about hiking in southwestern Ontario. The Bruce Trail Association also produces an excellent, detailed book of maps which is available at most outfitters and bookstores.

General Information
- Hike Ontario, #411, 1185 Eglinton Ave. East, Toronto ON M3C 3C6; 416-426-7362, Fax: 416-426-7045; Email: ay625@torfree.net, Website: www3.sympatico.ca/hikers.net/hike ont.htm

Trails

- The Avon Trail, PO Box 20018, Stratford ON N5A 7V3; Website: www.golden.net/~wlindsch/avon/avon.htm
- The Bruce Trail Association, PO Box 857, Hamilton ON L8N 3N9; 905-529-6821, Toll Free: 1-800-665-4453, Fax: 905-529-6823; Email: Bruce.Trail@freenet.hamilton.on.ca, Website: www.brucetrail.org
- Cambridge Trails, c/o Grand River Conservation Authority, 400 Clyde Rd., PO Box 729, Cambridge ON N1R 5W6; 519-621-2761, Fax: 519-621-4844; Website: www.grandriver.on.ca
- Guelph Trail: c/o Hike Ontario, above
- Niagara Trail: c/o Hike Ontario, above
- Point Pelee National Park; RR#1, Leamington ON N8H 3V4; 519-322-2365
- Thames Valley Trail Association, Grosvenor Lodge, 1017 Western Rd., London ON N6G 1G5; 519-645-2845, Fax: 519-645-0981

KIDS' STUFF

Ten of the sites covered in the main body of the guide are listed below, giving a balance of nature, science, and history excursions which will appeal to all ages, but particularly young ones.

- African Lion Safari, RR #1, Cambridge ON N1R 5S2; 519-623-2620, Toll Free: 1-800-461-9453, Fax: 519-623-9542; Email: admin@lionsafari.com, Website: www.lionsafari.com
- Fifties Streamliner, c/o Waterloo-St. Jacobs Railway Ltd., PO Box 40103, Stn. Waterloo Square, Waterloo ON N2J 4V1; 519-746-1950, Fax: 519-746-3521
- The Great Gorge Adventure, c/o Niagara Parks Commission, PO Box 150, Niagara Falls ON L2E 6T2; 905-354-1221; Website: www.tourismniagara.com/npc/
- Hume Cronyn Memorial Observatory, Dept. of Physics & Astronomy, University of Western Ontario, London ON N6A 3K7; 519-661-3183, Fax: 519-661-2033; Website:

phobos.astro.uwo.ca/dept/observatories.html
- Huron County Gaol, 181 Victoria St., Goderich ON N7A 2S9; 519-524-2686, Fax: 519-524-5677
- London Museum of Archaeology & Iroquoian Village Site, Lawson-Jury Bldg., University of Western Ontario, 1600 Attawandaron Rd., London ON N6G 3M6; 519-473-1360, Fax: 519-473-1363; Email: brigutto@julian.uwo.ca, Website: www.uwo.ca/museum/index.html
- Marineland, 7657 Portage Rd., Niagara Falls ON L2E 6X8; 905-356-8250, Fax: 905-374-6652
- Mountsberg Conservation Area, RR#2, Milton ON L9T 2X6; 905-336-1158
- Ska Nah Doht Indian Village, RR#1, Mt. Brydges ON N0L 1W0; 519-264-2420; Fax: 519-264-1562

MUSEUMS AND HISTORIC SITES

Each community in southwestern Ontario has its own story to tell, and usually a museum to tell it through. Historic plaques are also strung along the heritage highways enabling you to make history part of your drive. The Ontario Museum Association maintains a comprehensive listing of all local museums on their website.

General Information

- Ontario Museum Association (OMA), George Brown House, 50 Baldwin St., Toronto ON M5T 1L4; 416-348-8672, Fax: 416-348-0438; Email: omachin@planeteer.com, Website: www.museumassn.on.ca

Sites

- Annandale House, 30 Tillson Ave., Tillsonburg ON N4G 2Z8; 519-842-2294, Fax: 519-842-9431
- Canadian Warplane Heritage Museum, #300, 9300 Airport Rd., Mount Hope ON L0R 1W0; 905-679-4183, Fax: 905-679-4186; Email: museum@warplane.com, Website: www.warplane.com
- Crawford Lake Conservation Area, c/o Halton Region Conservation Authority, 2596 Britannia Rd. West, RR#2, Milton ON L9T 2X6; 905-227-1013, Fax: 905-336-7014;

Email: crawlake@hrca.on.ca, Website: hrca.on.ca/crawford.htm
- Doon Heritage Crossroads, RR#2, Kitchener ON N2G 3W5; 519-748-1914, Fax: 519-748-0009, Email: rtom@region.waterloo.on.ca, Website: www.region.waterloo.on.ca/doon
- Dundurn Castle, Dundurn Park, York Blvd., Hamilton ON L8R 3H1; 905-546-2872, Fax: 905-522-4535
- Fort George, c/o Niagara National Historic Sites, Parks Canada, PO Box 787, Niagara-on-the-Lake ON L0S 1J0; 905-468-4257, Fax: 905-468-4638
- Huron County Museum, 110 North St., Goderich ON N7A 2T8; 519-524-2686, Fax: 519-524-5677
- Joseph Schneider Haus Museum, 466 Queen St. South, Kitchener ON N2G 1W7; 519-742-7752, Fax: 519-742-0089
- McCrae House, c/o Guelph Museums, 6 Dublin St. South, Guelph ON N1H 4L5; 519-836-1482, Fax: 519-836-5280; Email: gcmchin@wat.hookup.net, Website: www.freespace.net/~museum/welco me.html
- Willistead Manor, 1899 Niagara St., Windsor ON N8Y 1K3; 519-255-6545

SHOPPING

Most of the shops mentioned in the main body of the Colourguide are listed here.

NIAGARA PENINSULA

- Maple Leaf Fudge, 114 Queen St., Niagara-on-the-Lake ON L0S 1J0; 905-468-2211
- Silly Old Bear Shop, 80 Queen St., Niagara-on-the-Lake ON L0S 1J0; 905-468-5411
- Wee Scottish Loft, 13 Queen St., Niagara-on-the-Lake ON L0S 1J0; 905-468-0965

CALEDON AND HALTON HILLS

- Recovering Nicely, 8 Thompson Cres., Erin ON N0B 1T0; 519-833-0225
- Tintagel, 50 Main St., Erin ON N0B 1T0; 519-833-0019

KITCHENER-WATERLOO AND AREA

- Baba Yaga, 9 Quebec St., Guelph ON N1H 2T1; 519-767-2001
- Canadian Clay and Glass Gallery, 25 Caroline St. North, Waterloo ON N2L 2Y5; 519-746-1882
- Duncan-McPhee, 1 Quebec St., Guelph ON N1H 2T1; 519-821-1260
- John M. Hall "The House of Quality Linens," 43 Grand River St. North Paris ON N3L 2M3; 519-442-4242
- La Maison de Madelaine, 38 Quebec St., Guelph ON N1H 2T4; 519-763-5023
- Mary Maxim, 75 Scott Ave. Paris ON N3L 3K4; 519-442-6342
- Mill Street Mews, Elora ON; 519-846-9160, Fax: 905-891-3073
- St. Jacobs Mennonite Quilts, 46 King St., St. Jacobs ON N0B 2N0; 519-664-1817
- The Southworks, Cambridge ON; 519-740-0110, Fax: 519-740-8616
- The Village Silos, 10 King St., St. Jacobs ON N0B 2N0; 519-664-2421

STRATFORD AND AREA

- Anything Grows, 10 Ontario St., Stratford ON N5A 3G8; 519-272-1100
- Bradshaws, 129 Ontario St., Stratford ON N5A 3H1; 519-271-6283
- Dressing Room, 20 Ontario St., Stratford ON N5A 3G8; 519-273-2392
- Family and Company, 6 Ontario St., Stratford ON N5A 3G8; 519-273-7060
- The Shakespearean Gift Shop, 7 George St. West, Stratford ON N5A 1A6; 519-271-9491

WINDSOR AND AREA

- Colasanti's, PO Box 40, Ruthven ON N0P 2G0; 519-326-3287,

Fax: 519-322-2302; Email: tropical@colasanti.com; Website: www.colasanti.com
- Hummingbird Gift Shop, 3502 St. Clair Pkwy., Sombra ON N0P 2H0; 519-892-3245\

LAKE HURON AND GEORGIAN BAY

- Penhale's, Bayfield ON N0M 1G0; 519-565-2107
- Times & Places, Bayfield ON N0M 1G0; 519-565-2700
- Wardrobe, Bayfield ON N0M 1G0; 519-565-2996

SNOW SPORTS

Any Ontario Travel Information Centre (1-800-ONTARIO) will carry copies of the *Winter Experience* guide; in addition, the three associations listed below each provide winter activity information. Some of the more notable ski clubs follow.

General Information
- Ontario Ski Resorts Association (OSRA), #10, 110 Saunders Rd., Barrie ON L4M 6E7; 705-727-0351, Fax: 705-727-0321
- Ontario Federation of Snowmobile Clubs (OFSC), PO Box 94, Barrie ON L4M 4S9; 705-739-7669, Fax: 705-739-5005; Email: ofsc@mail.transdata.ca, Website: www.transdata.ca/~ofsc/~ofsc.htm
- Resorts Ontario, 29 Albert St. North, Orillia ON L3V 5J9; 705-325-9115, Toll Free: 1-800-363-7227, Fax: 705-325-7999; Email: escapes@resorts-ontario.com, Website: http://www.resorts-ontario.com

Resorts
- Beaver Valley Ski Club, RR#4, Markdale ON N0C 1H0; 519-986-2520
- Blue Mountain Resort, RR#3, Collingwood ON L9Y 3Z2; Location:11 km. west of Collingwood; from Hwy 26, take Blue Mountain Rd.; 705-445-0231, Fax: 705-444-1751

- Chicopee Ski Club, 396 Morrison Rd., Kitchener ON N2A 2Z6; 519-894-5610
- Glen Eden Ski Area, Milton ON; 905-878-5011
- London Ski Club, 689 Griffith St., London ON N6K 2S5; 519-657-8822
- Talisman Mountain Resort, Thornbury ON; 519-599-2520, Toll Free: 1-800-265-3759, Website: http://www.talisman.ca

SWIMMING

Since southwestern Ontario is surrounded by water, swimming opportunities are everywhere. *The Ontario Bluewater Visitor Guide* or the *Ontario South Central Trip Planner*, available at any Ontario Travel Information Centre (1-800-ONTARIO), can be of further assistance.

The Bluewater Guide will take you along Ontario's Bluewater Trail, stretching from the north shore of Lake Erie to Manitoulin Island. *The Trip Planner* lists swimming opportunities for each major community in the region.

THEATRE

Opportunities to enjoy live theatre abound in southwestern Ontario. Contact each theatre individually for production information and reservations. Most theatres also post brochures at Ontario Travel Information Centres.

General Information
Theatre Ontario, #1500, 415 Yonge St., Toronto ON M5B 2E7; 416-408-4556, Fax: 416-408-3402

Theatres
- Blyth Festival, Blyth Centre for the Arts, PO Box 10, Blyth ON N0M 1H0; 519-523-9300; Email: blyth.festival@odyssey.on.ca
- Drayton Festival Theatre, PO Box 10, Drayton ON N0G 1P0; 519-638-5555, Fax: 519-638-5575
- Grand Theatre, 471 Richmond St. London ON N6A 3E4; 519-672-8800, Toll Free: 1-800-265-1593, Fax: 519-672-2620; Email: GrandInfo@graystone.com

Website: www.grandtheatre.com
- Huron County Playhouse, RR#1, Grand Bend ON N0M 1T0; 519-238-6000, Fax: 519-238-6587; Email: hcplay@hay.net, Website: www.hay.net/~hcplay/
- Lighthouse Festival Theatre, PO Box 1208, Port Dover ON N0A 1N0; 519-583-2221
- Shaw Festival, PO Box 774, Niagara-on-the-Lake ON L0S 1J0; 1-800-511-7429, Fax: 905-468-5438; Email: bxoffice@shawfest.com, Website: shawfest.sympatico.ca
- Stage Door Southwestern Ontario Theatre Website: stage-door.org/sw-ont.html
- Stratford Festival, PO Box 520, Stratford ON N5A 6V2; 1-800-567-1600, Fax: 705-271-2734; Website: www.stratford-festival.on.ca
- Theatre Aquarius, 190 King William St., Hamilton ON L8R 1A8; 905-522-7529; Toll Free: 1-800-465-7529, Fax: 905-522-7825; Email: aquarius@theatreaquarius.org Website: www.theatreaquarius.org
- Theatre and Company, 20 Queen St. North, Kitchener ON N2H 2G8; 519-571-0928, Fax: 519-571-9051; Email: kholt@wchat.on.ca
- Theatre Orangeville, 87 Broadway, Orangeville ON L9W 1K1; 519-942-3423, Fax: 519-942-9978; Website: www.headwaters.com/theatre.orangeville
- Waterloo Stage Theatre, 24 King St. North, Waterloo ON N2J 2W7; 519/888-0000, Fax: 519/888-7599; Email: theatre@golden.net

WINE TASTING

The wineries listed below are located on the Niagara Peninsula, Pelee Island, and in the Windsor area.

General Infromation
- The Wine Council of Ontario #B205, 110 Hannover Dr., St. Catharines ON L2W 1A4; 905-684-8070, Fax: 905-684-2993; Website: www.wineroute.com

Wineries
- Andrés Wines, 697 South Service Rd., Grimsby ON L3M 4E8; 905-643-8687, Toll Free: 1-800-836-3555. Tastings from 11 am to 4 pm. Tours are offered.
- Cave Spring Cellars, 3836 Main St., Jordan ON L0R 1S0; 905-562-3581. Open Monday to Saturday, 10 am to 5 pm, and Sundays from 11 am - 5 pm. Tours at 1 pm and 3 pm daily.
- Château des Charmes Wines, 1025 York Rd., Niagara-on-the-Lake ON L0S 1J0; 905-262-4219. Open 10 am to 6 pm daily; tours every hour on the hour from 11 am to 4 pm.
- Colio Estate Wines, 1 Colio Dr., PO Box 372, Harrow ON N0R 1G0; 519-738-2241; Email: colio@1sol.com. Open year-round; tours at 1 pm, 2 pm, and 3 pm.
- Hillebrand Estates Winery, Hwy. 55, Niagara-on-the-Lake ON L0S 1J0; 905-468-7123, Toll Free: 1-800-582-8412. Open from 10 am to 6 pm; tours on the hour throughout the day.
- Inniskillin Wines, Niagara Pkwy at Line 3, RR #1, Niagara-on-the-Lake ON L0S 1J0; 905-468-3554.
- Pelee Island Wine Pavilion, West Shore Rd., General Delivery, Pelee Island ON N0R 1M0; 519-724-2469; Toll Free: 1-800-597-3533. Open seven days a week; tours at 11 am, 1 pm, 2 pm, and 4 pm.
- Reif Estate Winery, 15608 Niagara Pkwy., RR#1, Niagara-on-the-Lake ON L0S 1J0; 905-468-7738. Open daily, May to October from 10 am to 6 pm, November to April from 10 am to 5 pm; tours at 1:30 pm, May to September.
- Stoney Ridge Winery, 3201 King St., PO Box 566, Vineland ON L0R 2C0; 905-562-1324. Open daily from 10 am to 5 pm; tours at 11 am and 2 pm.
- Thirty Bench Wines, 4281 Mountainview Rd., Beamsville ON L0R 1B2; 905-563-1698. Open Wednesdays to Sundays from 11 am to 5 pm; tours by appointment.
- Willow Heights Estate Winery, 3679 Cherry Ave., Vineland ON L0R 2C0; 905-562-4945. Open year round; call for tour times.

INDEX

accommodation, 12, 173-76
 See also bed and breakfast
Acton, 33-34, 122, 187
Adams Golden Acres Motel, 175
African Lion Safari, 133, 188
airports, international, 170
Albright-Knox Art Gallery, 29, 80
alcoholic beverages, tax on, 171
Alliston, 92
Alton, 174, 181-82
Amherstburg, 65, 114, 136, 168, 184
Andrés Wines, 165, 191
Angie Strauss Gallery, 79
Annandale House, 142, 188
Anthony's Seafood Bistro, 113, 183
Antique Emporium, The, 177
Antique Warehouse, 177
antiquing, 74-77, 176-77
Antiquities Shoppe, The, 177
Anything Grows, 148, 189
Art by the Falls craft show, 95
art galleries, 177
  Art Gallery of Hamilton, 79, 95-96,
    177
  Art Gallery of Windsor, 62, 82, 177
  Canadian Clay and Glass Gallery,
    134, 145, 177
  Gallery/Stratford, 177
  Homer Watson House and Gallery,
    38, 80, 177
  Kitchener-Waterloo Art Gallery,
    177
  Macdonald Stewart Art Centre, 81,
    177
  McMaster Museum of Art, 79, 177
  Preservation Fine Art Gallery, 78,
    177
  Tom Thompson Memorial Art
    Gallery, 72, 82, 177
Artistry by the Lake, 95
Art in the Park, 96
Arts in Bloom craft show, 95-96
Arts and Craft Spring Show, 97
A Small Book Shop, 145
At the Bay craft show, 99
Avon Trail, 52 130, 188

Baba Yaga, 146, 189
Backus Mills Conservation Area, 59,
  142
Baden, 41, 141
Bailey's Restaurant, 185
Bansaree, 181
Barber Gallery, 146
baseball, 134
Bayfield, 69
  accommodation, 176

art and craft show, 98-99
beaches, 69
boating, 89
dining, 115, 150, 184-85
fall fair, 108
marinas, 69
shopping, 150
strawberry festival, 107
Bayfield Premier Art & Craft Show,
  179
Bayfield Village Inn, 176
Beamer Memorial Conservation Area,
  83-84
Beamsville, 165-66
Beaver Valley Ski Club, 153, 190
bed and breakfast
  Idlewynd Inn, 175
  Kingswood Inn, 175
  Stratford and Area Bed & Breakfast
    Association, 175-76
  Woods Villa, 175
   See also accommodation
Bedford Hotel, 176
Beild House Country Inn, 185
Benmiller Inn, 70, 152, 176
Bentley's Inn, 112, 183
Best Western Brant Park Inn
  (Brantford), 174
Best Western Continental Motor Inn
  (Windsor), 176
Best Western Wheels Inn Resort &
  Conference Centre (Chatham),176
Bhima's Warung, 111, 183
birding, 83-86, 177-78
Bistro, The, 114
black experience
  North American Black Historical
    Museum, 66
  Uncle Tom's Cabin Historic Site,
    136
  underground railway settlements,
    42, 65-66
Blackshop Restaurant & Lounge, 182
Blair, 37
Bluebird Cafe, 182
Blue Mountain, 124, 152-53, 190
Blue Springs Golf Club, 122, 187
Bluewater Ferry, 150
Bluewater Summer Playhouse, 162
Blyth Festival, 159-60, 190
Boating, 178
  Lake Erie, 88-89
  Lake Huron, 89-90
  Lake Ontario, 87-88
  Lake St. Clair/Detroit River, 89-90
Boler Mountain, 153
Bonnie Doone Manor, 176

Bookshelf, The, 146
bookstores, 34, 145, 148
Boston Mills Press, 35
Bradshaws, 148-49, 189
Brantford, 96, 119, 174
Brantford North Ridge golf course, 123
Breadalbane Inn, 174
Breslau, 122
breweries, 111, 146
Bruce Nuclear Power Development, 70
Bruce Peninsula, 71-72
Bruce Peninsula National Park, 71
Bruce Trail, 126-29
Bruce Trial Association, 188
Buffalo, 29, 80
butterfly conservatory. See Niagara Parks Butterfly Conservatory

Cadillac Motel, 176
Cafe Grand, 147
Caledon and Halton Hills, 31-35, 181
  accommodation, 174
  Acton, 33-34
  antiquing, 75
  birding, 84
  Campbellville, 33
  camping, 92
  conservation areas, 32
  cycling, 102, 180
  dining, 181
  Erin, 145
  golf, 187
  hiking, 127, 133
  historic sites, 140
  kids' stuff, 132-33
  maps, 4-5, 31
  Orangeville, 34-35
  shopping, 145
  skiing, 153
Caledon Rail Trail, 180
Cambridge, 37
  accommodation, 174
  African Lion Safari, 133, 188
  cycling, 102, 180
  dining, 37, 111-12, 147, 182
  farmers' market, 37
  golf, 122, 187
  hiking, 129-30
  shopping, 37, 147
Cambridge Golf and Country Club, 187
Cambridge-Paris Trail, 180
Cambridge Trails, 188
Campbellville, 33
  antiquing, 75, 177
  birding, 84
camping, 91-94, 178-79

Canadian Antique Dealers Association (CADA), 177
Canadian Clay and Glass Gallery, 40, 134, 145, 177, 189
Canadian Heritage (for National Parks), 179
Carden Street Café, 112, 182
Cardinal Court Motel, 175
Carlisle golf course, 123
Carriages & Cannery Dining, 181
casinos
  Niagara Falls, 22
  Windsor, 62-63, 89
Castle Kilbride, 41, 133, 140-41
Cataract Inn, The, 181
Caves Conservation Area, 72
Cave Spring Cellars, 110, 166, 191
Cedar Highlands Ski Club, 153
Chantry Dunes, 71, 155
Château des Charmes Wines, 167, 191
Chatham, 98, 123, 136, 176, 179
Chatham Festival of Crafts, 98, 179
Chatham Street Grill, 184
Chi-cheemaun ferry, 72
Chicopee Ski Club, 190
children. See kids' stuff
Chimney Reefs, 90
Chippewa golf course, 124
Christmas
  Christmas Craft Festival, 97
  Christmas Craft Show (Lucan), 97
  Deck the Halls craft show (Ingersoll), 97
  Potters Guild Christmas Show and Sale, 97
  tree decorating (Grand Bend), 99
  Victorian Christmas Antique and Craft Show, 97
Christmas Craft Festival, 97
Christopher's, 115, 185
Church, The (restaurant), 112, 183
C.J.'s Antiques and Refinishing, 177
climate, 172
Colasanti's Tropical Gardens, 120, 186, 189-90
Colio Estate Wines, 114, 168, 191
Collingwood
  camping, 94
  dining, 115, 185
  golf, 124
  skiing, 152-53
Comfort Inn (Chatham), 176
Comfort Inn (Owen Sound), 176
Comfort Inn (Windsor), 176
Conservation Ontario (for Conservation Areas), 179
Countryside Motel & Restaurant, 176
craft shows, 95-99, 179-80

Craftworld Arts & Crafts Show, 96, 97, 98, 179
Craigleith Provincial Park, 94, 156
Cranberry Resort, 124
Crawford Lake Conservation Area, 32, 178
  birding, 84
  hiking, 127
  historic site, 132-33, 140, 188
cultural festivals, 186
  Eden Mills Festival, 146
  Mennonite Relief Sale, 106
  Oktoberfest, 106-7, 146
  Scottish festival and Highland Games, 106
  See also theatre
currencies, 170
customs, 171
cycling, 100-3, 180

da Caruso Ristorante, 181
D'Angelo Estate Winery, 114, 168
Deliciously Different Creative Cuisine, 112, 182
Delta London Armouries Hotel, 175
DeSousa Wine Cellars, 166
Destination Inn, 174
Detroit, 65
Detroit River, 89-90
dining, 110-15, 180-85
Donald Forster Sculpture Park, 81
Doon Heritage Crossroads, 38, 133
Doon Valley golf course, 122
Down the Street Bar and Cafe, 112, 183
Drawbridge Inn, The, 176
Drayton Festival Theatre, 162, 190
Dressing Room, 148, 189
driver's license, 172
du Maurier Ltd. Centre, 160
Duncan-McPhee, 145, 189
Dundurn Castle, 139-40
Dunnville, 92, 178

Earl Rowe Provincial Park, 92, 179
East Town Pizza, 113, 184
Eaton, Timothy, 50
Eden Mills Festival, 146
Edgewater Manor, 87
Eigensinn Farm, 115
Eldon House, 54, 141
Elm Hurst Inn, 175
Elmira, 43, 122
Elora, 43-44
  accommodation, 174
  antiquing, 75
  cross-country skiing, 152
  dining, 44, 182
  golf, 122
  maple sugar festival, 107
  music festival, 105, 185
  shopping, 146
Elora Mill Inn, 44, 146, 174, 182
Empress Garden Restaurant(s), 114, 184
Epicurean, The, 181
Erin, 35, 145
Essex, 114, 185
Essex Courtyard, The, 114, 184
Essex Region Conservation Authority, 178
Fair November, 96
fairs. *See* festivals
fall festivals, 186
Falls Incline Railway, 131
Family and Company, 148, 189
Fanshawe Pioneer Village, 120, 141
Fanthom Five Natl. Marine Park, 71
farmers' markets, 37, 38, 40, 146, 185
Federation of Ontario Naturalists (FON), 178
Feminist theatre, 161
Fergus, 44, 174, 186
  fishing, 44
  Scottish Festival and Highland Games, 106, 186
  theatre, 44, 162
Festival of Arts and Crafts, 98
festivals, 146, 185
  cultural, 106-7, 186
  fall, 108-9, 186
  food, 96, 107
  music, 105-6, 185-86
  winter, 109, 152, 186
Fifties Steamliner, 133, 188
Fifty Point Marina, 87, 178
Fine Art and Crafts Fair, 98
First Nations people and culture
  Crawford Lake historic site, 140
  Grand River Champion of Champions Powwow, 107
  history, 13
  Independent Indian Handcrafters Bazaar, 96, 179
  London Museum of Archaeology and Iroquoian Village Site, 141, 188
  Long Point archaeological site, 61
  N'Amerind Powwow, 186
  Saugeen First Nations Reserve, 71
  Ska Nah Doht Indian Village, 134, 138
  Woodland Cultural Centre, 96
Flesherton, 115, 185
floral clock
  Guelph, 118
  Niagara Falls, 116, 186-87
Fonthill, 74
food festivals, 96, 107, 108
food. *See* dining

food service, tax, 171
Forks of the Credit Provincial Park, 35
Fort Erie, 28-29
  camping, 92
  historic, 29
  travel information centre, 171
Fort George, 26-27, 139
Fort Malden National Historic Park, 136
Four Points Hotel Kitchener, 174
Foxwood golf course, 122
François Baby House, 64

Gage Park, 117, 186
Gallery/Stratford, 81, 177
gardens, 116-20, 186-87
Georgian Theatre Festival, 162
Giardino, 181
gifts, duty-free, 171
Gingerbread House (restaurant), 113-14, 184
Glen Eden, 153
Glen Eden Ski Area, 190
Glen Manor Galleries, 177
Goderich, 69-70
  accommodation, 176
  beaches, 69, 155
  boating, 89
  camping, 94
  dining, 185
  Festival of Arts and Crafts, 98
  Governor's House, 70, 143
  Huron Historic Gaol, 70, 143
  Huron Tract Spinners and Weavers sale, 98
  kids' stuff, 137
  skiing, 152
Goderich Festival of Arts & Crafts, 179
golf, 121-24, 187
Goods and Services Tax (GST), 171
Governor's House, 137, 143
Grand Bend, 68-69
  accommodation, 176
  beaches, 69, 136-37, 155
  boating, 89
  Christmas sale and tree decorating, 99
  Lambton Heritage Museum, 69
  winter festival, 152, 186
Grand Bend Sport Parachuting Centre, 68
Grand River, 90
Grand River Conservation Authority, 178
Grand Victorian Bed and Breakfast, 168
Great Gorge Adventure, The, 132, 188
Greenwood Golf Club, 187

Greyhound Canada, 170
Grey Rose, The, 185
Grey Rose, The (restaurant), 115
Grimsby, 83, 165
Grosvenor's, 115, 185
Guelph
  accommodation, 174
  art galleries, 81, 177
  bookstores, 146
  cycling, 102
  dining, 182
  Donald Forster Sculpture Park, 81
  Fair November, 96
  floral clock, 118
  gardens, 118, 186-87
  golf, 122, 187
  hiking, 129
  McCrae House, 141
  Macdonald Stewart Art Centre, 81, 177
  music festival, 106
  shopping, 145-46
Guelph Trail, 188

Halton Hills. See Caledon and Halton Hills
Halton Region Conservation Authority, 178
Hamilton
  art galleries, 79, 177
  Arts in Bloom craft show, 95-96
  botanical gardens, 118, 132
  Canadian Warplane Heritage Museum, 132, 139
  craft shows, 180
  cycling, 101, 180
  Gage Park, 117
  gardens, 118, 186-87
  McMaster Museum of Art, 79
  marinas, 87, 178
  music, 106
  Sam Lawrence Park, 118
  theatre, 160-61
  Winter Festival of Friends, 106
Hamilton to Brantford Rail Trail, 180
Hanover, 77, 115
Harrow, 168
Hawkesville, 42
Heidelberg Restaurant & Brew Pub, 111, 182
Henry of Pelham Family Estate Winery, 166-67
Hepworth, 151
Hernder Estate Wines, 166
Highland Games. See Scottish Festival and Highland Games
Hike Ontario, 187
hiking, 187-88
  Avon Trail, 130, 187
  Bruce Trail, 126-29, 188
  Cambridge Trail, 129, 188

Guelph Trail, 129, 188
Niagara Trail, 129, 188
Point Pelee National Park, 130, 188
Thames Valley Trail, 130, 188
Hillebrand Estates Winery, 106, 167, 191
Hillebrand Vineyard Cafe, 167, 181
Hillside Festival (music), 106
historic sites and buildings
　Annandale House, 142, 188
　Backus Mills Conservation Area, 59-60, 142
　Castle Kilbride, 41, 133, 140-41
　Doon Heritage Crossroads, 38, 140, 189
　Dundurn Castle, 139-40, 189
　Eldon House, 54, 141
　Fort Erie, 29
　Fort George, 26-27, 139
　Fort Malden National Historic Park, 65, 126
　Francois Baby House, 65
　Freeport Church, 38
　Gordon House, 65-66
　Laura Secord Homestead, 139
　Long Point, 61
　McCrae House, 141
　Port Burwell lighthouse, 142
　Queenston Heights Park, 25
　Uncle Tom's Cabin Historic Site, 136
　Willistead Manor, 142-43
　See also museums; native peoples and culture
Hockley Valley, 34, 153
Holiday Beach Conservation Area, 86
Holiday Inn (Guelph), 174
Home County Folk Festival, 97
Home (restaurant), 113, 183
Household China and Gifts, 145
Hume Cronyn Memorial Observatory, 135, 188
Hummingbird Gift Shop, 190
Huron County Playhouse, 68, 161, 162, 191
Huron Tract Spinners and Weavers sale and exhibition, 98

Idlewyld Inn, 175
Independent Indian Handcrafters Bazaar, 179
Indian Creek golf course, 123
Indian Falls, 72, 137
Ingersoll, 97, 175
Inglis Falls, 72, 137
Inniskillen Wines, 25, 26, 168
interurban cycling trails, 101
Inverhuron Provincial Park, 86
Ironwood golf course, 124
Ivy Room at the Benmiller Inn, The, 185

Jack Miner Bird Sanctuary, 93, 135-36
Jackson Park Queen Elizabeth II Gardens, 186
Jakobstettel Guest House, 174
Janet Lynn's Bistro, 183
Jazz on the River, 48
John M. Hall "House of Quality Linens", 148, 189
Jonny's Antiques, 177
Jordan, 173
　antiquing, 74, 177
　dining, 110, 180
　wineries, 166
Jordan Antique Centre, 177
Joseph's Estate Wines, 167

Keppel Croft Farm and Gardens, 120
Keppel Croft Gardens, 72
Kettle Creek Clothing Co., 57
Kettle Creek Inn, 176, 184
Kettle Creek Valley, 135
Keystone Alley Cafe, 183
kids' stuff, 188
　African Lion Safari, 133, 188
　Beachville District Historical Society Museum, 134
　Canadian Clay and Glass Gallery, 132
　Canadian Warplane Heritage Museum, 132
　Chi Chi Maun, 137
　Crawford Lake Conservation Area, 132-33
　Doon Heritage Crossroads, 133
　East Park Golf Gardens, 134
　Falls Incline Railway, 131
　Fanshawe Pioneer Village, 134
　Fifties Steamliner, 133, 188
　Fort Malden National Historic Park, 136
　Governor's House, 137
　Grand Bend, 136-37
　Great Gorge Adventure, 131-32, 188
　Hume Cronyn Memorial Observatory, 135, 188
　Huron County Gaol, 137, 188
　Indian Falls, 137
　Inglis Falls, 137
　Island Stage Theatre, 134
　Jack Miner Bird Sanctuary, 135-36
　Jones Falls, 137
　London Museum of Archaeology and Iroquoian Village Site, 135, 188
　London Regional Children's Museum, 55, 135
　McManus Theatre, 55, 160
　Maid of the Mist cruise, 132
　Mennonite experience, 133-34

Mountsberg Conservation Area, 133, 188
Point Pelee National Park, 135
Port Burwell Marine Museum, 135
Port Stanley Terminal Railway, 135
Royal Botanical Gardens, 132
Sauble Beach, 136-37
Ska Nah Doht Indian Village, 134, 188
ski programs, 153
Sportsworld, 134
Storybook Garden, 134
Uncle Tom's Cabin Historic Site, 136
Wasaga Beach, 136-37
Wreck Exploration Tours, 136
Kiely Inn, The, 173
Kincardine, 70
    antiquing, 77
    theatre, 162
King's Forest golf course, 121
Kingsville, 107, 114, 135, 149, 175, 184
Kingswood Inn, 175
King, William Lyon Mackenzie, 38, 141
"kissing" bridge, 43
Kitchener, 37-39
    accommodation, 174
    art galleries, 177
    Craftworld Arts and Craft Show, 96
    Doon Heritage Crossroads, 38, 133, 140
    farmers' market, 38
    Freeport Church, 38
    gardens, 118, 186
    golf, 122, 187
    Joseph Schneider Haus Museum, 38, 140
    New Year's Eve celebration, 109
    Rockway Gardens, 118
    skiing, 152, 153
    Victoria Park, 39
    Woodside National Historic Park, 133, 141
Kitchener-Waterloo and area, 36-44
    accommodation, 174
    antiquing, 75-76
    art galleries, 80-81, 177
    Baden, 41
    birding, 84-85
    Blair, 37
    Cambridge, 37
    craft shows, 179-80
    cultural festivals, 146, 186
    cycling, 102
    dining, 111-12, 182-83
    Elmira, 43
    Elora, 43-44
    fairs, 107-8
    farmers' market, 185

Fergus, 44
    gardens, 118-19, 187
    golf, 122-23, 187
    Hawkesville, 42
    kids' stuff, 133-34
    Kitchener, 37-39
    maps, 4-5, 37
    museums, 140-41
    New Hamburg, 41
    Paris, 147-48
    shopping, 145-48
    St. Agatha, 40
    St. Clements, 42
    St. Jacobs, 42-43
    theatre, 161
    Waterloo, 39-40
    Wellesley, 41-42
    West Montrose, 43
    winter sports, 152, 153
Kitchener-Waterloo Oktoberfest, 106-7, 146, 186
Kitchener-Waterloo Symphony, 39
Kittling Ridge Estate, 165
Klassen's Blueberry Farm, 123
Konzelmann Estate Winery, 167
Kortright Waterfowl Park, 84

La Casa Ristorante, 113, 183
La Contessa, 114, 184
Lake Erie, boating, 88-89
Lake Erie shoreline, 58-61
    accommodation, 176
    antiquing, 76-77
    beaches, 154-55
    birding, 85, 85-86
    camping, 92-93
    craft shows, 97-98
    cycling, 103
    dining, 113-14, 184
    gardens, 120
    kids' stuff, 135
    Long Point, 60-61
    maps, 4-5, 58, 59
    marinas, 178
    museums, 141-42
    Port Burwell, 61
    Port Dover, 59
    Port Rowan, 59-60
    Turkey Point, 59
    wineries, 168
Lake Huron, boating, 89-90
Lake Huron and Georgian Bay
    accommodation, 176
    antiquing, 77
    Bayfield, 69
    beaches, 155-56
    birding, 86
    Bruce Peninsula, 71-72
    camping, 93-94
    craft shows, 98-99
    cycling, 103

dining, 115, 184-85
gardens, 120
Goderich, 69-79
golf, 122-23
Grand Bend, 68-69
kids' stuff, 136-37
Kincardine, 70
maps, 4-5, 67
marinas, 178
museums, 143
Owen Sound, 72
Sauble Beach, 71
shopping, 150
skiing, 151-53
Southampton, 71
theatre, 159-60
Lake Ontario, boating, 87-88
Lake St. Clair, boating, 89-90
Lakeview Cellars Estate Winery, 166
Lakewinds Country Manor, 173
La Maison de Madelaine, 146, 189
Lameth, 76
Langdon Hall, 37, 111, 174, 182
Laura Secord Homestead, 139
Laurel Creek Conservation Area, 152
Leamington, 85
Leblanc Estate Winery, 114
Lighthouse Festival Threatre, 161, 191
lighthouse, Point Clark, 70
Little Inn of Bayfield, The, 69, 115, 150, 176, 184
London, 53-56
  accommodation, 175
  antiquing, 76, 177
  Arts and Craft Spring Show, 97
  Banting House Museum, 54
  children's museum, 55, 135
  Christmas Craft Festival, 97
  Civic Garden Complex, 119
  craft shows, 179
  dining, 113, 183-84
  Eldon House, 54, 141
  Fanshawe Pioneer Village, 54, 134, 141
  gardens, 119, 186-87
  golf, 187
  Grand Theatre, 55, 160
  Guy Lombardo Museum, 54
  Home County Folk Festival, 97
  Island Stage Theatre, 134
  kids' stuff, 134-35
  McManus Theatre, 55, 160
  Middlesex County courthouse, 55
  Museum of Indian Archaeology, 135, 141, 188
  music festivals, 105-6, 185-86
  New Arts Festival, 97
  Potters Guild Christmas Show and Sale, 97
  shopping, 149
  skiing, 153

Storybook Gardens, 134
St. Paul's Cathedral, 55
St. Peter's Cathedral, 55
Talbot Theatre, 56
University of Western Ontario campus, 55-56
Victorian Christmas Antique and Craft Show, 97
Western Fair, 108
London and area, 53-57, 119-20
  accommodation, 175
  antiquing, 76
  craft shows, 97
  cycling, 102-3
  dining, 112-13, 183-84
  gardens, 119-20
  golf, 123
  kids' stuff, 134-35
  London, 53-56
  maps, 4-5, 53, 54
  museums, 141-42
  Port Stanley, 57
  shopping, 149, 149-50
  Sparta, 56-57
  St. Thomas, 56
London Arts & Crafts Spring Show, 179
London Civic Garden Complex, 186
London New Arts Festival, 180
London Regional Children's Museum, 55
London Ski Club, 190
London Winery, 114
Long Point
  archaeological site, 61
  beaches, 154
  biosphere reserve, 60-61
  birding, 86
  boating, 89
  camping, 92
  diving, 61
  provincial park, 92-93, 179
Longwoods Road Conservation Area, 134
Lorne Park, 119
Luther Marsh Wildlife Management Area, 84-85

McCrae House, 118, 141
McCrae, John, 141
McCully's Hill Farm, 52
Macdonald Stewart Art Centre, 81, 177
MacGregor Point Provincial Park, 70, 94, 178, 179
McMaster Museum of Art, 79, 177
McMaster University, 79
Magnotta Cellar, 166
Maid of the Mist cruise, 22, 132
Maitland Valley Marina, 178
Manitoulin Island, 72
Maplegrove Vinoteca Estate Winery, 166

Maple Leaf Fudge, 144, 189
maple sugar festivals, 43, 107
maps
  Caledon and Halton Hills, 4-5, 31
  Kitchener-Waterloo and area, 4-5, 37
  Lake Erie shoreline, 4-5
  Lake Huron and Georgian Bay, 4-5, 67
  London and area, 4-5, 53, 54
  Niagara Peninsula, 5, 20
  southwestern Ontario, 4-5
  Stratford and area, 4-5, 45, 46
  Windsor and area, 4
Marineland, 132, 188
Mary Maxim, 147-48, 189
Meaford, theatre, 162
Meetingplace, 140
Mennonite experience, 16, 140
  art, 81
  food, 111, 146
  handicrafts, 96, 147
  Hawkesville, 42
  New Hamburg, 41
  sightseeing, 133-34
  St. Jacobs, 42-43
  Wellesley, 41-42
Mennonite Relief Sale and Quilt Auction, 41, 96, 106, 180
metric conversion, 172
Michael's Inn-By the Falls, 173
Millcroft Inn Restaurant, 182
Millcroft Inn, The, 34, 174
Mill Street Mews, 146, 189
Mimosa Restaurant, 182
Minolta Tower, 22
Minosa, 112
Moffat Inn, 173
money. See currencies
Monterra golf course, 124
Mountsberg Conservation Area, 32, 84, 133, 188
movies, art, 146
Munshaw's Bistro, 115, 185
Murano, 113, 184
museums
  Banting House Museum, 54
  Beachville District Historical Society Museum, 134
  Billy Bishop Heritage Museum, 72
  Bruce County Museum and archives, 71
  Canadian Baseball Hall of Fame and Museum, 51
  Canadian Warplane Heritage Museum, 132, 139, 188
  County of Grey-Owen Sound Museum, 72, 143
  Guy Lombardo Museum, 141
  Huron County Gaol, 70, 137, 143, 188
  Huron County Museum, 70, 143

  Joseph Schneider Haus, 140
  Lambton Heritage Museum, 68, 143
  London Museum of Archaeology and Iroquoian Village Site, 135, 141, 188
  London Regional Children's Museum, 55
  Mackenzie Printery, 22, 25, 139
  Meetingplace, 140
  Niagara-on-the-Lake, 139
  North American Black Historical Museum, 66
  Ontario Museum Association, 188
  Owen Sound Marine and Rail Heritage Museum, 72
  Port Burwell Marine Museum and Lighthouse, 135
  Wellington County Museum and Archives, 44
  Wilmot Township museum, 141
  Woodside, 133, 141
    See also historic sites and buildings; First Nations people and culture
music festivals, 97, 186
  Home County Folk Festival, 97, 105-6
  Royal Canadian Big Band Music Festival, 105, 186

N'Amerind Powwow, 107, 186
National Marine Park, 72
native peoples. See First Nations people and culture
New Hamburg, 41, 106, 109
Newport Marina, 87, 178
New York state, 29
Niagara Falls, 20-23
  accommodation, 173
  Art by the Falls craft show, 95
  butterfly conservatory, 117, 132
  casino, 22
  dining, 22
  entertainment, 23
  Falls Incline Railway, 131
  floral clock, 116
  gardens, 116-17, 186-87
  Great Gorge Adventure, 131-32
  greenhouses, 23, 117
  Imax Theatre, 22
  International Festival of Lights, 109
  Maid of the Mist cruise, 22, 132
  Marineland, 132, 188
  travel information centre, 171
  waterfalls, viewing, 21-22
Niagara Golf Club, 121-22, 187
Niagara and Mid-Western Ontario Travel Association, 173
Niagara-on-the-Lake, 26-28
  accommodation, 27-28, 173-74

Angie Strauss Gallery, 79
antiquing, 74, 177
art galleries, 78-79, 177
Artistry by the Lake craft show, 95
boating, 88
dining, 110, 167, 181
golf, 187
historic sites and buildings, 26, 139
museum, 139
music festivals, 106
Preservation Fine Art Gallery, 78
  79
shopping, 28, 144-45
wineries, 25, 167-68
  See also Shaw Festival
Niagara Parks Botanical Gardens,
  24-25, 116, 132, 186
Niagara Parks Butterfly
  Conservatory, 24-25, 117, 187
Niagara Parks Commission
  Greenhouses, 22, 117, 187
Niagara Parks Marina, 178
Niagara Parkway, 23-26, 28-29, 84,
  117, 129
Niagara Peninsula, 20-30
  accommodation, 173-74
  antiquing, 28, 74-75
  art galleries, 177
  birding, 83-84
  camping, 92
  craft shows, 95-96
  cycling, 101-2, 180
  dining, 110-11, 180-81
  gardens, 116-18, 116-19, 186-87
  golf, 121-22
  hiking, 126-28, 129
  kids' stuff, 131-32
  map, 5, 20
  marinas, 178
  museums and historic sites, 139
  New York state, 29
  Niagara Falls, 20-23
  Niagara Gorge, 24
  Niagara-on-the-Lake, 26-28
  shopping, 144-45
  St. Catharines, 30
  wine festival, 108, 186
  wineries, 25-26, 30, 165-68
Niagara Peninsula Conservation
  Authority, 178
Niagara Region Wine Festival, 186
Niagara River Recreational Trail,
  180
Niagara Trail, 188
Norma Jean's, 115, 185

Oaks of St. George golf course, 123
Oakwood Inn Resort, 124
Oktoberfest. See Kitchener-
  Waterloo Oktoberfest
Old Bullock Tavern, The, 114, 184

Olde Hide House, 33
Old Fort Niagara (New York), 139
Old London South Antiques, 177
Old Prune, The, 112, 184
Ontario Accommodation
  Association, 173
Ontario Association of Agricultural
  Societies, 108, 185
Ontario Association of Art
  Galleries (OAAG), 177
Ontario Camping Association, 179
Ontario Crafts Council, 179
Ontario Cycling Association, 180
Ontario Federation of Snowmobile
  Clubs, 190
Ontario Field Ornithologists (OFO),
  178
Ontario Horticultural Association,
  186
Ontario Marina Operators
  Association, 178
Ontario Museum Association, 188
Ontario Parks Head Office, 179
Ontario Private Campground
  Association (OPCA), 179
Ontario Ski Resorts Association,
  190
Ontario South Central Trip Planner,
  173
Ontario Tourism, 173
Ontario Travel Information Centres,
  171
On The Twenty, 110, 180
Orangeville, 34-35
  dinning, 182
  shopping, 34
  skiing, 153
  theatre, 34, 162
Other Brother's Restaurant &
  Lounge, 112, 182
Overtures, 184
Owen Sound, 72, 177
  accommodation, 176
  art galleries, 177
  boating, 90
  County of Grey-Owen Sound
    Museum, 143
  dining, 115, 185
  kids' stuff, 137
  skiing, 151, 153
  theatre, 162
Owen Sound Marina, 178
Oxley Beach golf course, 123

Paris, 75-76, 102, 147-48
parks, provincial, 91-92
passports, 170-71
Pelee Island
  birding, 66
  dining, 66, 114
  winery, 25, 114, 168, 191

See also Point Pelee National
    Park
Peller Estates, 165
Pellitteri Estates, 167
Petrolia, 162
Pike Lake Golf Centre, 124, 187
Pillar & Post Inn, The, 173
Pinehurst Conservation Area, 152
Pinery Provincial Park, 179, 180
    birding, 86
    camping, 93-94
    Christmas sale and tree
        decorating, 99
    cross-country skiing, 152
    cycling, 103
    swimming, 69, 155
Pine Valley golf course, 123
Point Clark Lighthouse, 70
Point Farms Provincial Park, 94
Point Pelee National Park, 66
    birding, 85, 126, 135, 178
    camping, 93
    cycling, 103, 180
    hiking, 130, 188
    swimming, 155
    See also Pelee Island
Porcino's, 114, 184
Port Burwell, 61, 92, 135, 142, 154
Port Colborne, 88
Port Dalhousie, 30, 88
Port Dalhousie Pier Inc., 178
Port Dover, 59, 88
    beaches, 154
    dining, 113, 184
    Lighthouse Festival Threatre, 161
        62
Port Elgin, 70, 94, 187
Port Glasgow, 154
Port Rowan, 59-60
    beaches, 154
    pioneer village, 142
Port Stanley, 57
    accommodation, 176
    boating, 89
    dining, 57, 184
    hawk festival, 57
    railway, 135
Potters Guild Christmas Show and
    Sale, 97
powwow, 107
Prince of Wales Hotel, The, 174
pubs, 48, 111, 112

Quai du Vin winery, 56
Quality Inn, 175
Queen Elizabeth II Sunken Gardens,
    120, 187
Queen's Inn at Stratford, 175
Queen's Landing Inn, 174

Queenston
    antiquing, 74
    Bruce Trail, 126
    Laura Secord Homestead, 139
    Mackenzie Printery, 139
Queenston Heights Park, 25
Queen Victoria Park, 117
Radisson Hotel London Centre, 175
"rail trails", 100
Recovering Nicely, 145, 189
recreation
    camping, 91-94, 178-79
    cycling, 100-3, 180
    diving, 71
    golf, 121-24, 187
    hiking, 125-30, 187-88
    skydiving, 68
    snow sports, 151-53, 190
    swimming, 154-56, 190
Red Barn Antique Mall, 177
Regency House Antique Galleries,
    177
Reif Estate Winery, 25, 26, 168, 191
Relais & Chateaux Country House
    Hotel, 111
Resorts Ontario, 190
restaurants. *See* dining
Rinderlin's Dining Rooms, 181
Riverside Marina of Dunnville, 178
Riversong Herbals and Naturals, 115
Rock Gardens, 71
Rock Point Provincial Park, 92, 179
Rockway Gardens, 118, 187
Rockway Golf Club, 122, 187
Rondeau Provincial Park
    birding, 85-86, 178
    camping, 92, 180
    cycling, 103, 180
    hiking, 92
    swimming, 92
room tax, 171
Royal Botanical Gardens, 118, 132,
    187
Royal Canadian Big Band Music
    Festival, 105, 186
Royal Hamilton Yacht Club, 87, 178
Royals Dining Room, 181
Rundles, 112, 183

sales tax, provincial, 171
Sam Lawrence Park, 118
Sand Hill Park, 61, 154
Sarnia
    accommodation, 124-25, 176
    craft shows, 99
    golf, 187
    travel information centre, 171
Sauble Beach, 71, 136-37, 155-56
Sauble Falls Provincial Park, 94, 179
Saugeen Amphitheatre, 71

Saugeen First Nations Reserve, 71
Saugeen Golf Club, 124, 187
Scottish Festival and Highland
  Games, 106, 186
Seaforth, 99
seat belt use, 172
Sebastian's, 113, 184
Shakespeare, 52
  antiquing, 52, 76, 177
Shakespearean Festival Garden, 119
Shakespearean Gardens, 119
Shakespearean Gift Shop, The, 148,
  189
Shaw Festival, 27, 105, 159-60, 191
Sherkston Shores, 92, 179
shipwrecks, 61, 71, 136
shopping, 29, 144-50, 189
  See also antiquing
Sifton Bog, 119, 187
Silly Old Bear Shop, 144, 189
Simcoe Georgian Bay Marketing, 173
Singhampton, 115
Ska Nah Doht Indian Village, 134,
  188
skiing, 152-53
Skyline Brock Hotel, The, 173
Skylon Tower, 22
Sleeman Brewery, 111, 146
Sombra, 149-50
Southampton, 71, 90
  beaches, 155
  dining, 185
  golf, 124
  sand dunes, 155
southwestern Ontario
  accommodation, 12
  Amerindians, 13
  climate, 172
  cultural identity, 15-17
  economy, 17-18
  European settlement, 14-15
  history, 13-18
  language, 12
  maps, 4-5
  region, 8-9
  time zone, 172
  touring, 10-12
  travelling to, 8-9
Southwestern Ontario Travel
  Association, 173
Southworks, The, 147, 189
Spago Trattoria, 114, 184
Sparta, 56-57
speed limits, 172
Spencer's George Wilderness Area,
  127
sports, professional, 29
Sportsworld, 134
Springfield golf course, 122
Stage Door Southwestern Ontario

Theatre, 191
Stan's Marina Inc., 178
Starkey Hill, 129
Station Park Inn, 175
Stokes Seeds Trail Gardens, 117
Stonechurch Vineyards, 167
Stone Crock, 111, 183
Stone Maiden Inn, 175
Stoney Ridge Cellars, 165, 191
Storybook Garden, 134
Stratford
  art galleries, 81-82, 177
  Art in the Park craft show, 48, 96
    97
  Craftworld Arts & Crafts Show, 97
  dining, 48-49, 112, 183
  fall fairs, 109
  Gallery/Stratford, 81, 177
  gardens, 119, 187
  hiking, 187-88
  history, 45-46
  Jazz on the River, 48
  Shakespearean Gardens, 119
  shopping, 148-49
  theatre. *See* Stratford Festival
Stratford and area, 45-52, 119
  accommodation, 175
  antiquing, 76
  craft shows, 96-97
  cycling, 102
  dining, 112, 183
  gardens, 119
  hiking, 130
  kids' stuff, 134
  maps, 4-5, 45, 46
  Shakespeare, 52
  shopping, 148-49
  Stratford, 45-49
  St. Marys, 49-52
  visitors information, 174-75
Stratford and Area Bed & Breakfast
  Association, 174
Stratford Chefs School, 112
Stratford Festival, 46-47, 105, 157-58,
  191
Stratford Festival Inn, 175
Strathroy, 176
strawberry festivals, 107
St. Agatha, 40
St. Catharines, 30
  dining, 182
  Stokes *Seeds* Trial Gardens, 117
  travel information centre, 171
  wine festival, 108, 186
  wineries, 166-67
St. Clements, 42
St. Davids, 167
St. George, 75
St. Jacobs, 42-43
  accommodation, 174

antiquing, 75, 177
dining, 111, 146, 183
Fifties Streamliner, 133, 188
golf, 122
kids' stuff, 133-34
Meetingplace museum, 140
shopping, 42-43, 146-47
St. Jacobs Antique Market, 75, 177
St. Jacobs Farmers' Market, 134, 146, 185
St. Jacobs Mennonite Quilts, 147, 189
St. Marys, 49-52, 175
Canadian baseball hall of fame, 51
crafts, 97
dining, 183
golf, 51-52
hiking, 52, 130
historic sites and buildings, 50-52
Opera House, 50
St. Marys Farmers' Market Association, 185
St. Thomas, 56, 135, 175
Strewn Winery, 111, 167
Sugarloaf Harbour Marina Centre, 88, 178
Summer at the Roxy, 162
Sunnybrook Farm Estate, 167-68
Sunroom, The, 112
Swain Greenhouses, 120
Swan Motel, 175
swimming
Georgian Bay, 156
Lake Erie, 154-55
Lake Huron, 155-56

Talisman Mountain Resort, 153, 190
Tapas, 113, 184
Tapestries Restaurant, 181
Tecumseh, 114, 185
Terra Cotta, 33, 102, 182
Terra Cotta Inn, 33, 182
Thames Valley Golf Club, 187
Thames Valley Trail, 130
Thames Valley Trail Association, 188
theatre, 190-91
Blyth Festival, 159-60
regional, 160-61
Shaw Festival, 27, 158-59
smaller companies, 161
Stratford Festival, 105, 157-58
summer, 161-62
Theatre Alive, 161
Theatre Aquarius, 160-61, 191
Theatre and Company, 191
Theatre on the Grand, 162
Theatre Orangeville, 162, 191
Thirty Bench Winery, 165
Thorold, 30

Tiara Restaurant at the Queen's Landing Inn, 181
Tillsonburg, 142
time zone, 172
Tin Goose Inn, 114
Tintagel, 145, 189
Tobermory, 71, 90, 126, 128
Tottenham Summer theatre, 162
Tourism Stratford, 175
tourist information. See visitors information
travel
air, arrving by, 170
bus, arrival by, 170
bus, touring by, 10-11
car, touring by, 10, 170, 172
information centres, 171
by public transportation, 10
rail, arriving by, 170
See also accommodation
Travelodge Hotel Kitchener, 174
Turkey Point, 59
beaches, 59, 154
birding, 93
boating, 88
camping, 93
golf course, 59
hiking, 59
provincial park, 93, 179
swimming, 93
Twenty-Three Albert Place Hotel, 175

Uncle Tom's Cabin Historic Site, 136
universities, 17, 39, 55
University of Guelph Aboretum, 118, 129, 187
U.S. visitors, 170-71

Vase, 112, 182
Verandah, The, 113, 184
VIA Rail, 170
Victoria Park East Golf Club, 122, 187
Victoria Playhouse, 162
Victorian Inn on the Park, The, 175
Vincor-Niagara Cellars, 168
Vineland, 110-11, 181
Vineland Estates Winery Restaurant, 110-11, 181
Vineyard Café. See Hillebrand Vineyard Café
Vineyard Concert Series, 106
Vintage Goose, The, 114, 184
Vinter's Inn, 173
Vinters Quality Alliance (VQA), 163-64

Visitors information
  Ontario Travel Information
    Centres, 171
  Tourism Stratford, 175
    See also accommodation
V.P. Cellars Estate Winery, 166

Wah Court, 114, 184
Walters Estate, 165
Wasaga Beach, 136-37, 156
Waterford, 76, 108
Waterfront Trail, 180
Waterloo, 39-40
  accommodation, 174
  bookstores, 145
  Canadian Clay and Glass Gallery,
    40, 81, 134, 145, 189
  cross-country skiing, 152
  dining, 183
  farmers' market, 40
  Fifties Streamliner, 40, 133, 188
  map, 37
  shopping, 145, 189
  theatre, 39-40
  universities, 29
Waterloo Inn, 174
Waterloo Stage Theatre, 191
Wee Scottish Loft, 144, 189
Welland, 181
Welland Canal, 30, 88
Wellesley, 41-42, 96
Wellesley Apple Butter and Cheese
  Festival, 41-42, 96, 108
Wellington Court Restaurant, 181
West Lorne, 120
West Montrose, 43
Westover Inn, 175, 183
Wheatley Provincial Park, 93, 179
Whirlpool Jet Boat Tours, 24
White Oaks Inn and Racquet Club,
  174
Wiarton, 72, 94, 120
Wildwood Inn Restaurant, The, 112,
  183
Willistead Coach House Arts &
  Crafts Show, 98, 180
Willistead Manor, 142-43
Willow Heights Estate Winery, 166,
  191
Windsor
  accommodation, 176
  art galleries, 65, 82, 177
  casino, 62-63, 89
  classic and antique car show, 64
  Colasanti's Tropical Gardens, 120,
    189
  craft shows, 180
  cycling, 103, 180
  dining, 65, 114, 184
  François Baby House, 65

  gardens, 64, 120, 186
  golf, 123
  kids' stuff, 135-36
  Queen Elizabeth II Sunken
    Gardens, 120, 187
  shopping, 65, 149
  theatre, 161
  travel information centres, 171
  Willistead Coach House Arts and
    Craft Show, 98
  Willistead Manor, 64, 142-43
  Winter in the Park exhibition, 98
Windsor and area, 85, 123, 135-36
  accommodation, 176
  birding, 135-36
  boating, 89
  camping, 93
  craft shows, 98
  cycling, 103
  dining, 114, 184
  gardens, 120
  golf, 123
  Kingsville, 149
  map, 4
  museums, 142-43
  shopping, 149-50
  Sombra, 149-50
  wineries, 114
Windsor Hilton, 176
Windsor Light Opera, 161
Wine Country Cooking School, 167
wineries
  Lake Erie shoreline, 168
  Niagara Peninsula, 25-26, 30, 165-
    68
  Pelee Island, 168
  tour routes, 25-26, 164-65
wines
  festival, 108, 186
  Ontario, 163-64
  sample tastings, 164-65
Winnie the Pooh, 144
Winona, 165
Winter Festival of Friends, 106
Winter Festival of Lights, 186
winter festivals, 109, 152, 186
Winter in the Park exhibition, 98
Woodland Cultural Centre, 96
Woodside National Historic Park, 38,
  133, 141
Woodstock, 175
Woods Villa, 175
Words Worth, 145

York Street Kitchen, 112, 183

PHOTO CREDITS

We thank all the companies, associations, organizations, and other groups that contributed visual material to this guide. We also wish to thank the following photographers: Dwayne Coon, Terry Manzo, Jackie Noble, Glenn Ogilvie, David Smiley, Willy Waterton, and Scott Wishart. All maps in Niagara & Southwestern Ontario were created by Peggy McCalla. We regret any errors in crediting photographic material and will be pleased to make any necessary corrections in future editions.

Legend: T = Top; C = Centre; B = Bottom

African Lion Safari: 133C; Albright-Knox Art Gallery, Buffalo, courtesy of: 29T, 80T; Art Gallery of Hamilton, 79B (Prudence Heward [Canadian, 1896-1947], Girl Under a Tree 1931, oil on canvas, 122.5 x 193.7cm, collection of the Art Gallery of Hamilton, gift of the artist's family, 1961); Annandale House: 142T

Blue Mountain: 124T, 151T, 152B; Blyth Festival: 159; Bruce County Tourism: 154T, 155B

Caledon Rail Trail: 102; Canadian Heritage Parks (Niagara National Historic Sites): 14; Canoe Ontario: 90B; Casino Niagara: 22T; Castle Kilbride: 140B; Christopher's: 115; Coon, Dwayne: 6, 7, 9B, 11B, 12B, 19, 21, 22B, 23, 24T, 25T&B, 26, 27C&B, 29T, 29B, 30, 46, 73, 121B, 127T, 132B, 164T, 165T, C&B, 167B; Craftworld Crafts: 96T&B, 98T; Cranberry Resort Golf Club: 124B

Deliciously Different: 112T; Dreams-in-Mo-Tion (Lou-Ann Barnett Freelance Photography): 64B

Earl Rowe Provincial Park: 92T&B; Economic Development Corporation of Fort Erie: 28B, 139T; Einhorn Fine Chocolate: 146B; Elora Festival: 105

Fanshawe Pioneer Village: 54. 141; Fergus Festival and Highland Games: 107; Fort George (Niagara National Historic Parks): 138; Fort Malden National Historical Park: 65, 136

Greyhound Canada Transportion: 10; The Gallery Stratford: 81T&B;

Haldimand-Norfolk Economic Deveopment: 58-59, 60T, 61B, 86C; Halton Region Conservation Authority: 13, 133T; Hamilton Conservation Authority: 127B; Hernder Estates Winery: 166B; Hike Ontario: 11T, 125; Hillebrand Estates Winery: 106B, 164B, 167T; Hillside Festival: 106T; Hockley Valley Resort: 153; Home Country Folk Festival: 97, 106C; Huron County Museum: 143B

Jack Miner Sanctuary: 135; Ken Jantzi (Reflections), courtesy of: 95, 147B; Joseph Schneider Haus: 38T, 140T

Kitchener, Parks and Recreation: 122T; Kittling Ridge: 165C
Lambton Heritage Museum: 15B; Long Point Region Conservation Authority: 142B; Lower Thames Valley Conservation Authority: 134T

Maid of the Mist Corporation: 1; Manzo, Terry: 51; Marineland: 132T; McMaster Museum of Art, courtesy of, 78T, 79T; Munshaw's: 115T

Niagara Parks Commission: 24B, 100, 101, 116B, 117T, 117B, 129, 131;

Niagara Spanish Aerocar Ride: 20; Nothing New Antiques: 74; Jackie Noble: 14T, 18T, 53, 55-57, 134B, 154B, 160T

Oaks of St. George Golf Club: 123T; Odrohekta (Six Nations Cultural & Historical Assoc.): 16B; Ogilvie, Glenn: 18B; On the Twenty: 110; Ontario Parks (Long Point Provincial Park): 60B, 86C; Overtures: 114; Owen Sound Tourism: 151B, 152T; Oxley Beach Golf Course: 123B

Pinery Provincial Park: 83B, 84B, 85, 86B, 91, 94, 155C; Port Burwell Provincial Park: 61T, 93T; Port Dover Travel Co.: 87T, 88B, 155T; Preservation Gallery: 78; Peter Etril Snyder Studio, 80B

Red Barn Antiques: 74T; Reif Estate Winery: 168; Rondeau Provincial Park: 83T, 84T, 86T; Roseland Golf and Curling Club: 121T; Royal Botantical Gardens: 116T, 117C, 126; Royal Hamilton Yacht Club: 87B; Rundles: 112C&B; Rumner's Wobble: 75

Seaforth Craft Show: 98B, 99; Shakespearean Gift Shop: 148T; Shaw Festival: 27T (Andree Lanthier, photographer); 104B, 157T, 158B (David Cooper, photographer); Silly Old Bear Shop: 144B; Smiley, David: 12T, 16T, 17, 31-37, 38C&B, 39-44, 128C, 145T, 146T, 147T&C, 161C; Springfield Golf and Country Club: 122B; Stevens, Peter: 15T, 139B; St. Lawrence Seaway Authority: 88T; Stone Crock: 111B; Stratford Festival (all photographs Cylla von Tiedemann unless otherwise noted): 9T, 36, 37T&B, 45, 47(Terry Manzo, photographer), 104, 157B; Sun Room: 113

Times and Places: 77T&B; Thames Valley Trail: 120; Theatre and Company (Kate Holt, photographer): 161T; Theatre Aquarius (Roy Timm, photographer): 160B; Theatre on the Grand: 162; Tom Thomson Memorial Art Gallery: 82; Tourism Stratford: 119T&B; Trilife Sports International (Kokanee 24 Hrs of Adrenalin; Freeze Frame, photographers): 103; Turkey Point Provincial Park 93C

University of Guelph, The Arboretum: 118T&B

Vineland Estates Winery: 11T, 163, 166T; Vintage Goose: 66B

Waterloo, Regional Municipality of: 133B; Waterton, Willy: 8, 67-72, 90T, 128T, 128B, 137T & B, 150, 156; Wee Scottish Loft: 144T; Wellesley Apple Butter and Cheese Festival: 108T&B; Willistead Manor: 64, 143,; Windsor Light Opera Association: 161B; Words Worth Books: 145; Windsor, Essex County & Pelee Island Convention and Visitors Bureau: 62-63, 64T, 66T&C, 89, 120, 149; Winter Festival of Lights: 109; Wishart, Scott: 47C&B, 48- 50, 52, 76, 148

Canadian Cataloguing in Publication Data
Niagara & Southwestern Onatario
(Colourguide series)
Includes Index.

ISBN 0-88780-426-8

1. Niagara Peninsula (Ont.) — Guidebooks.   2. Ontario, Southwestern — Guidebooks.   I. Knowles, Paul.   II. Pietropaolo, Vincenzo.   III. Title: Niagara and Southwestern Ontario.   IV. Series.
FC3095.N5N44 1998   917.13'2044   C98-950164-7
F1059.N5N46 1998

CONTRIBUTORS

Ellen Ashton-Haiste is a features and travel writer who lives near London.

Mike Baginski is a veteran travel and features writer and editor who lives in Toronto—when he is not travelling.

Sue Bailey is an award-winning journalist who covers the casino beat and writes general news features for the *Windsor Star*. Her work has appeared in several Canadian magazines and daily newspapers.

Patricia Bow, of Kitchener, is a freelance writer and author of mystery novels (published in German) and children's books (published in English).

Rick Campbell is a Waterloo writer, editor, and golfer who was formerly publisher of the *Waterloo Chronicle*. He has written about golf for many publications.

Kelly Daynard is a features and travel writer and avid crafter and gardener who lives in Baden, Ontario.

Bret Evans has been the editor of *Collectibles Canada* and *Gift and Collectibiles Retailer* for the past seven years.

Anita Hanson lives in New Hamburg. Her stories have appeared in the *Toronto Star*, and in *Close to the Heart*, an anthology of Canadian literature. Summer weekends are spent on *Ten Forward*, the boat she shares with her husband, John.

Paul Knowles has written more than half a dozen books, including *Why Is This Doctor Smiling?* (1997), and *Castle Kilbride*, the story of a Victorian mansion. He edited and contributed to *Close to the Heart*, an anthology of Canadian literature (1996). He writes an award-winning column for a number of publications, and is also a travel writer specializing in the United Kingdom and southern Ontario. He has been published in the *Globe and Mail*, the *Toronto Star*, *Today's Seniors* and other major periodicals, has appeared frequently on CBC Radio, and is also in demand as a public speaker.

Jana Miller is editor of the Kitchener-Waterloo edition of *Today's Seniors*, and the *New Hamburg Independent* community newspaper. She is writing a book on the history of hockey in her community.

Henry Moore is a wine lover who writes and teaches about wine, and conducts wine tastings. He lives in Kitchener.

Robert Reid is theatre and entertainment critic at the *Record*, the daily newspaper in Kitchener-Waterloo.

Joyce Spring is a feature writer who lives in Cambridge. She contributes frequently to *Today's Seniors* newspaper.

Jim Ste. Marie is the garden writer for the *Record*, in Kichener-Waterloo. He also leads international garden tours and is a popular speaker on gardening.

Cathy Williams is a Waterloo-based freelance writer whose articles have appeared in dozens of publications; she is also a member of the renowned Renaissance Singers.